# POPULISM

BY *Margaret Canovan*

**HBJ** Harcourt Brace Jovanovich    New York and London

*Library of Congress Cataloging in Publication Data*

Canovan, Margaret
Populism.
Includes bibliographical references and index.
1. Populism. 2. Radicalism.
3. Rural conditions. 4. Peasantry.
5. Populism—United States. 6. Populism—Russia.
I. Title.
HN15.5.C36    303.4'84    80-22245
ISBN 0-15-173078-4

Printed in the United States of America

First edition

B C D E

For Jim and Cherry

# Contents

# POPULISM

modern Switzerland. Pointing to the
Scopes monkey trial and the political
success of Hitler, Mussolini, and George
Wallace, and to the institutions of direct
participation in government such as
referendum, initiative, and recall,
Canovan provides fresh insight into
populism's potential for social abuse and
social improvement.

*Populism* is a penetrating, illuminating,
and, above all, relevant political history.

MARGARET CANOVAN is Professor of
Politics at the University of Keele, England. She is the author of the critically
acclaimed *The Political Thought of Han-
nah Arendt* and *G. K. Chesterton: Radical Populist.*

# Introduction: What Is Populism?

## THE PROBLEM

The reader who opens a book entitled "Populism" can have very little idea what to expect. Although frequently used by historians, social scientists, and political commentators, the term is exceptionally vague and refers in different contexts to a bewildering variety of phenomena. It is used to describe techniques of direct democracy such as the referendum and popular initiative, but also certain kinds of dictatorships such as that of Peron in Argentina. Latin American parties with a loose ideology and a coalitional base share the label with grass-roots explosions of reactionary feeling such as the "white backlash." Often applied to peasant movements, the term was also appropriated by Jimmy Carter to describe his political outlook when first campaigning for President; while the two acknowledged classics of populism, the People's Party of the 1890s in the United States and the *narodnichestvo* of Russian intellectuals a little earlier, could hardly differ more from one another.

What, if anything, have all these "populist" phenomena in common? If we dig deep enough, can we find some central core, some esoteric essence uniting them? Scholars have made many valiant attempts to identify such an essence, but the results are not encouraging. Let us look for a moment at some of the conflicting definitions of populism that have emerged in the course of such discussions:

1. "The socialism which [emerges] in backward peasant countries facing the problems of modernization."[1]
2. "Basically the ideology of small rural people threatened by encroaching industrial and financial capital."[2]
3. "Basically . . . a rural movement seeking to realize traditional values in a changing society."[3]
4. "The belief that the majority opinion of the people is checked by an elitist minority."[4]
5. "Any creed or movement based on the following major premiss: *virtue resides in the simple people, who are the overwhelming majority, and in their collective traditions.*"[5]
6. "Populism proclaims that the will of the people as such is supreme over every other standard."[6]
7. "A political movement which enjoys the support of the mass of the urban working class and/or peasantry but which does not result from the autonomous organizational power of either of these two sectors."[7]

While some of these definitions are clearly concerned with more or less the same area, there are strange differences of focus. (1), (2), and (3), though by no means in agreement, seem close enough for negotiation, as do (4), (5), and (6): but it is not at all obvious how these sets are related to one another or to (7). The bewildering scope

1. Notes are on pages 302–344.

of the subject is amply illustrated by the only previous general study, *Populism: Its Meanings and National Characteristics*, a cooperative venture edited by Ghita Ionescu and Ernest Gellner that brought together the views of specialists in many different fields.[8] That book, and the conference "To Define Populism" upon which it was based, demonstrated that the term was being used to describe so many different things that some of the participants doubted whether it could be said to mean anything at all.[9]

Not that problems of this sort are unique to populism. A conference to define socialism, liberalism, or conservatism would probably have equal difficulty in reaching a conclusion, and would certainly generate a great deal more acrimony in the process. None of these terms represents a single, unified phenomenon; each stands for a family of related ideas and movements, some of them contradictory to others. Nevertheless, the range of diversity within socialism or liberalism is less than that within populism. One reason for this is that the uses of the former terms have been chiefly dictated by their adherents. It has on the whole been the socialists who have decided what socialism means, so that although they have disagreed spectacularly among themselves, their uses of the term are related to a common movement and tradition.

The case of populism is quite different. It is true that the term originated as self-description, most notably among the self-styled "Populists" of the People's Party in the United States. Unknown to the American farmers, however, a group of intellectuals within a totally different political tradition in Russia had already styled itself *narodniki*—a term that, for better or worse, has also been regularly translated as "populist." Since then many groups have called themselves, in one language or another, something translatable as "populist" without sharing in a common tradition, while even more have been labeled "populist" from outside by scholars claiming to see analogies between one group and another. There has been no self-conscious international populist movement which might have attempted to control or limit the term's reference, and as a result those who have used it have been able to attach to it a wide variety of meanings. The more flexible the word has become, the more tempted political scientists have been to label "populist" any movement or outlook that does not fit into any established category.

Ought we then to drop the term from academic discourse on the grounds that it is more confusing than helpful? Scholars have been reluctant to do this, partly because it does have comparatively clear and definite meanings in a number of specialist areas (notably U.S. and Russian history and Latin American politics), and partly from the sense that it provides a pointer, however shaky, to an interesting and largely unexplored area of political and social experience. While use of the term remains in its present state of confusion, however, identifying a movement as "populist" cannot help us to understand or place it. Clarification is urgently needed, and this book represents an attempt at providing it. Given the enormous scope of the subject and the range over which the term is used, any such attempt must lie open to charges of superficiality in the various fields touched on. If, however, we can contrive to sort out the bewildering phenomena of populism into a reasonably coherent pattern, the effort may be justified.

## TOWARD A STRATEGY

One thing which the existing literature makes clear is that we cannot hope to reduce all cases of populism to a single definition or find a single essence behind all established uses of the term. At the conference already mentioned, Sir Isaiah Berlin christened such an approach "the Cinderella complex,"

> by which I mean the following: that there exists a shoe—the word "populism"—for which somewhere there exists a foot. There are all kinds of feet which it *nearly* fits, but we must not be trapped by these nearly fitting feet. The prince is always wandering about with the shoe; and somewhere, we feel sure, there awaits a limb called pure populism. This is the nucleus of populism, its essence.[10]

Attempts to identify such an essence seem to result, as we have seen, in a series of conflicting statements about what populism "basically" is. If we are to characterize populism, therefore, it is clear that we shall be able to do so only in terms of a range of populisms with Wittgensteinian family resemblances between them.[11] It may help us in our efforts at clarification, however, if we begin by noting two of the sources of confusion that have regularly bedeviled the subject, both of them related to the analytical focus adopted by academic students of populism.

The first source of confusion will become apparent if we look back for a moment at our sample of conflicting definitions. The first three of these agree in thinking of populism as a feature of rural societies, particularly those being modernized. The next three, by contrast, have no particular reference to rural or backward societies, but seem to focus upon political problems of democracy, particularly the relation between the people and the elite. The last definition does not fit easily into either category, although it has certain links with both.

Generally speaking, it is true that scholars have looked at populism from two broadly different angles and that many of the confusions and contradictions in the literature result from the clash between these different perspectives. Remaining at a broad level of generalization for the moment, we can say that there are two families of populism to be found in the literature, corresponding to two different sorts of interest on the part of their analysts.

In the first place, there is agrarian populism, which is a kind of rural radicalism. Since the focus here is upon the rural character of the movements concerned, scholars who share this approach usually think of populism as a type of movement with a particular kind of socioeconomic base (peasants or farmers), liable to arise in particular socioeconomic circumstances (especially modernization of one sort or another), and perhaps sharing a particular socioeconomic program.

One broad way of thinking about populism, then, stresses its agrarian character and takes a sociological approach toward its roots and significance. As we shall see later, this line of approach does not in fact give rise to a unified and internally consistent picture of populism, for there are too many differences among the various agrarian movements usually so named. Nevertheless, it is possible to identify an extended family of rural populisms and to argue intelligibly about their similarities and differences.

However, discussion of the various types of rural radicalism does not exhaust the phenomena known as "populism"—not even if one manages to smuggle certain kinds of urban populist movements (such as Peronism) into the same category, on the grounds that they attract recent migrants from the countryside. Alongside the various species and subspecies of agrarian populisms, there appears another family of populisms that may overlap in places with the first, but that are in many ways quite different because seen in a different focus.

This second broad family of populisms is not necessarily rural; indeed, the emphasis here is much less upon any particular socioeconomic base or setting, and much more upon political characteristics. When the term is applied to devices of direct democracy like the referendum, to mobilization of mass passions, to idealizations of the man in the street, or to politicians' attempts to hold together shaky coalitions in the name of "the people," what those who talk of "populism" have in mind is a particular kind of political phenomenon where the tensions between the elite and the grass roots loom large.

It is possible, then, to distinguish between a broadly agrarian sociological focus on populism and a broadly political one, and the different emphases produce different lists of populist phenomena, and different views about what is essential to populism.

We must not exaggerate this distinction. For one thing,

there is no single, unified concept of either agrarian or political populism, but instead highly controversial differences within each broad category. Also, the distinction is far from watertight. After all, the paradigm case of populism for American scholars, the People's Party, can be seen both as an agrarian uprising traceable to a particular socioeconomic situation, and as a classic grass-roots revolt against the elite.

A second source of confusion is equally important. We have been talking about the difference between an agrarian "focus" and a more political "focus" on populism, instead of simply distinguishing between different types of populist movement, and this is not simply academic circumlocution. We need to remind ourselves of the role of analysts and commentators in identifying and labeling populist movements. When we set out to clarify the notion of populism, we are not simply faced with a pile of diverse movements out there in the real world waiting to be sorted into categories. How these movements have been interpreted, whether they are counted as "populist," and what the term means when applied to them—these matters are not determined solely by the features of the movements themselves, but also by the attitudes of the intellectual community that has been interpreting them.

This is, of course, a cliché: pure empiricism is never possible, least of all in the study of society. Historians do not find the Renaissance or the Industrial Revolution lying about with neat outlines waiting for their description: they must construct such concepts, and therefore force their interpretations upon their data even as they collect it. The same applies to sociologists studying classes and political scientists examining political systems. But this familiar general point has a special relevance to the case of populism, simply because one of the recurrent themes in this field concerns the relations between the populace and the elite, including the intellectual elite to which academics belong.

It is always hard for the social scientist to achieve his aim of being the detached, disinterested observer and analyst of events, and there are special difficulties in the case of movements that are hostile to intellectuals, as so many of the movements generally known as populist have been. Interpretations of populism have therefore been deeply influenced by the fears of some intellectuals who have dreaded the grass roots and the appalling things that might crawl out of them, and by the idealism of others who have exalted the common man and his simple virtues. Even those academic commentators less directly involved with populism have been affected by populistic upsurges in democratic states, where the views of ordinary people, if articulated, often turn out to be contrary to the liberal and progressive biases of intellectuals.[12]

Because of the intimate relevance that populist themes have for intellectuals, scholarly interpretations of populism have often been controversial to the point where one can hardly recognize the same movement in different accounts. The U.S. Populists, for instance, have been seen by some scholars as backwoods neurotics with dangerously fascist tendencies, and by others as heroic fighters for democracy against overwhelming odds: rival interpretations which reveal a great deal about the scholars' views of their own political situation and of the relations between the elite and the masses.

It follows that when the prevailing political outlook

in academic circles changes, interpretations of populism will also change, and with bewildering results. One of the reasons why the existing literature on populism is so baffling to the uninitiated is that it mirrors recent changes in outlook in Western universities, notably the immense swing from post–World War II distrust of the populace to post–1960s enthusiasm for participatory democracy. Interpretations of the more political aspects of populism are obviously most immediately affected, but portrayals of agrarian populist movements also show clear signs of the changing academic climate.

The implication of this symbiosis between populist phenomena and their intellectual interpreters is that a study of populism seeking to clarify the confusions that surround the subject cannot confine itself to looking at the actual movements generally described as populist. It must also be constantly aware of the relation between populism and its interpreters, and must look at the intellectual categories and the changes in the academic climate that have influenced estimates of "populism." For instance, we must look not only at populist dictatorships like that of Peron, but also at the "mass society" theories which have influenced judgments of the *Peronistas*; not only at reactionary populist outbreaks like the "white backlash," but at the relation of such grass-roots attitudes to more progressive views in intellectual circles; not only at populist devices like referendums, but also at intellectual idealizations of popular participation in politics.

The range and variety of movements lumped together under the general heading of populism make it clear that what we need is not a single essentialist definition, but rather a typology of populisms—one, moreover, which is capable of accommodating a wide range of different phenomena seen from different analytical viewpoints. Any scheme that we propose will inevitably be open to objection: nevertheless, we may be able to establish reasonably clear analytical categories, separate in theory even though they overlap in real life.

The classification suggested here rests upon the very broad distinction made earlier between "agrarian" and "political" populisms, with each group subdivided further. To anticipate, this yields seven types of populism as follows:

Agrarian Populisms

1. farmers' radicalism (e.g., the U.S. People's Party)
2. peasant movements (e.g., the East European Green Rising)
3. intellectual agrarian socialism (e.g., the *narodniki*)

Political Populisms

4. populist dictatorship (e.g., Peron)
5. populist democracy (i.e., calls for referendums and "participation")
6. reactionary populism (e.g., George Wallace and his followers)
7. politicians' populism (i.e., broad, nonideological coalition-building that draws on the unificatory appeal of "the people")

The justification for this classification must lie in the argument of this study as a whole. Since the types suggested are analytical constructs, real-life examples may well overlap several categories. This is true, for instance, of the familiar cases of U.S. Populism and Russian *narodnichestvo.* While we shall argue that these provide classic examples of two particular types of agrarian populism, they also overflow into other sections of our classification. Rather than confining ourselves within our typology immediately, therefore, we shall begin with two chapters providing brief introductions to these two movements, and then pause in Chapter 3 to discuss the problems of providing any general concept embracing both.

American and Russian populism were very different indeed: the fact that they share the same name is, in fact, accidental.[13] However, there have been frequent attempts to gather the two under one general concept of populism, particularly by scholars who have focused upon them as agrarian movements and identified populism in sociological terms. We shall therefore have to consider in more general terms the feasibility of establishing a coherent concept of agrarian populism. This becomes most plausible if we add to the Russian and American cases another group of movements that are also often thought of as populist: grass-roots peasant movements. Even with the peasants as a buffer and a link between the farmers and the intellectuals, however, we shall find that what we have is not *one* kind of agrarian populism but three characteristic types that overlap.

After Chapter 3 we shall turn away from the agrarian focus to consider populism in more specifically political terms. From this point on, the discussion becomes more relevant to modern Western societies, where there is now little room for agrarian movements, but plenty of scope for problematic relations between the populace and the elite. Consequently, the effects on "populism" of fashions in the intellectual community also become more obvious. Interpretations of populist dictatorships such as Peron's have been strongly influenced by intellectual antipopulism, while the topic of populist democracy (treated next) demands consideration not only of the practice of direct democracy, but also of the changes in theoretical views of democracy and populism which accompanied the recent vogue for "participation." As for the phenomena of reactionary populism, these can be understood only within the context of a political culture committed to democratic principles but riven by cleavages between the progressive culture of the elite and the reactionary instincts of the populace.

For our last subspecies, "politicians' populism," we turn from the agonizings of intellectuals to the manipulations of politicians, and consider the uses of populism as a political technique. Appeals to "the people" have an integrating and legitimating effect that can be immensely useful to campaigning politicians in a wide variety of political circumstances. Our final task will be to look back at our seven varieties of populism and to consider the interrelations between them and the extent to which they add up to a coherent area of political phenomena.

There are three obvious objections to which a book of this kind lies open. The first is that it is not comprehensive: many phenomena of populism are omitted altogether and many others are given cursory treatment. "What about the Levellers?" some readers will ask. "What about Gramsci?" "What about Australia and New Zealand?" The only possible defense is that, given the range of material interpreted as populism, nothing short of an encyclopedia could hope to cover it all. The second objection is that the book relies heavily upon secondary material and makes no claim to be based on empirical research. Our answer must be that, at present, the general usefulness of much of the specialist material available is impaired for want of the kind of conceptual clarification which this study aims to provide. Finally, it may be objected that the classification of types of populism offered here is arbitrary, since it would be possible in principle to invent an infinite number of alternative classifications. This is, of course, true. We must simply hope that the scheme suggested here will prove useful, if only in stimulating someone else to provide a better one.

# 1. *Populism in the United States*

What you farmers need to do is to raise less corn and more hell.—*Attributed to Mrs. Mary Elizabeth Lease*[1]

## *THE SETTING*

In the last decade of the nineteenth century a radical populist movement appeared with startling suddenness in the United States, lasted long enough to give the American political establishment a severe shock, and then faded away as quickly as it had come. The People's Party held its first national nominating convention at Omaha in July 1892. There they adopted a radical platform which contained demands ranging from government ownership of railroads to popular referendums and from monetary inflation to the banning of strikebreakers. The Populist candidate in the 1892 Presidential election, James Weaver, polled over one million votes. In the next Presidential election, however, the established parties fought back. The Democrats divided the People's Party by adopting some of their measures and nominating a semipopulist candidate, William Jennings Bryan, while the Republicans put on a massively financed campaign which defeated Bryan and, with him, hopes of a Populist victory. Support for the movement, which quickly flickered out, had been sectional, coming from Southern and Western states and overwhelmingly from farmers.

The modern reader's first reaction to American Populism is likely to be surprise that farmers should have been capable of so much political radicalism. Peasant unrest does not surprise us in this way: that villagers in Russia or Rumania or Mexico should have revolted against centuries of oppression may seem quite comprehensible. But commercial farmers in a democratic society taking to radical politics, allying themselves with strikers and tramps, and demanding "socialistic" extensions of governmental control, may seem positively bizarre. So much so, indeed, that (as we shall see later) some interpreters of American Populism have sought to explain it as an irrational phenomenon produced by a variety of dark bucolic urges. A closer look at the origins of the Populist movement, however, will make the farmers' actions seem considerably less baffling.

Nineteenth-century Americans were citizens of a self-consciously democratic state and heirs of a culture that stressed independence, self-help, and the ability of a man (or at any rate a white man) to get on in the world by enterprise and effort. In the years after the Civil War, however, farmers in the West and South increasingly found that experience contradicted these expectations. Members of the sovereign people they might be, but they nevertheless felt impotent before powers that seemed to them to have no right to control their lives.

Some of the most imposing of these powers, particularly in the West, were the railroad corporations. As

defenders of the railroads pointed out, farmers had reason to be grateful to them, for it was railroad building
(aided by the grant of vast tracts of government land to
the railroad companies) that had made possible the rapid
opening up of the American West. The railroads had
encouraged settlement by providing easy access to new
areas and by running advertising campaigns that recruited
settlers from far and wide.[2] Many of the farmers, however, took a more ambivalent view of this corporate fairy
godmother. The settlers were utterly dependent on the
railroad to bring them equipment and supplies and to
take their grain to market, so that the companies, having
captive customers, naturally charged monopoly rates.
Western freight charges were sometimes four times as
high as the rate for the same distance in the East.[3] Furthermore, many railroads in the wheat country refused to
quote rates for carrying grain to cities close to the farmer,
insisting, for instance, that the seller who wished to send
his crop to Minneapolis must pay the full "transit" rate
through to Chicago or Milwaukee. Railroads, in alliance
with elevator companies, refused to supply freight cars
for small quantities of grain, or made the small farmer
wait while the market was flooded and the price dropped.
"Equality before the law," wrote one critic, "is a canon
of political liberty; equality before the railways should
become the canon of industrial liberty."[4]

The farmers' impotent fury at the power of the railroad
corporations was increased by the latter's domination of
Western state politics. Railroad managers took care to
keep control of state legislatures and to ensure by bribery
and corruption that their interests would be safeguarded.

One of the commonest means was the liberal issue of free travel passes to public officials, editors of newspapers, and other persons of influence, but there were even more blatant examples of corruption, like the "oil rooms" set up in Lincoln, Nebraska, when the state legislature was in session: "Run by lawyers and other lobbyists for railroads, these rooms were for the purpose of 'oiling' legislators to vote correctly on pending legislation in which railroads were interested."[5] In the circumstances, bitterness against the railroad companies was not surprising, and neither was the Populist conviction, which gained strength as the companies combined into ever more gigantic corporations, that the only adequate solution lay in government control.

If the farmer's powerlessness before the local railroad company became apparent every harvest time, his subjection to creditors was a perpetual nightmare. Settlers on new land in the West needed capital for machinery, fencing, and seed grain, and they mortgaged their land to get it. As production rose, however, farm prices dropped, and the farmer found himself in a cleft stick. If the weather was favorable and the crop abundant, the market was glutted and prices were low; whereas in the years of drought on the frontier after 1887, the farmers saw their corn shriveled by burning winds or smothered by dust storms. Either way, however hard he worked, the farmer could not keep himself from falling more and more uncontrollably into debt. To make matters worse, many had borrowed recklessly to get in on the boom in Western lands that followed from railway building. Thousands loaded themselves with debt, assuming that land prices would continue to rise around mushrooming settlements like Beatrice, Nebraska, where a real estate firm's slogan read:

> Beatrice is not dead or dying,
> Real estate is simply flying,
> He who buys today is wise,
> For Beatrice dirt is on the rise.[6]

The inevitable crash, started by the droughts which sent settlers in their covered wagons streaming back toward the East, brought land prices tumbling down and left farmers with nothing but their mortgages.

To find the worst examples of the powerlessness of the debtor before his creditor, however, one must look at the Southern states and at farmers caught in the grip of the "crop lien" system.[7] The upheaval of the Civil War had left behind a mass of small farmers, both white and black, who were nominal landowners or share-cropping tenants, but often in a state of desperate poverty. The only source of credit available to them was the local storekeeper or "furnishing merchant," who would let them have implements, fertilizers, and provisions on credit—but only at the cost of mortgaging their crop in advance. This meant that the farmer could buy only from the merchant who held this lien on his crop, at whatever prices the merchant chose to ask. He could buy only what the merchant would let him have, and if at harvest time, as often happened, the price his crop brought in was not enough to clear the merchant's account, his only way of providing for himself and his family was to mortgage the next year's crop before it was even planted. The farmer was in no position to

complain of the merchant's high prices or to contest the
merchant's accounts; nor could he even choose what crop
to grow, for the merchant insisted that it should be cotton, which was always salable, and not corn or potatoes
which the farmer might eat himself. As a result, the many
small farmers who had been tempted into cotton-growing
by high prices after the Civil War were unable to switch
to more suitable crops as the price of cotton sank lower
and lower.[8] A recent historian describes the constant
humiliation the system inflicted upon the farmer every
time he went shopping: "The farmer, his eyes downcast
and his hat . . . in his hand, approached the merchant
with a list of his needs. The man behind the counter con-
sulted a ledger, and after a mumbled exchange, moved to
his shelves to select the goods that would satisfy at least a
part of his customer's wants. Rarely did the farmer receive the range of items or even the quantity of one item
he had requested."[9]

Indebtedness and the experience of subjection to the
creditor which it entailed were the regular experience of
Southern and Western farmers in the latter half of the
nineteenth century. Indebtedness is also a common experience among the masses in modern industrial societies
who buy their homes through mortgages and most of their
household goods by hire-purchase. But the modern execu-
tive who takes on such financial commitments is aided by
inflation and rising money incomes: in real terms, his
debts decline in value with every passing year, whether
he pays them off or not. The opposite was the case with
the debt-ridden farmers who formed the backbone of the
Populist movement. Return to the gold standard after the

Civil War had caused a contraction in the money supply which forced prices down and increased the value of the dollar. Consequently, while the farmer's debt was worth more to his creditors, paying the interest on it required more and more bushels of wheat or bales of cotton.

Between the Civil War and the heyday of Populism in the 1890s, the money question periodically emerged as a political issue. There were, roughly speaking, three distinct views of the subject, those of the Greenbackers, Goldbugs, and Silverites, although all kinds of combinations and qualifications were possible. Greenbackers, called after the inflationary paper money of the war years, maintained that since gold and silver have no intrinsic value, currency derives its value simply from official recognition and need not be tied to any metallic standard. They demanded a paper currency in sufficient supply to cater for population growth and commercial expansion. The Populist Ignatius Donnelly later devised a vivid metaphor to describe the effects of lack of money in an expanding economy: "Take a child a few years old; let a blacksmith weld around his waist an iron band. At first it causes him little inconvenience. He plays. As he grows older it becomes tighter; it causes him pain; he scarcely knows what ails him. He still grows. All his internal organs are cramped and displaced. He grows still larger; he has the head, shoulders and limbs of a man and the waist of a child. He is a monstrosity. He dies."[10]

Most of those who debated the currency issue, however, were "hard money" men, distrustful of paper not secured by precious metal. The question was, however, what precious metal should form the basis of the country's money? Should it be gold alone, or silver equally with gold? From 1792 until 1873 the United States had been officially bimetallic, with gold and silver dollars having equal standing as legal tender. It happened, however, that by the mid-century silver had become scarce and was fetching more in the bullion markets than its official worth in coin, with the result that the silver dollar had virtually gone out of circulation. Since most of the world's major trading nations were in the process of adopting the gold standard, this situation suited American financial leaders very well, and the demonetizing of silver was confirmed by a currency measure that passed Congress in 1873.

At the time, since silver dollars were not in any case in common use, this esoteric measure passed virtually unnoticed. Before long, however, it was to become infamous in silverite demonology as "the Crime of '73," supposedly perpetrated upon the American people by a cabal of English, Jewish, and Wall Street bankers. For no sooner had the measure gone through than a boom in Western silver mining increased the supply and reduced the price of silver. It would have been feasible once again to coin silver at the old ratio with gold, and to do so would have expanded the currency and helped the nation's debtors as well as benefited the inhabitants of the Western mining territories. This was blocked, however, by financial experts who had their eyes on international trade and who feared that if the United States were to adopt a bimetallic currency once more, cheap silver would drive out gold, leaving the country unable to meet her obligations to gold standard nations such as Britain.[11]

After considerable controversy in the 1870s over the position of silver, a compromise was reached which did not satisfy any of the parties but did something to defuse the silver issue for the time being. The Bland-Allison Act, passed in 1878 over a Presidential veto, made silver legal tender once more and authorized the coinage of a certain number of silver dollars. The amount to be coined was too low, however, to create the inflation hoped for by debtors and dreaded by creditors. Meanwhile the silver grievance rumbled on, to contribute a plank to the Populist platform and eventually, in 1896, to swamp the rest of it.

From the 1870s on, the themes that were to come together in Populism were finding various means of expression. Farmers were first organized by the Grange, founded primarily as a social and educational organization, but which nevertheless articulated some of the farmers' grievances, particularly against the railroads. Under Granger pressure, legislatures in some of the Western states made attempts to regulate the activities of the railroads, though without a great deal of success.[12] To find the true seedbed of Populism, however, we must turn to the Alliance movement.

## THE RISE OF THE FARMERS' ALLIANCE

The origins of a grass-roots movement are, in the nature of things, difficult to locate precisely. Nevertheless, historians have traced the beginnings of Populism to Texas, meeting place of the West and South, where in the early 1880s a Farmers' Alliance grew up, mobilized by lecturers who traveled around speaking to farmers.[13] The message they carried was that "the farmers of this country have labored, and others have made the laws," with the result that "the non-producer has thrived while the producer has grown poor."[14] The answer, proclaimed the lecturers, lay in combination. In unity was strength: if the farmers joined in cooperatives for buying and selling, they would be able to stand up to their creditors. The cooperative crusade spread like wildfire across the South and West, bringing to desperate farmers the hope expressed by a Georgian who wrote to the Alliance journal: "We are going to get out of debt and be free and independent people once more. Mr. Editor, we Georgia people are in earnest about this thing."[15]

The movement which sprang from Texas, and which later acquired the resounding title of the National Farmers' Alliance and Industrial Union, was not the only farmers' movement on the ground. There was, for instance, the flourishing Agricultural Wheel of Arkansas, with which the Alliance eventually negotiated a merger: and there was an independent Northern organization, also officially entitled the National Farmers' Alliance, which had been organized from Chicago by Milton George, editor of a farm journal there. The Southern Alliance, however, was by far the strongest, and it was within its fraternal organization that farmers first caught a heady glimpse of the power that might come from solidarity.

No doubt some of the exhilaration that sent Alliance membership soaring was generated by sheer community spirit and revivalist-style meetings,[16] but a more potent attraction was the vision of cooperation among producers to defeat the monopolists who controlled the market. The summit of Alliance efforts was reached in the Jute Bag Boycott of 1889, when the farmers took on a real live trust and won. A group of jute manufacturers had united to drive up the price of the bagging traditionally used for bales of cotton. Instead of paying the higher prices, members of the Alliance all across the South united to boycott jute and arranged to have cotton bagging manufactured instead. In Georgia the farmers' enthusiasm for the cause was symbolized by a double wedding of Alliance supporters at which both pairs of brides and grooms were dressed in cotton bagging.[17]

In spite of such moments of success, however, the history of the Alliance's attempts at cooperation is on the whole a melancholy record of enterprises begun with high hopes, sustained with great dedication[18] but doomed to ultimate failure. Often cooperative attempts at marketing crops or supplying fertilizers and machinery failed through the deliberate opposition of local merchants and bankers. The fact remains, nevertheless, that most collapsed because their financial basis was too shaky: their backers were simply too poor. The soundest and most longlasting were those which, like the South Carolina cooperative exchange, refused credit to members[19]; but these, clearly, were of no use to the innumerable farmers caught in the toils of the crop-lien system, who practically never saw cash from one year's end to another.

The nemesis which haunted more ambitious attempts to break out of the cycle of debt was illustrated by the disastrous history of the Texas Exchange, the brainchild of Charles Macune, who had emerged as leader of the

Alliance. The Exchange attempted not only to market the farmers' cotton on favorable terms, but also to provide the credit necessary to free debtors from their dependence upon the furnishing merchant. Unfortunately, the capital to do this was simply not available and in 1889, after only two years of operation, the Exchange collapsed. This failure, and others equally disheartening, drove many farmers out of the Alliance, their hopes dashed.

Those who did not give up, however—and this included Macune and most of the early leaders of the Alliance—turned to a new way of thinking. It was becoming clear that the farmers were not strong enough to tackle the problem of credit by themselves, any more than they could take on the railroads and win. But why should they not use their potential power as citizens and get the government to support them against the monopolists in charge of transport and money? Surely, with over a million members in the South and the support, by 1890, of two-fifths of the farmers of Kansas and the Dakotas, the Alliance must be able to exercise influence on a national scale.[20]

The attempt to make the government do for them what they could not do for themselves forced the farmers into politics and turned their movement into Populism. Going into politics, however, was not a simple matter. Some of the problems it was likely to present had long been obvious. The Texas Alliance had almost split in 1886 over differences between radical and "nonpartisan" groups,[21] while signs of the future divisiveness of the racial issue were already evident in the Alliance's ambiguous attitude toward black farmers. There was on the one hand some recognition that black and white farmers shared common economic interests, and a separate Colored Farmers' National Alliance had been organized under the wing of the white Alliance. At the same time, however, it was understood that it was out of the question for the Alliance actually to allow black members. If the Alliance were to involve itself in politics, then, it was going to run up instantly against the taboos and constraints of the South.[22]

By 1889, the potentialities and pitfalls of the emerging movement were both clearly visible. The Southern Alliance and its cooperative enterprises had spread all over the South and West, while the separate Northern Alliance was gaining strength farther north. When both of them held conventions simultaneously in St. Louis in December 1889, it was expected that they would unite into a single massive farmers' movement. Nor was the movement to be confined to farmers, for the Alliance men thought of themselves, in comprehensive Jacksonian terminology, as "producers." Even in the early days in Texas, Alliance men had sided with striking railway workers against the monopolistic railroad kings,[23] and the labor organization with which they had worked, the Knights of Labor, was also represented at St. Louis. Here, surely, was the basis for a grand coalition of farmers and laborers, South and West, the producers of America against the monopolists and financiers of the plutocratic East.

Although the St. Louis meeting presaged the emerging Populist movement, there were ominous signs. The Northern and Southern Alliances did not succeed in uniting, and although the representatives of Kansas and the Dakotas, where cooperative enterprises had gone furthest, came over to the Southern Alliance, sectional differences were evident. It was clear, however, that unity was going to be crucial, for the logic of the situation was pushing the Alliance men further toward political activity. At the St. Louis convention Charles Macune put forward the most radical scheme yet suggested for coping with the farmers' difficulties. This was the "subtreasury" plan, designed to provide cheap credit for the farmer and to enable him to hold back his crop instead of having to sell it at a rock-bottom price when the market was glutted. Macune proposed that in each of the agrarian states a government warehouse should be established to receive and store cotton, grain, etc., and to give the farmer in return, at a low rate of interest, a negotiable credit note.[24] The proposal was adopted by the Alliance and was even introduced into Congress,[25] but it was ignored by the country's legislators and ridiculed by journalists. It was becoming increasingly clear, in fact, that if the farmers were to achieve anything they would have to go into politics to an extent that most of them had not so far contemplated.

## THE PEOPLE'S PARTY

Going into politics, as the farmers of the Alliance soon learned, meant encountering two lions in the path. It meant, in the first place, running up against the sectional party loyalties of North and South. But even if this obvious hazard could be negotiated, it meant also that the locus and concerns of the farmers' movement would be changed. Control of the movement would pass inevitably from the farmers themselves to professional politicians, who would be less concerned with clear principles and grievances than with tactical alliances and compromises.[26]

While the tension between Populism and politics would loom large toward the end of the Populist saga, the immediate problem was the former one, sectional loyalties. Since the Civil War, politics had been drastically simplified along sectional lines, kept clear by exhortations at election time to "vote as you shot, boys!" Broadly speaking, the North (with the notable exception of the immigrant urban workers) was Republican and tended to regard Democrats as traitors, while in the South most whites were Democrats and Republicanism was for scalawags and blacks. In real life, of course, things were never as simple as that: for instance, the massive Democratic majorities of the "Solid South" rested partly upon bribed and coerced black voters, while the white hill farmers there, discontented with their local Bourbon oligarchies, sometimes broke Democratic ranks.[27] But although third parties occasionally managed to dent sectional loyalty even in the South, their members were never allowed to forget that Southern politics was a very serious business. Any breach in the hegemony of the white man's party brought back the specter of Reconstruction and blacks in power, with the result that (as Populists were to discover) a white opponent of the Democrats was liable to be regarded as an outcast and a criminal.

Since this was the background against which the Alliance farmers of the South and West were attempting to forge a new political movement, it is not surprising that they soon found themselves in trouble. Nevertheless, the élan of the farmers' eruption into politics in 1890 led many to believe that the impossible could be accomplished. Such were the political earthquakes in Kansas and parts of the South that only in retrospect did the warning signs become evident.

The most startling political advent of Populism was the campaign in Kansas in 1890. In spite of occasional bursts of third-party activity by Greenbackers and others, the state had long been controlled by a Republican Party which was more responsive to railroads than to farmers, and which kept the latter in line by recourse to the Civil War rhetoric of the "bloody shirt." By 1890, however, many Kansas farmers were in a mood to rebel against their traditional allegiance. In 1887, as drought scorched the crops, the speculative boom in Western land had collapsed. Between 1888 and 1892 half of the population of western Kansas, most of them only recently arrived, fled back to the East, while those who remained were left with poor crops, low farm prices, and terrifying mortgages.[28] In the fall of 1889 corn prices were so low that farmers were burning corn in their stoves. As a farm boy recalled: "Many a time have I warmed myself by the kitchen stove in which ears were burning briskly, popping and crackling in the jolliest fashion. And if, as we sat around such a fire watching the year's crop go up the chimney, the talk sometimes became bitter . . . who will wonder?"[29]

After futile efforts to gain recognition and redress for their grievances through the Republican Party, the Alliance farmers at last revolted. In March 1890 a meeting of County Alliance presidents resolved that in the coming elections "we will no longer divide on party lines and

will only cast our votes for candidates of the people, by
the people and for the people."[30] By midsummer, the
logic of their activities had carried the farmers into the
formation of a new party, the People's Party.[31]

The campaign in Kansas that summer generated enormous enthusiasm. Popular orators emerged from the grass
roots, including "Sockless Jerry" Simpson, whose sou-
briquet followed an exchange in which he had jeered at
a political opponent for his silk stockings and excessively
gentlemanly appearance, and had been accused in return
of wearing no socks at all. Many of the speakers were
women, like Mrs. Mary Elizabeth Lease, mother of four
and a fiery speaker: "Wall Street owns the country. It is
no longer a government of the people, by the people and
for the people, but a government of Wall Street, by Wall
Street and for Wall Street. The great common people of
this country are slaves, and monopoly is the master."[32]

But there was no shortage of Populist preachers. According to one historian: "The farmers, the country
merchants, the cattle-herders, they of the long chin-
whiskers, and they of the broad-brimmed hats and heavy
boots, had . . . heard the word and could preach the
gospel of Populism. . . . Women with skins tanned to
parchment by the hot winds, with bony hands of toil and
clad in faded calico, could talk in meeting, and could talk
straight to the point."[33]

The orators spoke to crowds of farmers who had jolted
for miles over rough tracks to join the processions of carts
with their banners, their brass bands, their floats with
girls knitting socks for "Sockless Jerry," and their Populist songs. The upshot of the campaign was a severe shock

for the Kansas Republican Party, as Alliance candidates
captured the state legislature and five of the seven Congressional seats, and a Populist senator, William Peffer,
was sent to Washington. The campaign was sustained by
the exhilaration of a genuinely grass-roots movement.
The "people" had emerged into politics, and one of the
constant themes of their meetings was hostility to professional politicians and their maneuverings.[34] The heady
vision of a national popular uprising against the elite was
perfectly expressed by one of the speakers at a July Fourth
gathering that summer: "I will tell you what you are going to see. . . . You will see arrayed on one side the
great magnates of the country, and Wall Street brokers,
and the plutocratic power; and on the other you will see
the people."[35] The extent of this revolt against traditional
politics was appropriately symbolized by the fact that the
speaker who so succinctly presented the Populist outlook,
Leonidas Polk, national president of the Farmers' Alliance, was a North Carolinian and former Confederate
soldier, a Southerner preaching Populism in the heart of
Republican territory.

While the Kansas farmers had been trying their
strength against the Republican politicians, Southern
Alliance men had not been idle. But as those who dreamed
of a national farmers' uprising were soon to be reminded,
politics was different in the South. Even in Kansas, many
a farmer must have wrestled with his old party loyalties
before deciding to vote for the People's Party: but the
ties holding voters to Republicanism in the North were as
nothing compared with the strength of Democracy in the
South. Since the end of Reconstruction, most Southern

states were virtually one-party states, so that the natural tactic for the insurgent Alliance men of 1890 was not to confront the taboos by forming a new People's Party, but simply to capture the Democracy from within. As one Alliance man saw the matter, "Being Democrats and in the majority, we took possession of the Democratic Party."[36] The organized farmers gained control of Democratic nominating conventions in several states and applied the "Alliance Yardstick" to candidates, supporting only those who backed their cause. The most dramatic results came in Georgia, where the governor, three-quarters of the senators, and four-fifths of the representatives were all pledged to the Alliance.[37]

When the Alliance held its annual convention at Ocala, Florida, in December 1890, its leaders were faced with the problems of their own success. The farmers had undoubtedly arrived in politics, but in ways that promised endless contradictions. In the South they had scored many successes within the Democratic Party, but just how solid were these successes? Would the Democratic politicians who had promised to uphold Alliance interests remember their promises when in office? And would the prosperous farmers who headed the Alliances in many states try to hold them to radical schemes like the subtreasury plan?[38] Even more serious, however, was the question of relations between Northern and Southern Alliance men. The farmers' representatives who had succeeded with their new People's Party in Kansas wished to convert their Southern colleagues to third-party activity: otherwise, they would be open to the charge in their home states of splitting the Republican vote and letting the Democrats in.[39] What, then, was the Alliance to do in the next Presidential election year, 1892? Was it or was it not to back a national People's Party? A split was avoided only by postponing the question to a conference to be held in February 1892, leaving the crucial battles to be fought locally in the intervening period.

Although a People's Party did emerge from the Alliance to fight the Presidential election of 1892, the path that led to its formation was a long and thorny one, and many of the farmers who had previously supported the Alliance fell by the wayside. Failures in the cooperative enterprises were in any case taking their toll of the membership, but the strains of breaking with old party loyalties alienated many more. It did not take long for Southern farmers to realize that most of the Democrats they had elected in 1890 would do nothing for them; but to leave the white man's party and split the Solid South was not a tactic to be undertaken lightly. Nevertheless, a surprising number of Alliance radicals brought themselves to do just that. Texas, the original home of the Alliance, formed a People's Party in 1891,[40] and (not without hesitation) took the dramatic step of including black members on equal terms.[41] There were soon vigorous People's Parties in Alabama, Georgia, and North Carolina as well.

Meanwhile, enthusiastic Northern third-party men had been busy, and the emergence of Populism on a national scale was consummated at the party's first nominating convention, held in Omaha in July 1892, when James Weaver was nominated as the Populist Presidential candidate and the Populist platform was established. Its concrete demands were prefaced by a ringing preamble written by Ignatius Donnelly, a reformer of long-standing and author of the radical novel, *Caesar's Column*. After describing the miserable condition to which the American people had been reduced by the power of plutocrats, the preamble declared: "We seek to restore the government of the Republic to the hands of 'the plain people' with whose class it originated."[42] In view of the need for action to remedy the sufferings of "the producing class," the Populists declared: "We believe that the powers of government—in other words, of the people—should be expanded (as in the case of the postal service) as rapidly and as far as the good sense of an intelligent people and the teachings of experience shall justify, to the end that oppression, injustice and poverty shall eventually cease in the land."

According to the Omaha platform, "wealth belongs to him who creates it. . . . The interests of rural and civic labor are the same; their enemies are identical." The Party called for a "safe, sound, and flexible" currency in increased supply to be advanced to the people at a low rate of interest by means of the subtreasury plan for storage of agricultural produce, and also for free coinage of silver. Their demands included a graduated income tax, government-established postal savings banks, and state ownership of railroads and telegraph and telephone systems. Land monopolized by railways and other corporations, or in the hands of aliens, should be reclaimed by the government for grant to genuine settlers. Appended to this formal platform were resolutions on a variety of other matters, including a demand for an effective secret ballot, restriction of immigrant labor, shorter working hours in industry, the banning of Pinkerton strikebreakers, direct election of U.S. senators, and the adoption of the initiative and referendum.

The People's Party entered the elections of 1892 with high hopes, but although their Presidential candidate, General Weaver, received over a million votes—a very creditable showing for a new third party—the results were disquieting. In the first place, Weaver had clearly failed to make much impression in the South. His war record with the Union army did not help, and perhaps if Leonidas Polk of North Carolina, head of the Southern Alliance, had lived long enough to head the ticket, instead of dying suddenly in 1892, more Southern Alliance men might have torn themselves away from the Democratic Party.

As it was, however, the People's Party evidently lacked the allegiance of many of the people, while those who did support it found themselves in contradictory positions. In Kansas, for instance, a Populist governor, L. D. Lewelling, and a Populist-dominated senate had been elected, but only at the price of an electoral alliance with the Democrats. This tactic of "fusion" generated much heat among Kansas Populists, many of whom had seen their movement partly as a protest against shady political deals,[43] and it was very hard to reconcile with what was happening in the South. For those radical and brave enough to come out for Populism below the Mason-Dixon line were engaged in warfare with the Democratic Party that far surpassed ordinary politics in bitterness. Southern Populists like Tom Watson of Georgia represented a threat to the established Democratic oligarchy: worse still, they threatened the bastion of white supremacy. When Populists argued that the interests of poor white and poor black farmers were the same, and when, more dramatically, Watson and his supporters saved a black Populist from a lynch mob,[44] they earned the implacable hostility of those who were determined to keep the blacks down at all costs. Although many small farmers in the South did support the Populist cause, their strength was never reflected in election results. The local bosses stopped at nothing: they bribed or intimidated voters, flooded the polls with illegal supporters brought in from the next county (so that in Tom Watson's own district the total recorded vote was double the number of qualified voters),[45] or, since the local officials were all Democrats, simply falsified the returns. As a result, the areas where Populism was strongest and most passionately supported never had many elected representatives. One Democratic paper in Louisiana stated the case with the utmost frankness: "It is the religious duty of Democrats to rob Populists and Republicans of their votes whenever the opportunity presents itself. . . . Rob them! You bet! What are we here for?"[46]

Some of the most effective electoral support for Populism came from the silver-mining states of the West. This was a mixed blessing, however. As time was to show, the silver states, miners and mine owners alike, were concerned with one overriding issue, free coinage of silver, and they fixed their eyes on this to the exclusion of the rest of the Omaha platform.

Populists might be disappointed and politicians unnerved by the results of the 1892 elections, but neither could doubt that the People's Party had arrived in politics. Having done so, however, where was it to go? Between then and the next Presidential election year, 1896, the Populists found themselves caught in the classic radical dilemma. Should they stick to their whole platform, recognizing that they had no immediate prospect of political success, and that to convert the nation to their beliefs must take many years? Or should they be willing to compromise, to give up some of their policies in order to attract allies who would give them a chance of power in the near future? Different elements in the party, ex-Republicans and ex-Democrats, professional politicians and grass-roots Alliance men, radicals and silverites, naturally gave very different answers. The tactical dilemma, upon the horns of which the People's Party eventually tore itself to pieces, was made more acute by events which strengthened the arguments on both sides of the question. These were the economic depression of 1893 and the enormously costly financial strategy to which the government resorted in order to maintain its gold reserves.

In many ways the crisis strengthened the radical argument that the interests of the people—that is, of the producers—were being sacrificed for the sake of orthodox financial policies that benefited none except bankers and plutocrats. Farm prices for cotton, corn, and wheat fell below the cost of production, driving more and more farmers into debt, foreclosure, and misery. Unemployment in the cities gave rise to armies of tramps, like those led to Washington in 1894 by the Populist Jacob Coxey. Coxey attempted to deliver an address to Congress "on

behalf of millions of toilers," and called for a program
of public works to provide employment, to be financed by
the issue of paper money. He declared in an oration before the Capitol, "We choose this place of assemblage
because it is the property of the people"—only to be
arrested for "walking on the grass."[47]

One of the few Populists in office, Governor Lewelling
of Kansas, expressed official sympathy with the unem-
ployed in what came to be known as his "Tramp Circular"
of 1893, addressed to the boards of police commissioners
in his state, in which he exhorted the police to stop har-
rassing vagrants, declaring, "Let simple poverty cease to
be a crime."[48]

During the bitterly fought industrial conflicts of the
depression years, such as the Pullman strike of 1894,
Populists supported the labor leaders and denounced
government action against them. For good measure, they
balanced their support for productive workers of all
descriptions by attacks on the heartless extravagance of
the rich. There was a description, for instance, in James
Weaver's book, *A Call to Action*, of a "swan dinner" cost-
ing ten thousand dollars given at Delmonico's in New
York, at which the centerpiece was a real lake thirty feet
long, with real swans swimming in it.[49] Evidently the
Populist view of politics as a struggle between the producers and the idle rich was sufficiently widely shared to
give some of the upper crust a fright: "In Indianapolis, a
ruche-collared lady measured the political situation and
went off to see the cathedrals of Europe. 'I am going to
spend my money,' she said, 'before those crazy people
take it.' "[50]

But the lady need not have worried. The radical alliance between rural and urban producers never came to much, partly through lack of response from the most powerful labor leaders of the time.[51] Meanwhile, a quite different alliance was becoming increasingly likely. For that same depression and that same goldbug strategy which appeared at first sight to support the rhetoric of the radical Populists also strengthened and united the silver lobby, and made elements within the Democratic Party more ready to respond to it.

Ever since the "Crime of '73," when silver had been demonetized, there had been pressure from the silver-mining states of the West for the restoration of a silver currency, and governments had periodically passed relief acts of a limited kind. One of these, the Sherman Silver Purchase Act of 1890, which required the government to buy 54 million ounces of silver a year, was repealed by President Cleveland and Congress at the height of the gold panic in 1893, after a Congressional battle in which the opposition was led by the Populist William Allen in the Senate and the Democrat William Jennings Bryan in the House.

Already in 1889 the silver-mine owners had founded the American Bimetallic League to press for free coinage of silver, and after the repeal of the Sherman Act they stepped up their agitation. On the silver payroll was a talented publicist named William Harvey, whose pamphlet, *Coin's Financial School*, published in 1894, was a brilliant tour de force of popularization. Harvey harnessed Populist sentiments to the cause of free silver, having his young "Professor Coin" argue, for instance,

that silver "was so much handled by the people and preferred by them, that it was called the people's money.
Gold was considered the money of the rich."[52]

Free silver was, of course, one of the many planks in
the Populists' Omaha platform, and was a version of inflationary money policy that many farmers found easier to
swallow than Greenback theories. Consequently, when
their candidates in Western states performed disappoint-
ingly in the elections of 1894, some influential Populists
began to argue in favor of dropping the party's more controversial policies and forming a common front with all
silverites, who were becoming particularly conspicuous
in the Democratic Party. This strategy appealed particularly to the officeholders in the party who were naturally
more concerned about the short-term objective of winning
the next election than were the rank and file.[53] From a
tactical point of view, however, it could reasonably be
argued that this was the most promising way toward the
formation of an effective reforming coalition.

More radical Populists fought hard against the strategy
of fusion, predicting (correctly) that it would destroy the
party:

O, come into my party, said the spider to the fly—
Then he sharpened up his pencil and winked the other eye.
The way into my party is across a single plank—
You can take it from your platform, the rest can go to—blank.[54]

The issue of whether or not to engage in tactical fusion
with the old parties was one that had continually confronted Populists at state level, and had been resolved in
various ways, with Southern Populists sometimes fusing

with Republicans, and Westerners with Democrats, while purists who called themselves "midroaders"[55] tried to avoid deals of any kind. Fusion at national level with Democrats was a much more difficult proposition. While it might seem eminently sensible to Westerners, it was anathema to Southern Populists. Men like Tom Watson of Georgia had created their party in bitter conflict with their local Democratic oligarchies, daring ostracism and violence to do so. It was not to be expected that they would take kindly to cooperating with their enemies for nothing more than free silver.

The whole problem came to a head in July 1896 when the Democratic Party, meeting in Chicago, unexpectedly nominated William Jennings Bryan as its Presidential candidate on a free silver platform. The Populist convention met in St. Louis immediately afterward to face an agonizing decision. For the Democrats had stolen the Populists' clothes. In the course of their fight to keep the South out of Populist hands, they had veered in a Populist direction. Not only had they adopted the free silver plank and added to their platform various Populist items such as support for an income tax and federal control of railways; above all, they had chosen a candidate of Populist style and sympathies. Bryan, later to become known as the Great Commoner, had a long record of cooperation with the People's Party. In the Presidential campaign of 1892, indeed, he had campaigned for Weaver rather than for Cleveland, the leader of his own party, while Weaver and Mrs. Lease had helped him in his campaign for Congress.[56] Himself the product of a Western rural background, sharing the evangelical Protestantism and faith in the common people that were strong elements in Populism, Bryan's rhetoric was indistinguishable from that of genuine members of the People's Party: "I am proud to have on my side in this campaign the support of those who call themselves the common people. If I had behind me the great trusts and combinations, I know that I would no sooner take my seat than they would demand that I use my power to rob the people on their behalf."[57]

Should the Populists support Bryan, too? But the Omaha platform, which was the clearest expression of Populist principles, contained a great deal besides free silver, while all that Populists distrusted about the Democratic Party was symbolized by Bryan's chosen running mate Arthur Sewall, an Eastern bank president and railway director—a plutocrat whose only redeeming feature was his support for silver.

After a bitter struggle the Populist convention arrived at an awkward solution, giving its Presidential nomination to Bryan but nominating Tom Watson for Vice-President instead of Sewall, in spite of Bryan's known lack of enthusiasm for such an arrangement. The resulting confusion and recriminations did nothing to help Bryan's campaign. Many Western Populists worked for him enthusiastically, but most Southerners balked at helping the Democrats who had so often robbed them of votes, while in Texas, the original home of Populism, intransigent midroaders threatened to vote for the Republican McKinley rather than compromise with the Democrats.[58]

Meanwhile, the Republicans fought a massively financed and unscrupulous campaign, in which the danger of support for Bryan among industrial workers was averted by tactics such as threatening to close down businesses and sack workers if he should win.[59] In the event Bryan lost the election, so that the Populists discovered that they had destroyed their party for nothing. Arguments about whether Populism was betrayed by its leaders have continued ever since.[60] Ironically, the years after 1896, when the remnants of the People's Party were limping into obscurity, saw a revival of economic prosperity, caused partly by the very thing Populists had been demanding— a rise in the volume of the currency. The cause, however, was neither free coinage of silver nor the issue of Greenbacks, but a sudden rise in gold production consequent upon the discoveries of new gold fields and new extraction processes.[61]

## POPULISM AND THE HISTORIANS

Interpretation of the U.S. Populist movement is deeply controversial. It is true, though trite, that each age rewrites its history to suit its preoccupations, and Populist historiography was dramatically affected by McCarthyism and the shock it gave to the American academic world.[62] The classic history of Populism, which held the field for many years, was John D. Hicks's generally sympathetic study, *The Populist Revolt*, which appeared in 1931.[63] Hicks interpreted Populism as a response to real agrarian grievances in the West and South, and maintained that although the movement failed, the Populists had been vindicated by history. Many of their policies, though too advanced for the 1890s, had been implemented since. Hicks gave the impression that the movement was a healthy political phenomenon, entitled to praise from the point of view of a more advanced age.

This sort of relaxed and rather patronizing attitude to the Populists became more difficult as American intellectuals reeled under the impact of mid-twentieth-century mass movements. Even before World War II, liberal democrats had been forced to recognize that totalitarian movements like Nazism and fascism could attract a great deal of popular support. But until the advent of Senator Joseph McCarthy such problems seemed, on the whole, rather distant. It was the reign of terror carried on by the Senator in the early 1950s, apparently with popular approval, that forced upon many American intellectuals a sense of acute separation between their own liberal cultural milieu and the gullible, intolerant masses.[64] This new fear of the masses generated new and hostile interpretations of Populism, which was now seen as a dangerously proto-fascist mass movement.[65]

The most influential revised version of Populism was that put forward in Richard Hofstadter's widely read book, *The Age of Reform*.[66] While conceding much good in the movement, Hofstadter chose to concentrate his attention on blemishes in the Populist outlook which he enumerated as "the idea of a golden age; the concept of natural harmonies; the dualistic version of social struggle; the conspiracy theory of history; and the doctrine of the primacy of money."[67] Populists, according to Hofstadter, were haunted, terrified people, left behind by industrialization, who seized eagerly upon the notion of a financial conspiracy as the explanation for their ills, and on free silver as the panacea to cure them. When their hopes of the People's Party were dashed, they were easily converted to the jingoistic nationalism of the nineties.

Hofstadter's unflattering picture of Populism seemed

to regard the movement as a kind of political neurosis, and to reduce the patients' statements and programs to symptoms unworthy of rational attention. His views, and those of other hostile critics, provoked sharp reactions from scholars more favorable to Populism. Some demonstrated that the Populists had not evinced irrational hostilities, and had an unusually liberal record on matters like racism.[68] Others pointed out that, far from harking back to the agrarian and antistate traditions of Jefferson and Jackson, Populist programs were radical if not socialist in their demands for government action. Norman Pollack argued, for instance,[69] that the Populists should be regarded as notable progressives, since they offered a critique of modern industrial society comparable with Marxism.

Much of the controversy has concerned itself with the question of whether Populism was "progressive" or "reactionary." One scholar states the issues thus:

> Was Populism on the whole a rational and forward-looking response to the end of the frontier and the rise of industrialism, thrusting crucial issues upon the reluctant major parties and advancing remedies that for the most part eventually won acceptance? Or was it a preposterous rustic mutiny infested with cranks and visionaries, looking back to a mythical golden (or silver) age of the Jackson era and offering only wild monetary schemes or scapegoats as the response to exaggerated evils?[70]

More recently the terms of debate have shifted, reflecting the changing preoccupations of a new generation of scholars. Belief in progress and fondness for irrationalist sociological explanations have simultaneously gone out of favor, while the participationist enthusiasms of the 1960s and 1970s have cast a new aura of dignity over grass-roots movements of the past. Some recent studies of American Populism show the effects of these new perspectives. Robert C. McMath, Jr.'s history of the Southern Alliance, *Populist Vanguard,* explicitly adopts the rationalist viewpoint of Mancur Olson in discussing the rise and fall of the Alliance,[71] while Peter H. Argersinger in *Populism and Politics* and Lawrence Goodwyn in *Democratic Promise* both focus on the contrast between the participatory grass-roots origins of Populism and the elite politicking in which it expired.

Goodwyn's interpretation is particularly significant because his book is a full-length study designed to supplant Hicks as the standard work on the subject. He claims that most accounts have followed Hicks in placing too much emphasis on the movement in Northern states such as Nebraska and on what he calls the "shadow movement" which emerged in that region. This Bryanite, silver-oriented faction was, he maintains, only the shadow of the real substance of Populism, which was concentrated in the South and in Kansas. The significance of this "real" Populism lay not in the activities of its leaders, not even in its official programs, but rather in the experience of democratic politics which ordinary farmers gained in their Alliances and cooperatives: "To describe the origins of Populism in one sentence, the cooperative movement recruited American farmers, and their subsequent experience within the cooperatives radically altered their political consciousness."[72] Participation in this "cooperative crusade" opened the farmers' eyes and altered their views.

It made them aware, for one thing, of the structure of economic power in American society. Goodwyn considered that there was nothing paranoid about the "conspiratorial tendencies" discovered by Hofstadter in Populist rhetoric. The farmers were quite right: financial power *was* becoming increasingly concentrated in the hands of those who headed the great new corporate monopolies. And when farmers found their cooperative schemes opposed or thwarted by banking or railroad interests, they discovered for themselves where power lay.

But those who participated in Alliances and cooperatives, those who trooped to Populist rallies and participated in Populist parades, also discovered something else. They discovered the self-respect and sense of power that can come from seeing oneself not just as a helpless individual, but as a citizen among others, with collective power to act:

> In its deepest meaning, Populism was . . . a cooperative movement that imparted a sense of self-worth to individual people and provided them with the instruments of self-education about the world they lived in. The movement gave them hope—a shared hope—that they were not impersonal victims of a gigantic industrial engine ruled by others but that they were, instead, people who could perform specific political acts of self-determination. . . . Populism was, at bottom, a movement of ordinary Americans to gain control over their own lives and futures, a massive democratic effort to gain that most central component of human freedom—dignity.[73]

According to this interpretation, the most significant feature of Populism was not an ideology or even a specific set of proposals, but an *experience* of democratic participation in politics. This movement, springing from the grass roots and gradually articulating a political world view, brought to thousands of ordinary Americans the sense that they, "the plain people," were capable of acting together to free themselves from the bonds they felt so oppressively in their individual lives. As they acted in this way their view of the world changed, they acquired a different sense of what was possible and what was or was not inevitable.

It is clear that, like its rivals, Goodwyn's interpretation has a political ax to grind. His account of Populism as the grass-roots rediscovery of what democracy means stands at the opposite end of the spectrum from those accounts dating from the McCarthy era which presented it as a proto-fascist rising of the irrational and dangerous masses. As we shall constantly have occasion to note, the same range of variation occurs in the interpretation of populism in general, not just of the American case.

## THE POPULIST OUTLOOK

Let us now sum up the U.S. Populists' outlook and comment on it. The first point to be stressed is that the choice of "the People's Party" as a label was not accidental. The heart of the Populist case was their claim to speak for the people, the "plain people" of America. Over and over again they presented their campaign as a struggle between the mass of the people on one side and a few millionaires on the other—or, as one of Governor Lewelling's constituents put it, "the plutocrats, the aristocrats and all the other rats."[74]

The Populists did not think of their movement as a

rural or sectional interest group, but as an uprising of all honest working people. They constantly expressed their sympathy with industrial workers during the bitter labor disputes of the time, and sometimes gave practical support, like the provisions which Kansas farmers sent to the locked-out workers at Andrew Carnegie's Homestead plant.[75] They liked to point out the impossibility of earning a plutocrat's fortune by honest labor. One Populist calculated that even if a working man could manage to save ten cents from his earnings every day without fail, it would take him 3,750,000 years to accumulate the wealth of John D. Rockefeller, the oil magnate.[76] In their rhetoric, society is divided into two unequal parts, the honest toilers and the parasites who rob them of their reward:

> There are ninety and nine who live and die
>   In want, and hunger, and cold,
> That one may live in luxury,
>   And be wrapped in a silken fold.
> The ninety and nine in hovels bare,
> The one in a palace with riches rare.[77]

Although the demonic figures of millionaires brood over their rhetoric, Populists always stressed that the impersonal monetary system, rather than any individual villain, was their real oppressor. Isolated farmers and workers were helpless in the face of this system: but by uniting and wielding political power, they believed they could change it. One of the most striking features of their outlook was their faith in the potentialities of a "people's government" and their willingness to contemplate great increases in federal power. A prominent Kansas Populist, Frank Doster, revealed the workings of the Populist mind when he called for monopolistic enterprises such as the railroads to be taken over by "the government, that is, the people."[78] "Cyclone" Davis, the Texas lecturer whose speciality it was to ascend the platform loaded down with the works of Jefferson, managed by ingenious reinterpretation to find support for increased governmental activity even in his patron saint.[79] To alarmed observers, their ideas seemed nothing short of socialism.

The claim to speak for the whole people, millionaires apart; the stress on oppression by a system; and the faith in a "people's government," using "socialistic" measures, to put things right—these are the most pervasive features of American Populist ideology. Let us consider now some of the implications of these ideas.

One of Tom Watson's editorials in the *People's Party Paper*, published in Atlanta in 1892, gives away some of the fundamental ambiguity of Populism. Watson portrays the coming election as a contest between Democracy and Plutocracy: "And on which side shall you be found who read these lines? Will you stand with the people, within the party of the people, by the side of the other wealth producers of the nation—from city and country?"[80] This is stirring stuff, but its echoes of epic battles against the forces of darkness seem somewhat misplaced. After all, if the People's Party really *did* represent the bulk of the American people as solidly and exclusively as Populists liked to claim, the result must be a foregone conclusion, with scarcely any need to exhort the party's followers to heroic choices. The hard fact is that the People's Party never did gain the support of anything approaching the whole people. Even in the West and South many stuck to their old sectional loyalties.

Recent historians have clarified the picture of which groups in the susceptible regions actually went Populist. In Kansas, not surprisingly, there was a high correlation between the proportion of farm mortgages in a county and the strength of the Populist upsurge in 1890,[81] while in Nebraska the typical Populist was, it seems, "a pietistic Protestant who lived on a farm in the central part of the State."[82] Robert McMath maintains that Southern farmers were most strongly disposed to radicalism in frontier or quasi-frontier regions; it was in the more recently settled upland areas of the older states that the Alliance was strongest.[83] Whether or not Alliance membership was translated into political Populism in the South was of course another matter, depending a great deal on local conditions and personalities. Lawrence Goodwyn suggests, however, that the most important variable was the extent to which farmers had participated in the cooperative movement.[84] In the East, and in the cities everywhere, Populism never did make much headway, while pure middle-of-the-road Populism was even less generally popular than the watered-down silverite version of 1896. Whether they liked it or not, Populists were a collection of minority groups, not "the people" itself.

Their rhetoric presented a picture of society divided not along ordinary lines of interest or class, but between workers and parasites. This was appealing, but entailed a host of snags. It was, for instance, difficult to apply to actual cases (millionaires apart). The Kansas Farmers' Alliance tried to use such a criterion in drawing up their rules for membership. They were prepared to admit any who "really worked"—a category which apparently included not only farmers, laborers, and mechanics but also doctors, preachers, and teachers. But they excluded those who "lived off the labor of others"—under which heading they included bankers, lawyers, speculators, peddlers, commission merchants, etc. Clearly, any such classification must run into impossible distinctions.

The Populist insistence that farmers and industrial workers had the same interests was fraught with similar problems, which were pointed out bluntly by Samuel Gompers, president of the American Federation of Labor: "To support the People's Party under the belief that it is a *labor* party is to act under misapprehension . . . composed, as the People's Party is, mainly of *employing* farmers . . . there must of necessity be a divergence of purposes, methods and interests."[85] Gompers was not, perhaps, entirely fair. Many Populists, on family farms with no hired labor, threatened with foreclosure and eviction, cannot have felt much like capitalists, and in some areas there were alliances between farmers and workers.[86] Nevertheless, it is true that the farmers were bound to have different interests from industrial workers in some crucial respects, with farm prices and the cost of food foremost among them. If the American Populists had succeeded in creating a coalition with organized labor, it might not have held together for long.

Above all, the Populist attempt to draw the significant line of division between workers and producers foundered upon sectional and ethnic hostilities. Although many Southern Populists, black and white, made heroic efforts to unite "the people" across racial lines against "the monopolies," prevailing taboos were too strong for them, and it is not altogether incomprehensible that Tom Watson, the Georgia Populist leader, should have declined into a racialist in his embittered later years.[87] As populists in other times and places have found, the definition of "the people" that carries most resonance as a rallying cry is very often an ethnic, not an economic one.

The combination of attempted alliances with labor and demands for government intervention in the economy naturally led to the Populists being charged with "social-ism." This is not, however, a very appropriate desig-nation. It is true that there were some in the movement to whom the label really could be applied, notably Henry Demarest Lloyd, the radical intellectual who was one of the main forces behind the attempt in 1894 to capture Chicago with a Populist-labor alliance.[88] Even in Lloyd's case, however, the ideological stress was less upon the collectivist charms of a socialist utopia than on the fa-miliar Populist battle between people and plutocrats. His celebrated book, *Wealth against Commonwealth*, first published in 1894, is a massively documented muckraking account of the evil practices of monopolist corporations, especially Standard Oil.[89]

Where the rank and file of the movement were con-cerned, the scope and limits of their "socialism" were quite clear. They grew staples—wheat or cotton—for international markets, and their dependence upon a market over which they had no control perfectly explains their intense concern with monetary systems, transport, and government regulation. Inextricably involved in a vast commercial network, they thought of a people's government as the only agency strong enough to defend their interests. Collectivism on any more extensive scale did not appeal to them, however. Their ideal was still the independent proprietor, hard-working but secure on his farm. They desired a large measure of government action to protect this independent producer, but not to replace him with any more large-scale and collective system of production.

It is interesting to look at the Populist utopia with which Ignatius Donnelly concluded his apocalyptic novel, *Caesar's Column.* After the entire civilized world has been destroyed in the last war between the plutocrats and the people, a remnant survive, walled up in an idyllic republic in the mountains of Uganda. The government there owns all the roads, rails, mines, and telegraph, provides education, health care, and entertainment ("concerts and lectures"), settles wages and prevents usury—a fairly socialistic program. However, Donnelly emphasizes that land and business remain in private hands, subject only to upper limits to prevent the emergence of the plutocrats who had wrecked America.

The American Populists were not, therefore, socialist in their view of private property, although they showed a remarkable enthusiasm for action by the central government, provided that government were kept in the hands of the people. The devices they proposed to ensure this included direct election of senators by the people, an effective secret ballot, and the use of popular initiatives and referendums. Once these were in operation, there would be no need to restrict unduly the powers of government. To quote the self-styled Jeffersonian, Cyclone Davis: "There is a proper limit at which government should stop. But in a government which is organized as ours, by the people for their own good, there need be no fear so long as the power is kept in the hands of the people."[90]

Although the Populist movement was of course both an economic and a political phenomenon, it is possible to distinguish between two different aspects of it which correspond to the two basic perspectives adopted by analysts of populism in general. It was, on the one hand, a particular kind of agrarian movement with a rather specific socioeconomic base and a distinctive program: it was, in fact, a classic case of farmers' radicalism.[91] Besides being a socioeconomic phenomenon, however, Populism also had a prominent political aspect as a grass-roots revolt against the elite of plutocrats, politicians, and experts. Populists were passionately democratic, evincing a Jacksonian faith in the common man and a stress on popular control over government. As we have seen, interpretations of the movement have been strongly colored by reactions in intellectual circles to this kind of radical democracy.

We shall return later to these political aspects of populism and the problems to which the relation between people and elite gives rise. For the moment, however, let us turn to another classic populist movement that was also, in its very different way, a form of agrarian radicalism: Russian revolutionary populism. As we shall see, *narodnichestvo* also raised questions about the relation between the people and the elite, though from an entirely different angle.

# 2. *Russian Populism*

Before each revolutionary socialist stands the practical demand: sacrifice yourself, sacrifice everything in order to create the kingdom of justice: sacrifice yourself, sacrifice everything in order to bring its existence one day nearer.—*Lavrov*[1]

Go to the people, there is your way, your life, your learning. . . . Young men of education must become not the people's benefactors, not its dictators and guides, but merely a lever for the people to free itself, the unifier of the people's own energies and forces. To gain the ability and right to serve the cause, youth must submerge itself and drown in the people.—*Bakunin*[2]

## THE SETTING

The notion of "the people" as distinct from a collection of individuals or groups is one of those collective ideas that make sense only through an implied contrast with something else. In the United States, for instance, while cooperation and political activity might generate a feeling of solidarity among those who took part in them, it was above all the contrast between the Eastern strongholds of politicians and plutocrats and the peripheral regions of the South and West that made "the people" effective as a rallying cry. This kind of contrast between the people and the elite may seem salient not only from below but from above: "the people" can appear as a solid, homogeneous group from the viewpoint of a privileged minority. Throughout history, indeed, aristocrats have contrasted themselves with "the people" in this way and have often felt contemptuous or suspicious of the dark, undifferentiated mass they perceived. Occasionally, however, members of such a privileged elite have turned against their situation and, while still seeing "the people" from outside, have idealized them, exalted their virtues and dedicated themselves to their interests. Nowhere has this romantic populism been taken further than among the radical intelligentsia of nineteenth-century Russia.

The essential feature of Russian populism is that it was in no sense a movement of "the people," that is, of the peasantry who made up the overwhelming majority of Russia's vast population. The populists dedicated themselves to the welfare of the people; their aim was an ideal society built upon peasant traditions; they hoped and agitated for a popular revolution. But prior to World War I, they never had popular support. Russian populism was the movement of a tiny group of radical intellectuals, alienated from the regime but also from the people on to whom they projected their hopes and dreams. It is not surprising that the history of so romantically idealistic a movement should be, to a certain extent, a tragicomedy of illusions and failures. Nevertheless, the Russian populists remain interesting not only as classic examples of the characteristic populism of intellectuals, but also for the clarity with which they faced genuine and continuing dilemmas, notably the problem of relations between radical intellectuals and the masses, and problems of economic and social development in backward countries.

Who were the Russian populists? The proper use of the term *narodnichestvo* and the question of who should or should not be regarded as a populist are matters of considerable scholarly dispute.[3] The problem cannot be solved by producing a simple, overt criterion of Russian populism, such as membership in a party. In the political atmosphere of the Tsarist regime, political parties with open organization and recruitment were out of the question. Radical activities could be carried on only in small, conspiratorial circles of personal friends, and these revolutionary groups were short-lived, constantly forming, splitting, being crushed by the authorities, and reemerging. As Richard Pipes has pointed out, the Russian intelligentsia themselves used the term *narodnik* or "populist" in a narrowly specific sense, to refer to a particular group, active in the late 1870s, who geared their revolutionary activity to the felt needs of the people rather than to what the intelligentsia believed to be their long-term interests. However, "populism" is commonly used in a range of much wider senses, often to refer to the entire non-Marxist Russian revolutionary movement from the pioneer writings of Alexander Herzen to the 1890s and beyond. We shall adopt this wider sense as a preliminary strategy, although we shall pay particular attention to the self-styled *narodniki* of the 1870s.

Russian society in the nineteenth century was torn by a fundamental contradiction. In spite of the attempts of Peter the Great and his successors to assimilate their country to the rest of Europe, mid-century Russia seemed more backward than ever. At a time when even the more reactionary regimes farther West felt it necessary to pay lip service to constitutional forms and due process of law, the Russian government remained a byword for autocratic tyranny. Meanwhile, in spite of occasional improvements and regional variations,[4] the vast rural population labored in a condition of misery and subjection unparalleled in Europe. Until 1861 they remained serfs, chattels without rights, quite at the mercy of their owners, who could have them flogged, send them into the army for life, tell them whom to marry, and generally tyrannize over them.

When emancipation came it proved a grave disappointment for many, for although the peasants were no longer serfs, they found that the land which they farmed, to which they believed they had a sacred right, was not to be theirs without the payment of high redemption fees. The imperial government, uneasily aware of the disappointment likely to be engendered by this half-measure, prepared for emancipation not only by organizing "spontaneous" demonstrations of gratitude to the Tsar-Liberator, but also by laying in extra supplies of flogging sticks—a prudent precaution, as it turned out, for there were two thousand separate peasant disturbances in the next two years.[5] As the suppression of these outbreaks demonstrated, the Tsarist military-bureaucratic machine was well able to cope with popular expressions of discontent. But between the autocratic state on the one hand and the peasants on the other stood a third force, a tiny but vitally important educated elite, increasingly oriented toward Western modes of thought that were utterly at odds with Russian conditions.[6]

The gap between the Westernized social elite and the system in which they had to live first manifested itself in the Decembrist Revolt of 1825. This attempted coup by liberal aristocratic officers baffled the military governor of Moscow, who wrote: "I can understand the French bourgeois bringing about the Revolution to get rights, but how am I to comprehend the Russian nobleman making a revolution to lose them?"[7] Although this first revolutionary attempt was easily suppressed, to be followed by a long period of intense political repression, the Russian government throughout the nineteenth century was faced increasingly often with the same problem of revolutionary attempts that did not come from the masses themselves, but from a minority of the comparatively privileged who were appalled by the injustice of their society and unable to bear their guilt at benefiting from it.

Many Russian intellectuals perceived the faults of their own country in the light of Western democratic and socialist ideals. Few of them, however, thought simply of setting out to catch up with the West. On the contrary, contact with these ideals led many to reject Western institutions, and to construct an image of a specifically Russian future which would be as much superior to France or England as it was to the Russia they knew. In doing so, the radicals drew on the ideas of the conservative Slavophiles.[8]

During the reign of Nicholas I a number of Slavophile writers and thinkers had provided a defense of Russian traditions and institutions against the Western-oriented criticisms which had fueled the Decembrist rising. They maintained that where Western society was atomized and rationalistic, Russian traditions preserved social harmony and spiritual wholeness. They drew a contrast, flattering to the national ego, between the atmosphere and practices of the Russian village and the competitive individualism of Western urban life. In particular, they praised the *obshchina*, the peasant commune.[9] According to traditional practice in much of Russia, peasant land was held not by the individual but by the commune, and although it was cultivated in separate strips by the various households, it was periodically repartitioned in order to maintain a rough equality in the village.

The Slavophiles stressed the cooperation and fraternity within the commune, which cared for its weaker members and managed its own affairs in an amicable manner. They deplored the military and bureaucratic expansion of the Russian state, which they saw as an alien import, an outcome of Peter's misguided attempt to Westernize Russia. Instead they emphasized what seemed to them the home-grown virtues of the Russian people, their communal instincts as well as their religious faith. These writers were conservatives, defending autocracy, orthodoxy, and tradition, but by one of the dialectical twists so characteristic of the history of ideas, their theories were turned into building blocks for a new and specifically Russian form of radicalism. The transformation was accomplished by Alexander Herzen.[10]

## THE FORERUNNERS OF POPULISM

Herzen, the illegitimate son of an aristocratic serf-owner, was born in 1812, and grew up during the repressive reign of Nicholas I. A youthful attraction to radical ideals was hardened by his experience of the police state. In 1834 he was arrested and subjected to five years of internal exile as a minor clerk in the bureaucracy, on the strength of a tenuous link with persons suspected of singing "seditious songs." Herzen's encounters with the Tsarist authorities illustrate the seesaw between privilege and humiliation that drove so many from the Russian upper classes into radicalism. He languished for several years in a remote corner of the provincial administration until his father's influence at court procured him not only a pardon but promotion within the bureaucratic apparatus. Shortly after his return to Moscow, an incautious remark about the police in a private letter sent him into exile again, but this time his connections pulled strings in such a way that he found himself head of the department that supervised political exiles in the area, and thus in the preposterous position of having to countersign the quarterly reports on his own behavior submitted to St. Petersburg by the local police chief! He remained in exile until 1842, when he was allowed to live in Moscow under police surveillance and to join in the literary controversies raging between Westernizers and Slavophiles.

Herzen had already filled out his early radicalism by becoming a vague kind of socialist, having picked up ideas from the French writers of the time, the Saint-Simonians and Fourierists, Proudhon, and Louis Blanc. Accepting their denunciations of bourgeois and capitalist society, he could not adopt a simple Westernizing stance and desire that Russia should copy France or England. Instead, he gradually worked his way toward a synthesis of the fraternal ideals of Western socialism and the Slavophile vision of cooperation in the peasant commune. He came to believe that, although everything else about Russian society was deplorable, the saving exception of the commune could provide a basis upon which the Western ideal of socialism might be constructed.

In 1847 Herzen at last obtained a passport to leave Russia and departed for the West, never to return. But in spite of his relief at escaping into a freer atmosphere, his impressions of Europe paradoxically strengthened his conviction that the future of mankind lay with Russia. He drew frequent comparisons between his own time and the fall of Rome, with the bourgeois civilization of Western Europe playing the role of the Roman Empire and socialism that of Christianity, while the key role of the barbarians who would destroy and renew civilization was shared by the proletariat and the Russian people.[11]

When the revolutions of 1848 broke out with high hopes, only to end with defeat for the radicals all over Europe, Herzen was confirmed in his belief that the best hope for social regeneration lay with "young" Russia rather than with "old" Europe. Apart from the implied contrast between decadence and barbarism, his point in talking about the "youth" of Russia was that the very evils of Russian society made Russians of all classes less conservative than Western Europeans, simply because they had less to lose. In the West, almost all groups had some stake in the existing order, some traditions and loyalties which they would hesitate to risk in a social revolution. But Russia, said Herzen, had no past, in the sense that (with the exception of the protosocialist commune) there was nothing to be loyal to, no institution which had any command on the people's affections, no one except government functionaries who had a stake in society as it existed. Even the aristocracy were alienated from the system. His hope was that since the Tsarist state rested on force and force alone, the time would come when it would be overthrown and society reconstructed as a federation of self-governing peasant communes, themselves liberalized to provide more individual freedom.

In the early 1850s Herzen established a Free Russian Press in London, and from the early years of Alexander II's reign his journal *Kolokol* (The Bell) found its way into Russia. It was read avidly—even, so the rumor went, by the Emperor himself—and it made his writings an important influence upon his successors. Herzen cannot himself be called a populist—his outlook was too aristocratic for that; but he created the characteristic outlook of Russian populism:

> The people suffer much, their life is burdensome, they harbour deep hatreds, and feel passionately that there will soon be a change. . . . They are waiting not for ready-made works but for the revelation of what is secretly stirring in their spirits. They are not waiting for books but for apostles—men who combine faith, will, conviction and energy; men who will never divorce themselves from them; men who do not necessarily spring from them, but who act within them and with them, with a dedicated and steady faith. The man who feels himself to be so near the people that he has been virtually freed by them from the atmosphere of artificial civilisation; the man who has achieved the unity and intensity of which we are speaking —he will be able to speak to the people and must do so.[12]

The dedicated servants of the Russian people whom Herzen had so vividly invoked did not take long to appear. One of the features of the political thaw authorized

by Nicholas's successor, Alexander II, was a large increase
in the student population, including a number of intellectuals coming from nonaristocratic backgrounds—the
so-called *raznochintsy*. Few of these men were genuine
peasants; many were priests' sons, like the most notable
of them, Nicolas Chernyshevsky. Nevertheless, they were
certainly a step closer to the common people than the
writers of Herzen's generation, to whom they often
seemed deplorably plebeian.[13] Indeed, Herzen declared—
using his social superiority in a most unpopulist manner—
that they retained too many traits of the "servants' room,
the theological seminary and the barracks."[14]

What disturbed Herzen was Chernyshevsky's single-
minded political fanaticism, the unwelcome by-product
of unswerving devotion to the people. Chernyshevsky's
views on all subjects were unflinchingly radical. As a
literary critic he was prepared to maintain a utilitarian
theory of art which made literature entirely the servant
of political ends. He commented on a love story by Tur-
genev: "Take them away, these questions of love. They
are not for the reader of our times, who is occupied with
administration and improvement of the courts, financial
reforms, and liberation of the peasants."[15] He attacked
liberals who aimed at a constitution for Russia, on the
grounds that political liberties are useless to starving
peasants, and on one occasion went so far as to maintain
that Siberia was a more democratic country than England:
the vaunted rights of Englishmen meant nothing to starving
proletarians, who would have been better off as members
of a peasant commune in the backwoods of the Russian
empire.[16] This hostility to political reforms and liberal

half-measures was to become characteristic of the whole
Russian populist movement, with unfortunate results.

During the brief period around 1860 when Chernyshevsky was prominent as a writer for *The Contemporary*,
everything he wrote was geared toward his goal, the
welfare of the people. He did not idealize the peasants'
character, however, or credit them with any clear understanding of their own interests.[17] Before the emancipation
of the serfs, reformist writers often tried to strengthen
their case by portraying peasant society as a rural idyll,
but Chernyshevsky deplored such romanticism. Instead,
he praised the brutal realism of writers like Nicolas
Uspensky, whose fictional peasants have been described
as "brutish, base, alcoholic, ignorant and dull-witted."[18]
Chernyshevsky declared that Uspensky's willingness to
tell the unvarnished truth about the people was an indication of his sincere devotion to their cause: "Only a few
clear-sighted persons like Uspensky who love the people
fiercely could muster the resolution to lay before us these
traits without mitigation."[19]

The hope which Chernyshevsky held out to these be-
nighted peasant masses rested upon the village commune,
the "sacred and redeeming heritage bequeathed to us by
our past life, the poverty of which is atoned for by this
one invaluable heritage."[20] The commune as it existed at
the time was by no means ideal—Chernyshevsky was considerably further than Herzen from Slavophile romanticism—but it had the enormous virtue of providing a
bulwark against the capitalist modernization of Russia.
Western Europe had achieved industrial progress and
scientific enlightenment, but at a terrible cost: the cost of

expropriating its producers, of turning peasants with land into proletarians with nothing at all, and of making competitive egoism respectable and accumulated property sacred. If Russia were to follow the Western example of economic development, the condition of the people would become even more wretched than it already was. But Chernyshevsky, echoing Herzen, claimed that there were advantages in economic backwardness: "History, like a grandmother, is very fond of its grandchildren."[21] Perhaps Russia could learn from the experience of the West, and achieve a better society without having to go through the stage of rampant expropriation and capitalism which had been unavoidable in Western development. On the basis of the commune, which over the centuries had kept alive ancient egalitarian traditions, a new socialist society could be built when the popular revolution came. Their ancient tradition of communal ownership would enable the peasants to develop cooperative production, so that they could modernize their agriculture and ultimately, Chernyshevsky believed, progress to a fully communist society.[22]

Although Chernyshevsky's views were expressed in roundabout ways in journals scrutinized by the censors before publication, it eventually became apparent to the authorities that he was a dangerously radical influence. He was arrested in 1862 and sent to Siberia, to spend the rest of his life in exile. Ironically, as part of his harsh, realistic, "scientific" attitude to life he had preached a philosophy of rational egoism. He belied his own doctrine by his willingness to sacrifice everything for his political ideals.

## *NARODNICHESTVO*

In the decade following Chernyshevsky's arrest and exile, the motif of sacrifice for the people became increasingly dominant in radical circles. It found its classic form in the *Historical Letters* published in 1869 by "P. Mirtov," the pseudonym of Peter Lavrov. The most influential section of this work was a chapter entitled "The Price of Progress," in which Lavrov pointed out that the precious development of civilization, which had made possible education and self-development for a privileged few, had been bought with the labor and suffering of all the rest, the mass of the people. The cultivated classes must therefore recognize that they owed a vast moral debt to the people. The impression this point made on sensitive consciences was described later by one of Lavrov's readers:

> Reading this book convinced me that in our present social organisation . . . the members of society itself were inevitably distributed in two unequal groups. One of these, numerically very small, was in a privileged position and able to enjoy—to the detriment of the others—all the good things of life. Whereas the second, which made up the great majority, was destined to eternal misery and to labours beyond the scope of human capacity. Mirtov eloquently pointed out the vastness of the unpaid debt which weighs on the conscience of the privileged group towards the millions of workers in this generation and those of the past. . . . I accepted these ideas which were new to me, and felt myself in the position—so much ridiculed at the time—of a "repentant noble."[23]

By the early 1870s the radical youth of the Russian universities were deeply convinced of the injustice of Russian

society, of the possibility of its regeneration in a new
socialistic order based on the peasant commune, and of
the debt they owed the people for their own privileged
existence. But what were they to do? What action should
they take? They found what seemed to be an answer to
their perplexities in the pronouncements of Michael
Bakunin.

Bakunin, best known as one of the founding fathers of
anarchism, had been out of Russian society for some
years, dividing his time between imprisonment and exile
in Russia and Siberia and fomenting international revolution in Europe. He was convinced, however, that the
Russian people were ripe for revolution. Pointing not
only to the numerous disturbances of the 1860s but to the
unruly history of peasant revolts, many of them led by
brigands like Stenka Razin and Pugachev, he maintained
that only a spark was needed to start the revolutionary
conflagrations: "In such a situation, what can be done by
our intellectual proletariat, our honourable, sincere Russian youth, devoted to socialism to the bitter end? They
must, without doubt, go to the people."[24]

Urged on by this kind of exhortation, the radical intelligentsia "went to the people." In the summer of 1874
thousands of young people, girls as well as young men,
abandoned their books and set off into the countryside,
full of high hopes and ready for any sacrifice. In order to
get closer to the people, they dressed in peasant clothes
and took up manual labor. Some of them even adopted
the peasants' religion, Orthodoxy. One Jewish intellectual
reported, "I was baptized and felt myself literally renewed. . . . So I had drawn near the peasants, among
whom I was to live."[25]

This mass pilgrimage to the people was doomed from the start. The more experienced and prudent radicals saw the dangers of such an impulsive movement and tried to organize it, urging the young people at least to settle in one place and work at a trade rather than wandering about like friars preaching revolution.[26] But the thousands who flocked into the countryside were beyond control. For one thing, they were very young indeed. So many were teenagers that those in their early twenties were nicknamed "the old ones."[27] For another, some of these young ladies and gentlemen were too carried away by the sheer romantic excitement of it all to do anything more practical than play at revolution. Vera Zasulich, later to become world famous as the first woman terrorist, went to the people as part of a group who opened a village tea shop. Humdrum chores, however, did not suit her notions of revolutionary activity. She refused to cook or to make the tea, preferring "to ride around the countryside with a pistol strapped to her belt."[28] Many of the revolutionaries made no attempt to guard against arrest. They walked into the villages and told the peasants openly that all the land belonged to them and that they should rise against the state.

The peasants' response was disappointing. Revolutionary zeal seemed to be in short supply, and instead the people were indifferent, suspicious, or actively hostile. Where the preaching of the youthful missionaries did seem to strike a chord, it was not always the one they intended. One revolutionary described later how he had been telling a group of peasants what life would be like after the revolution, when the land belonged to the people. One of them jumped up, shouting, "Oh, how wonder-

ful when we shall redistribute land! I shall hire two
workers and live like a lord!"²⁹

The net results of the venture were 770 arrested and,
for those who had escaped or were released after questioning, a sobered awareness of the difficulties of revolution, and especially of the differences in outlook between
intellectuals and peasants. It was clear that, contrary to
what Bakunin and others had led them to expect, the
Russian peasant was not ready for an immediate socialist
revolution. Nevertheless, repression only strengthened
the radicals' dedication to revolutionary change and their
devotion to an ultimate socialist society based upon free
peasant communes. But how were they to work toward
this aim?

Two alternatives presented themselves, two conflicting
paths between which the revolutionary movement was to
be fatally torn, one of them elitist and conspiratorial, the
other "populist" in the strict sense of the word. It could
be persuasively argued, on the one hand, that since the
people were not ready for revolution, and since the
regime was capable of repressing any open attempt to
build a wide popular movement, the only hope of revolution lay in the organization of a tightly knit conspiratorial
party which would strike at the government by the only
means available to a small group, acts of individual terrorism, with the ultimate aim of seizing political power
and building a socialist society.

But although both the logic of their situation and the
sheer glamor of terrorism were to draw most of the revolutionaries toward this alternative by the end of the
1870s, during the period immediately after the pilgrimage

to the people most of them found it repugnant. It was too elitist, too much removed from "the people"; further-more, it strongly recalled the Machiavellian tactics of the notorious Nechaev, a psychopathic power-seeker who had mesmerized and deceived radical circles in the late 1860s, and who had recently been tried for the cold-blooded murder of a fellow revolutionary.

For the moment, therefore, the failure of their efforts to stir up peasant revolution did not drive the revolu-tionaries in the direction of terrorism, but into a new deference toward the people. Many of the radicals came to the conclusion that the reason for their failure lay in their own presumption. They had come out from the city full of confidence in their own ideas, expecting the peas-ants to accept them as leaders, whereas they should have been willing to *learn* from the peasant and to accept his homely wisdom. Some writers took this view to extrava-gant lengths. Peter Chervinsky, for example, maintained that the peasant lived on a higher moral level than the intelligentsia: "How pitiful the *intellectual* humanity and love for 'man' is before the direct feeling of some downtrodden peasant woman."[30]

Not everyone was prepared to go as far as this. Never-theless, following the debacle of 1874 there was for a time a consensus that if there was to be a revolution based on the peasantry, it would have to be guided by the actual needs and attitudes of the people. Under the leadership of Mark Natanson and Alexander Mikhailov, the revolu-tionary intellectuals formulated a new policy, the policy of *narodnichestvo* or "populism." The emergence of this policy was described later by one of those who lived through it, Andrew Zhelyabov, one of the leaders of the group that assassinated Alexander II:

> Having come to the conclusion that the difficulties which the government created made it impossible to imbue the conscience of the people entirely with socialism, the socialists went over to the populists. . . . We decided to act in the name of the interests of which the people have already become aware—no longer in the name of pure doctrine, but on the basis of interests rooted in the life of the people, interests of which it was conscious. This was the characteristic quality of *narodnichestvo*.[31]

The policy of the self-styled *narodniki* meant giving up the rarified world of the intellectual elite and its abstract theories, and adapting oneself to the outlook and interests of the people. This new movement "to the people" took a variety of forms. For instance, some of those inspired by the *narodnik* vision went off to be trained for peasant life at the curious academy run by Alexander Engel'gardt, whose own ideals and failures encapsulate much of the experience of the Russian populist movement.

Engel'gardt was a scientist, the ex-rector of the St. Petersburg Agricultural Institute, who had fallen foul of the authorities by allegedly condoning the spread of subversive ideas among his students. When he was removed from his post in 1870 and sent into internal exile on his own estate, he resolved to turn his punishment into an opportunity to participate in the simple rural life of the people. The difficulties inherent in this program became apparent right at the start, on his train journey into the country. Engel'gardt had begun his new life by denying himself the comforts of the first-class railway carriage and climbing into the unheated car reserved for peasants. But it was January, and 30 degrees below zero. Even though, unlike the peasants in the carriage, Engel'gardt was well wrapped up in his thick suit, fur coat and cap, scarf, and felt boots, he found himself shivering uncontrollably. As he sat in misery, the temptation of first-class warmth just along the corridor became irresistible. He paid the difference and moved to the aristocratic carriage to spend the rest of the journey in physical comfort but agony of mind.[32]

Coming home to the estate which he had not seen for years was a still more chastening experience. He found that while he had been a celebrated agronomist in St. Petersburg lecturing on chemical fertilizers, his own land had been going to rack and ruin for want of the most elementary cultivation. Guilt-stricken, he set himself to create a model farm and succeeded—but only, as unsympathetic fellow radicals pointed out, by perpetuating the exploitation of the people through wage labor. Anxious to find some way of showing the peasants how to better their own lot, and eager at the same time to unite manual and intellectual labor, he offered to train members of the intelligentsia to set up agrarian communes which would provide the local villagers with models of efficient self-sufficiency.[33]

In the exalted moral atmosphere of the 1870s, it was not difficult for Engel'gardt to find recruits, but the young men and women who joined his "practical academy" found rural life harder than they had bargained for. They lived with the real peasant workers on the estate in a common hut, slept on hard benches, ate revoltingly

fatty peasant food, and struggled with exhausting, un-
familiar labor. When they were incompetent, the peasants
laughed at their physical weakness, their ineptitude in
milking cows or plowing furrows; yet if they did show
promise, the peasants resented competition from their
labor.[34] Those who stayed the course and established
themselves on collective farms found that communal living was not so easy or idyllic as they had supposed. Fraternal harmony seemed hard to come by in the endless
clash of individual personalities. Disillusioned, they
gradually drifted back to the city.

While some of the *narodniki* were seeking union with
the people by sweating over the milk pail, others chose
more devious means of closing the gap between their
revolutionary ideals and the people's point of view. In
the region round Chigirin near Kiev, where there had
already been manifestations of peasant discontent over
the way in which land had been divided, Jacob Stefano-
vich decided that the peasants' traditional loyalty to the
Tsar, generally regarded by radicals as a stumbling block,
might be turned into a revolutionary instrument. He
brought them a document purporting to be a Secret Imperial Charter, telling them that the Tsar had ordered
the equal division of land among his subjects, but that the
nobles had prevented this. The "Tsar" called on the peasants to organize and prepare for an insurrection against
the nobles and officials. A remarkable number of them
obeyed the bogus imperial call. During 1877 the organization spread rapidly, leading inevitably to discovery and
repression.[35]

Meanwhile, in the urban centers a new populist revolutionary organization was taking shape. The party which emerged in 1876 eventually took the name *Zemlya i Volya*, "Land and Liberty," a slogan chosen to represent the historic demands of the Russian peasantry and to recall a revolutionary group of the same name which had appeared briefly in the 1860s. In its first statement the group announced: "We restrict our demands to objectives which really can be achieved in the most immediate future, i.e. to those claims and demands of the people which exist at this given moment."[36] The demands were, first, division of all Russian land equally among the peasantry, who would organize its cultivation by means of village communes; second, freedom for the subject peoples of the Russian empire; and third, local self-government by the various *obshchinas*. These demands could be brought about only by violent revolution, which the group proposed to promote by means of agitation among the people and "the disorganisation of the state."

Many of this group's members also went to the people, but in a more organized way than in 1874, as teachers, doctors, or clerks, settling in the villages and trying to win the confidence of the peasants. The first number of their periodical, *Zemlya i Volya*, dated October 1878, declared that the revolution could be brought about only by the people themselves, and urged the revolutionaries to strip away their veneer of civilization and come closer to the peasants: "Steep yourself in the great sea of the people. Throw open your eyes and your ears."[37]

This policy was a logical one, but it had a serious disadvantage: it was clearly going to take a long time. In profound contrast to Marxists, the Russian populists were anxiously aware that time was not on their side. Their ideal was a socialist Russia stripped of its autocratic state and its social and economic inequalities, in which harmony and brotherhood would reign. They believed that such harmony and brotherhood were deeply embedded in the traditions of the Russian village, particularly the practice of communal landholding, whereby there was no absolute, exclusive ownership of land within the village, and plots were periodically equalized by repartition. But whether or not their view of the *obshchinas* was idealized (a matter about which there was a good deal of argument inside the radical camp[38]), there could be no doubt that the commune was threatened. Since the emancipation of the serfs there had been more scope for individualism, enterprise, and the consolidation of private property. Engel-'gardt, who actually lived in the country for a long period, admitted gloomily that "the ideals of the *kulak* reign among the peasantry; every peasant is proud to be the pike who gobbles up the carp."[39]

Egoism rampant in the village; industrialism getting under way in the towns: it seemed to the populists that Russia was on the point of following the West into the horrors of capitalist modernization. Time was short if they were to stem the tide of history. Could they afford to wait until the masses were ready to rise of their own accord? Some of the members of *Zemlya i Volya* began to advocate more drastic means. The revolutionaries themselves were few: without mass support they could not change society. But perhaps if they could strike at the autocratic state by acts of terrorism—if, above all, they could assassinate the Tsar—they would give the signal

for a popular uprising and terrify the authorities into
collapse.

Adam Ulam has noted the "schizophrenic character"
of *Zemlya i Volya*: "Intellectually it remained committed
to education and agitation among the peasants and the
growing industrial proletariat of the big cities; emotionally most of its members became obsessed with terror."[40]
What tipped the scale was less a matter of prudential cal-
culation than intoxication with the sheer glamor of terrorist acts. The crucial event was Vera Zasulich's attack
on General Trepov in January 1878. Trepov, governor of
St. Petersburg, had ordered the flogging of one of the
revolutionaries in jail, and Zasulich proposed to avenge
this act of brutality. Having approached the general in
the guise of a petitioner, she shot him at point-blank
range, though, with the inefficiency characteristic of the
revolutionaries of the period, she failed even to wound
him seriously. Under the newly reformed judicial system
she was tried by a jury, and such was the dislike of Trepov
and the sympathy for his assailant that the jury brought
in the unlikely verdict of not guilty. Europe rang with
praises of the revolutionary heroine, and direct action
appeared to be vindicated.

Within *Zemlya i Volya*, arguments for and against the
use of terrorist methods raged until in 1879 the party split
in two. One section stuck to work among the people, calling itself *Cherny Peredel*, "Black Repartition," to signify
its primary demand for equal partition of the land
among the "blacks," or servile class.[41] This faction was
led by Plekhanov, who was later converted to Marxism.
But the stronger faction, calling itself *Narodnaya Volya*,

"The People's Will," while still proclaiming their devotion to the people, decided to concentrate on a terroristic struggle with the autocracy. After many failures this led ultimately, on March 1, 1881, to the assassination of Alexander II. At his trial, one of the conspirators, Zhelyabov, looked back over the way in which populist ideas had developed:

> We have tried in several different ways to act on behalf of the people. At the beginning of the seventies we chose to live like workers and peacefully propagate our Socialist ideas. The movement was absolutely harmless. But how did it end? . . . A movement, which was unstained by blood and which repudiated violence, was crushed. . . . The short time that we lived among the people showed us how bookish and doctrinaire were our ideas. We then decided to act on behalf of the interests created by the people. . . . Instead of spreading Socialist ideas, we gave first place to our determination to reawaken the people by agitation in the name of the interest that it felt; instead of a peaceful fight we applied ourselves to a fight with deeds. We began with small deeds. . . . It was in 1878 that the idea of a more radical fight made its appearance—the idea of cutting the Gordian knot.[42]

But, as in their movement to the people in 1874, the revolutionaries had misjudged the situation. The Tsar's death did nothing to weaken the autocracy: on the contrary, it merely strengthened the hand of reactionaries at the court of Alexander's successor. Above all, it did nothing to set off a popular insurrection. According to police reports, some peasants believed that the Tsar had been murdered by the landlords because he had abolished serfdom.[43] In any event, the catastrophe did nothing to shake popular loyalty to Tsarism. All that the populists had demonstrated was their utter remoteness from the people they desperately longed to serve.

## POPULISM AND MARXISM

By the time of Alexander II's assassination, the main features of Russian populism had become apparent. Devoted to what they supposed to be the interests of the peasantry, the populists were inclined to idealize "the people." They aimed at a form of agrarian socialism based on a federation of peasant communes, and they deliberately stressed social goals rather than political ones, believing that liberal hopes of a constitution were irrelevant to the needs of the peasantry. Lacking any clear political strategy, they relied on hopes of a peasant revolution on the one hand, and on spectacular but counterproductive acts of terrorism on the other. Unlike the Marxists, they had no theory of historical determinism, but instead a great deal of faith in the power of dedicated and high-minded individuals to change the course of history. Where Marxism emphasized science, objectivity, and discipline, the characteristic atmosphere of Russian populism was profoundly romantic.[44]

The differences between populism and Marxism became more salient in the latter years of the century, for the débacle of revolutionary populism led in many radical circles to disillusionment with the idea of a peasant revolution and to an accelerated drift toward Marxism. One of the first to switch his revolutionary hopes from the peasant masses to the still-embryonic proletariat was George Plekhanov, former leader of the Black Repartition faction of *Zemlya i Volya*. It was, curiously enough, his populist distrust of the elitist tactics of *Narodnaya Volya* that led him away from the populist tradition. Socialism meant to him a revolution brought about by the people themselves, not imposed by a dictatorial elite, but he became convinced that the peasants would never be a revolutionary force. In exile, however, he found among the workers' social democratic parties of Western Europe the kind of authentic popular socialism that he was looking for, and he adopted Marxism and its corollary that only an industrial proletariat, not a peasantry, could produce a socialist society. For Russia, as for the West, the way to socialism must lie through capitalist modernization, which would eventually provoke a proletarian revolution.

For those who could achieve such a reconciliation with the historical process, there were great gains in certainty. As Plekhanov put it, the Marxists felt that they were "seated in that historical train which at full speed takes us to our goal."[45] Toward the end of the century, as government-sponsored industrialism got under way and the capitalist transformation of Russia gathered pace, the attractions of Marxism were obvious. Its disadvantages, particularly for radicals brought up on the high-minded ideals of populism, were moral and psychological. For how could avowed revolutionaries and friends of the people sit calmly by, counseling patience with the historical process, while peasants were being turned into proletarians and subjected to the worst rigors of an industrial revolution? To some populists, Marxist determinism seemed nothing short of collaboration with the enemies of the people.

During the 1880s and 1890s, revolutionary manifestations of populism were rare, but the so-called Legal Populists kept up a constant running battle in their periodicals
against government policies of industrialization on the
one hand, and Marxist approval of such policies on the
other. The concerns of writers like Mikhailovsky and
Vorontsov were still those of the populist tradition. They
wished to better the lot of the peasantry and to build
socialism on the basis of the commune. The situation in
which they were writing, however, forced them to give
their attention to questions of economic development and
historical inevitability. Was the only way to prosperity,
as the government assumed, to copy the industry of the
West and turn most of the peasants into landless proletarians? Even more crucially, was that the only way to
socialism?

The Legal Populists denied these claims. In striking
anticipation of the arguments of some Third World econ-
omists at the present day, they drew attention to the
terrible price paid by the rural population for "development," and to the weakness of a backward country like
Russia as a competitor in international markets. Instead,
they urged the adoption of an alternative path which
would concentrate on aid to the peasantry and small-scale
local handicrafts, and build a prosperous—and socialist—
society upon a rural base.[46]

For all the increasing dominance of Marxist ideas
among the intelligentsia, therefore, the tradition of
agrarian socialism survived the turn of the century to give
birth to another revolutionary populist movement: the
Socialist Revolutionary Party, led by a disciple of Mik-

hailovsky, Victor Chernov. Faith in the revolutionary potential of the peasantry, which had been in abeyance since the failures of the 1870s, was revived by the agrarian disturbances of 1902, for in that year the peasants rose spontaneously to burn down the houses of the gentry, execute rough justice on unpopular local officials, and seize the nobles' land to add to their own village holdings.

While reassured by these revolutionary stirrings among the peasantry, however, the neopopulists of the Socialist Revolutionary Party found it almost as hard to achieve rapport with the *narod* as had their predecessors in the 1870s. It is typical of Chernov's ambivalent attitude to land reform that he termed the peasant movement of 1902 "semisocialist." He and his fellow Socialist Revolutionaries believed, in true populist fashion, that deeply ingrained in the Russian peasant mind was the knowledge that land belonged to the people as a whole and should be held equally by those who cultivated it. On the basis of this tradition, they maintained, a fully collectivized system of production could eventually be built. They had less faith, however, in spontaneous self-help on the part of the peasants. Fearing that unorganized land seizures would give rise to vested interests, they wished to postpone land reform and redistribution until after the revolution, to be carried out then by new administrative organs. They doubted, with some justification, whether the peasants' tradition of fraternity would stretch to giving up newly acquired land in order to make possible an equal distribution over the whole country.[47]

The very fact that the peasants were by this time becoming more radical and articulate helped to make obvious the gulf between them and the intellectuals who formed the bulk of the Socialist Revolutionaries. *Revolyutsionnaya Rossiya*, the Socialist Revolutionary journal, published a letter from a peasant revolutionary in 1903 that sheds a vivid light upon the problem:

> To work among the peasantry, it's best to be a peasant yourself, or to have studied properly the life of the peasants, and to live among them not as a master but as a peasant. Only then will they understand you and trust you fully. I know from experience of several examples of unsuccessful work among the peasants by students. . . . And no wonder. The student, living in the countryside, gives the peasants literature and talks to them about liberty, equality, fraternity and so on. At the same time he himself is frittering away thirty to fifty roubles a month on trifles. Meanwhile the peasants, to whom he's explaining that each of them should help the needy with their last crumb, and sacrifice themselves for the benefit of others, are shivering with cold, and their children are dying of hunger. . . . How can the peasants trust such people?[48]

As the most influential historian of the Socialist Revolutionary party, Oliver Radkey, has acidly remarked, "This was only nominally a peasants' party; in essence it was a party of doctrinaire intellectuals."[49]

The relation between the populist movement and the Revolution of 1917 is a paradoxical one. Although the Socialist Revolutionaries were utterly defeated by Lenin and the Bolsheviks, it could be argued that the Revolution vindicated populism and refuted Marxism, and that Lenin succeeded largely because he was prepared to adopt a good deal of populist doctrine for purely Machiavellian purposes.

Ever since the 1880s, Marxists had been arguing that Russia was following the West on the path of capitalist development and that socialist revolution must come in the orthodox manner, on the basis of a proletarian uprising. It was a Marxist axiom that the peasants were not a revolutionary class, and indeed not really a class at all, since the impact of an increasingly commercial economy was presumed to be sorting them out into distinct classes of kulaks, middle peasants, and rural proletarians. Others besides Marxists found this account persuasive, particularly when (in the wake of the abortive 1905 revolution) the government, directed by Stolypin, deliberately set out to disrupt the village commune and to create a conservative class of yeomen farmers with enclosed farms.

In 1917, however, the peasantry—that supposedly inert and divided mass—rose in spontaneous revolution, seizing the gentry's lands without waiting to be stirred up by socialist agitators. The way in which they did this, furthermore, was a vindication of populism, for there was a tremendous resurgence of the traditional communal egalitarianism that the *narodniki* had so long celebrated.[50] The village commune, supposedly defunct, acquired new life as an organ of local self-government and land division, while those who had left communes to farm on their own were frequently forced back into the traditional pattern. The general feeling among the peasants, as expressed in their actions, appeared to correspond to the populist slogan that the land belonged to the people as a whole and that each cultivator had the right to possess what he could till. The "Black Repartition," *Cherny Peredel*, of which the populists of the 1870s had dreamed, appeared

to be accomplished by the peasants' own hands. One of
Lenin's most effective tactical maneuvers was simply to
approve this, thus swallowing the populist land program
whole.

If, however, the populists had been right about the
peasants' revolutionary potential and the Marxists wrong,
why did ultimate victory go to the Bolsheviks? The answer
seems to lie mainly in the realms of political skill and
tactics: in the application of the maxims—as distasteful
to most Marxists as to most populists—that political
power grows out of the barrel of a gun, or that an organized minority can always rule a disorganized majority.
Certainly the Socialist Revolutionary Party of 1917 was
unfitted for leadership in a critical situation.[51] Already
split between factions and soon to split again, it was riven
with disagreement over the vital questions of what attitude to take to the war with Germany, whether to cooperate with other parties in the coalition government,
and whether to approve the land seizures, which threatened to jeopardize any attempt at orderly land reform.
With no leader of Lenin's stature, and no organized and
mobilized following to match the Bolsheviks, the Socialist
Revolutionaries were hopelessly weak in spite of the vast
amount of diffuse peasant sentiment they represented.
Ironically, it was populist doctrine—in opposition to the
Marxist theory of historical inevitability—that stressed
the importance of individual decisions and actions in the
making of history.

While both the Socialist Revolutionaries and the peasants themselves were defeated by the outcome of the
Revolution, the degree to which the Socialist Revolu-

tionaries actually represented the rural masses should not be exaggerated. All Russian populists were socialists, just as much as Marxists were, while the egalitarian and communal traditions of peasants in some parts of Russia did not amount to a desire for collective cultivation, as subsequent Russian history was to demonstrate. If the Socialist Revolutionaries had been in power in the 1920s, therefore, they would have faced much the same ideological problem as the Bolsheviks: namely, the gulf between socialist ideals and peasant inclinations, not to mention the urgent practical problem of food crises and shortages in the towns. Given the populist tradition of deference to the peasants, it is unlikely that a hypothetical Socialist Revolutionary government would have been as ruthless in setting about these problems as the Bolsheviks. It is difficult to imagine, however, that any political party with such scruples, and with the generally anarchistic leanings of the Socialist Revolutionaries, could ever in any case have conquered power in the chaotic circumstances of the Russian Revolution.

Ever since the polemics between Marxists and populists at the turn of the century, it has been customary for Marxists to dismiss populism as the typically reactionary and self-deluding ideology of the peasantry, in contrast to the scientific and progressive viewpoint of the proletariat. According to Lenin, the populists' attachment to the peasant commune, their hostility to Westernization, and their belief that expropriation of the peasantry could be avoided, were all indications that populism was a "petty-bourgeois" ideology, the typical backward-looking view of small proprietors whom history was leaving behind.

More recently, a version of Lenin's thesis has been vigorously argued by Dr. Andrzej Walicki, who claims: "Populism was a broad current of Russian democratic thought which reflected the class standpoint of small producers (mainly peasants), willing to get rid of the remnants of serfdom, but, at the same time, endangered by the development of capitalism."[52] Walicki admits that Russian populism was not formulated by the peasants but by the intelligentsia, but he maintains nevertheless that it was the peasants' standpoint which the intelligentsia expressed. However, he makes another claim which leads in a rather different direction. Besides being the ideology of small producers threatened with the loss of their property, Russian populism "reflected *also* specific problems of a backward peasant country in confrontation with the highly developed capitalist states."[53]

There are in fact two separate lines of argument here: on the one hand an analysis of Russian populism as the ideology of small peasant producers, and on the other hand an account of it as an intellectual response to the problems of economic backwardness. It will make for greater clarity if we look at these two suggestions in turn.

The claim that populism represented the standpoint of the small producer is not a very convincing one. As we have seen, genuine peasants had remarkably little to do with populism even as supporters, let alone as sources of its ideas. This is not to deny that intellectuals do on occasion succeed in speaking for an inarticulate group by expressing its interests and outlook. To what extent, however, was this the case in Russia? If the populists had confined themselves to attempts to conserve existing peasant institutions and to give the peasants the land, the argument would be stronger. In fact, however, they wished to graft on to the *obshchina* a higher socialist society whose ideals were clearly derived from Western radicalism.

The *narodniki* of the 1870s were probably right when they concentrated on Land and Liberty as the two great "felt needs" of the peasantry. It is less certain, however, that their interpretation of these values would have been endorsed by the peasants. During the revolution in the countryside the peasants demonstrated their attachment to the village community and to a rough equality between heads of households within it. What they completely lacked, however, was any inclination toward socialism, agrarian and otherwise.[54] The fully collectivized culti- vation and consumption that the intellectuals aimed at held no charm for them, nor did they share the intel- ligentsia's views on religion or on that particularly crucial issue in intelligentsia circles, the emancipation of women.

It seems clear, therefore, that neither in its original form nor in its Socialist Revolutionary revival was Rus- sian populism precisely "the ideology of the small pro- ducer." It was an ideology of intellectuals oriented *toward* the peasantry, which is not at all the same thing. Marxism, of course, is in similar fashion an ideology of intellectuals oriented toward the industrial proletariat, whereas the workers themselves, as Lenin shrewdly remarked, gener- ate only "trade-union consciousness."[55]

Perhaps the strongest objection, indeed, to the Leninist view of populism as the ideology of the small producer, is that it ignores perhaps the most conspicuous feature of Russian populism. This is the pathos of *distance* between the populists and the people, the gulf between the "small producers" and their supposed representatives, and the effects that this gulf had on the populists: the sense of guilt on the part of the privileged; the heroic sacrifice by so many young people of their lives, liberty, and worldly prospects in what they believed to be the people's cause; the atmosphere of exalted idealism and utter lack of self-interest that clothed even their terroristic campaigns, and that makes Russian populism in retrospect seem both attractive and bizarre.

If we seek a socioeconomic basis for the characteristic features of Russian populism, therefore, we may do better to take up Walicki's other suggestion, which links populism to the situation of intellectuals in an under-developed country. This line of explanation has in fact been frequently adopted by students of *narodnichestvo*, though with two rather different emphases.

One common view presents populism as, in effect, a symptom of the neurotic alienation of the Russian intelligentsia. That intelligentsia was, after all, in an acutely uncomfortable position. Isolated from the majority of their compatriots and from Russian traditions by their Western education, members of the intelligentsia were not compensated for these losses by recognition as part of the elite. Yet in their relations with the outside world the intelligentsia, though constantly geared toward Western culture, were profoundly ambivalent about it.[56] Herzen's original invention of "Russian Socialism" has been convincingly connected with his hypersensitive national pride. It was very comforting, after all, for one moving in an international intellectual milieu and conscious of Western condescension, to be able to convince himself that his own backward country was destined to be the pathfinder of socialism. More generally, scholars have found in the rootlessness of so many Russian intellectuals, in their dissociation from family and class, the explanation for their impulse to "drown themselves in the people."[57]

While this kind of account is plausible in many ways, it adds up to a rather derogatory picture of Russian populism as the characteristic self-delusion of intellectuals. Lenin (who had little patience with the intelligentsia as a group) derided the populist as "a Janus, looking with one face to the past and the other to the future."[58] Secure in his knowledge of the objective course of history, Lenin meant this as a sneer. It is not obvious, however, that it need be accepted as such.

For there is surely something to be said for the populists' ambivalent attitude to history. As intellectuals in a developing country, they were at least able to take a self-conscious and critical view of the process of modernization. They had some awareness both of the costs of industrialization and of the advantages of traditional society; of modern ideas like socialism as well as modern inventions like capitalism. From any point of view except that of a historical determinist, there was nothing inherently unreasonable in their attempt to combine the best of past and future. While it could hardly be claimed that most populists had a balanced and rational view of the problems and prospects of rural society, their views, and particularly those of the Legal Populists toward the end of the century, were by no means as empty as their Marxist opponents maintained.[59]

It is perhaps a little facile, then, to dismiss all the ideas of the Russian populists as the delusions of an alienated intelligentsia. The main charge of which they cannot be cleared is that of excessive romanticizing of the *narod*. They undoubtedly projected on to "the people" and their traditional institutions much that was not really there, and visualized the people in excessively generalized terms, talking, for instance, of the simple feelings of the Russian peasant woman without apparently noticing the differences between different Russian peasant women. Their deference to the common man was of a generalized and slightly ludicrous kind: though even here, it might be reasonable to prefer such deference to the Bolshevik's willingness to ride roughshod over the wishes and interests of the masses. As we shall see in Chapter 6, some of the populists explored with considerable sensitivity the difficult question of how to respect the dignity of ordinary men while striving for progress and advanced ideas.

How can we sum up Russian populism? The first point that needs to be underlined is that in its conventional wide usage the term covers a very long period, roughly from 1870 to 1917, and takes in a great variety of writers and activists, many of them forceful personalities with their own ideas. We can hardly expect, therefore, to state a set of clear propositions that all populists would have accepted. If we use the term in its narrower sense, to refer to the self-styled *narodniki* of the 1870s, its meaning is of course clearer. The stress here is on "going to the people," deferring to the people's wishes and striving to further their interests—above all, for land and liberty: peasant land, and liberty from landowners and the state.

In its wider sense, while Russian populism has a

central core of commitment to agrarian socialism, based (in some way which was never made clear) upon the peasant commune, the term takes in a large variety of other things that were historically but not always logically connected with this: revolutionary terrorism and a disdain for gradual constitutional reform; opposition to historical determinism, and a stress on the possibility of alternative historical paths and on the role of ideas and individual actions in bringing these about; and last but not least, a tremendous moral high-mindedness. These elements do not constitute a fully coherent ideology, but they certainly add up to a very characteristic style of thought, and one that forms a striking contrast to U.S. Populism. Compare, for instance, the Russian's contempt for liberal constitutional forms and high-minded adoption of terrorism with the U.S. Populists' commitment to political processes and search for laws and institutions to protect their interests.

It is quite clear, in fact, even from this exceedingly cursory look at the two acknowledged classics of populism, that Russian and American populism were very different from each other. True, both were in a sense forms of agrarian radicalism, but they can only very loosely be comprehended within such a term. Both undoubtedly idealized "the people" and aimed at grassroots control of society: but the difference between such an impulse coming from within "the people" themselves and one coming from a conscience-stricken intelligentsia is obvious. Each of the two paradigm cases raises problems to which we shall return in the course of our argument. *Can* there be such a thing as a "people's government"? And what happens to the role of intellectuals as pathfinders of progress if "the people's will" is really put into effect? For the moment, however, let us narrow our focus and see whether, if we concentrate upon the aspect of agrarian radicalism that is common to both our cases, we can identify a general phenomenon, "agrarian populism."

# 3. *Agrarian Populism in Perspective*

No-one must have more land than he and his family can work. Everyone must have enough land to provide work for his family and to be self-supporting.—*Raiko Daskalov of the Bulgarian Agrarian National Union*[1]

"Tierra y Libertad"—*Slogan of the Zapatistas in the Mexican Revolution*[2]

Any attempt to generalize about populism, even restricting the term to its agrarian senses, must begin by recognizing that the whole subject of such generalization is problematic. The fact that the U.S. People's Party and *narodnichestvo* are both called "populism" is a matter of historical accident,[3] and it is clear from our brief surveys of them in the preceding chapters that they differed greatly. Nevertheless, the literature on the subject is haunted by the conviction that this accidental conjunction is not meaningless, and that, different as the two cases are, they are nevertheless in some sense instances of the same general phenomenon. They were, after all, both cases of rural radicalism: of radicalism, that is, not based upon the conventional modern urban classes, bourgeoisie and proletariat, from whom we have been taught to expect such behavior. Both movements have in some sense earned the title of "socialist"; both were related to problems of modernization and the effects on rural life of a wider market economy; and last but not least, both idealized "the people."

These persuasive similarities have, it is true, a tendency to dissolve upon closer inspection. U.S. Populism and *narodnichestvo* were perhaps both rural radicalisms, but they arose among two very different classes of people, farmers on the one hand and an intelligentsia on the other, and the difference in their roots is apparent in every line of their programs. As we have seen, "socialism" for the U.S. Populists meant control by a people's government of key aspects of commodity marketing and finance, whereas for the *narodniki* it meant a communal and regenerated life at the level of the village. Again, while it could be said that both were concerned with problems of modernization, there is not really much in common between the farmers' extremely concrete worries about railroad corporations and the gold standard, and the much more diffuse anxieties of intellectuals with an ambivalent attitude toward Westernization. Both groups, certainly, exalted "the people"; but even here, a grass-roots uprising of "the producers" is a different matter from the romantic yearnings of an alienated intelligentsia.

Reflection upon our cases seems to suggest, therefore, that the project of establishing a clear concept of agrarian populism is not a very hopeful one. Two reasons can be given, however, for resisting the impulse to take a nominalist position and to dismiss the two cases as unique historical phenomena about which nothing more general can be said. The first is that, while U.S. and Russian populism may not seem to have much in common, neither is unique. In each case, parallels can be found which are sufficiently close to suggest that we are at any rate dealing with two characteristic types of agrarian populism, those of farmers and of intelligentsias, if not with "populism" in general. The second reason is that these two distinct types of agrarian radicalism can be persuasively linked together by means of another kind, peasant radicalism, which fits neatly between the two and which is also frequently given the name of "populism." Our task in this chapter will be to explore this line of argument and to see whether it leads us to a clearer understanding of "agrarian populism" as a general category.

## FARMERS' POPULISM

The U.S. People's Party of the 1890s is by no means the only case of grass-roots radicalism among commodity farmers, focusing their hostility against plutocrats and corporations and calling for regulation by a people's government. There are in fact several other strikingly similar examples, based in each case on the clash between a political tradition which led farmers to expect to be able to control their own destiny, and their actual economic thralldom to outside corporate and financial interests. Such movements have clear family resemblances, although they do not necessarily share the same economic program or the same political style. This point can be illustrated by contrasting the different movements that emerged out of very similar social and economic conditions in two adjacent Canadian provinces in the 1930s: the Cooperative Commonwealth Federation in Saskatchewan and Social Credit in Alberta.

In both cases, the circumstances that gave rise to radicalism were directly analogous to those in the American West in the 1890s. In Saskatchewan the farmers of the province depended upon wheat, and therefore upon elevators and transport, and above all on the remote and uncontrollable international wheat market. Spurred by their situation to cooperative action, by the 1930s they had established a cooperative network that had successfully taken on the elevator companies and the Canadian Pacific Railway. The slump in the wheat market during the world depression was too much for them, however. A combination of rock-bottom prices and searing droughts reduced them to such a condition that two-thirds of the rural population of the province were living on government relief.[4]

The result was the rise of the socialist Cooperative Commonwealth Federation, which was radical to the point of advocating nationalization of the land. The spectacle of farmers supporting such a policy becomes intelligible when one realizes what nationalization meant to them. The farmers were to become government tenants with long leases and security of tenure—a situation preferable to that of a nominal "owner" threatened with eviction on the foreclosure of his mortgage. Government action had come to seem the only possible bulwark of the farmers' independence.

The Cooperative Commonwealth Federation was notable not only for its socialist program but also for its

record of internal democracy. S. M. Lipset, who studied
the movement not long after it gained control of the
province, was struck by the level of political awareness
to which it had given rise among quite ordinary farmers:

> Winter after winter, when the wheat crop is in, thousands
> of meetings are held throughout the province by political
> parties, churches, farmers' educational associations, and
> cooperatives. There are informal gatherings, also, in which
> farmers discuss economic and political problems. . . .
> The farmers . . . have frequent sessions in which they
> consider the ideas of Adam Smith, Karl Marx, William
> Morris, Henry George, James Kier Hardie, William
> Jennings Bryan, Thorstein Veblen, and others.[5]

Meanwhile the next-door province, Alberta, having much
the same type of society and range of economic problems,
generated a populist movement of a different kind. In
1932 a local headmaster, William Aberhard, who was
well-known in the province as a spell-binding fundamentalist preacher, became convinced that the answer
to the economic distress in which the province was sunk
lay in Major Douglas's reflationary "Social Credit" System.[6] Aberhard began to preach Social Credit as well as
salvation on his regular religious broadcasts, and quickly
converted his already large personal following. A charismatic and authoritarian figure, he built up a movement
amazingly quickly, until in 1935 his party gained 89
percent of the seats in the provincial legislature. Aberhard claimed that he represented the will of the people,
but he took great care to keep control of the party in his
own hands, and managed to survive the widespread disappointment when he did not, after all, implement his

Social Credit doctrines. The measure of his dominance over the party is that he could pass a Recall Act in 1936 enabling the people to recall their representatives if they were not satisfied, and then get it repealed, retroactively, a year later, because a petition was circulating in his constituency to recall Aberhard himself.

Other notable North American outbreaks of "farmers' populism" include the rise of the "socialistic" Non-Partisan League in North Dakota at the time of World War I,[7] and also—though here there are complicating factors—the rural support given in the American South to radical demagogues like Huey Long, whose career we shall view later from another perspective.

An interesting variant of farmers' populism, arising in similar economic circumstances but a quite different political context, is provided by the German agrarian movement of the 1890s, which Kenneth Barkin has compared to U.S. Populism.[8] Like North American farmers, the Prussian Junkers grew grain for international markets, and saw their prices drop and their debts rise. They responded by forming the German Farmers' League, a group which, in spite of its Junker leadership and hierarchical structure, was militantly radical in defense of rural interests. Given the German context, the antiplutocratic and antiurban rhetoric of the agrarians was heavily laced with anti-Semitism, and there was no parallel to the American *rapprochement* between farmers and industrial workers. The tone of the movement was in fact strongly right-wing. Nevertheless, the Germans, like their American counterparts, looked to government intervention in the economy to help them and supported an

income tax, control of speculation in grain futures, bi-
metallism, and a system of government warehouses somewhat along the lines of the U.S. Populists' Subtreasury
proposals.

One of the notable features of this type of populism,
indeed, is that it seems invariably to include calls for extensive government intervention in the economy coming
from people who own property. In terms of ordinary
Right/Left dichotomies this seems confusing, for it has
often been assumed that the natural allies of state intervention will be those who possess no property and have
nothing to lose. Commercial farmers, however, insofar
as they are dependent upon market forces over which
they have no more control than they have over the
weather, tend to welcome a good deal of government protection, in spite of their determination to remain autonomous on their own land. The situation of the modern
European small farmer, protected from the risks of
agricultural production by the umbrella of the European
Community's Common Agricultural Policy, is typical of
this development.

Besides giving rise to economic policies that do not fit
easily into the Right/Left spectrum, farmers' populism
seems to harbor another ambivalence vividly illustrated
in the two Canadian cases mentioned. The attempt to
recapture control of the economy for "the people" (i.e.,
the producers) is a constant where these movements arise
in a democratic context,[9] but this sort of populism can
apparently run just as easily to charismatic demagoguery
à la Aberhard in Alberta as to participatory democracy
in the mode of Saskatchewan. The original U.S. Populist

movement was, as we have seen, deeply committed to grass-roots democracy: but it is clear that a similar socio-economic base and program can coexist with a much more demagogic political style—a point that we shall take up later.

## THE POPULISM OF THE INTELLIGENTSIA

If the U.S. Populist movement can be seen not just as a unique historical occurrence but as an example of a genre, so too can *narodnichestvo*. The parallels in this case are less clear and more controversial, partly because there is no precise equivalent to the farmers' economic problems, which governed the solutions they sought. Nevertheless, there are suggestive similarities (which have often been pointed out) between *narodnik* ideas and the views of some revolutionary intellectuals in contemporary developing countries. These recurrent themes cluster round the "Janus-faced" attitude to modernization shared with the Russians by many Third World spokesmen: their habit of looking back to the traditions of their own countries as well as forward to a developed society; their focus upon the countryside rather than the towns; their desire to avoid repeating the experience and the mistakes of more advanced countries; their stress upon building their own road to socialism upon indigenous political traditions, and their idealization of "the people" while stressing the vital role of an intellectual elite.

Quasi-*narodnik* ideas are conspicuous, for instance, in the work of Frantz Fanon, the West Indian psychiatrist who became involved in the Algerian revolution. His book *Les Damnés de la Terre*, published in 1961,[10] did much to create for a while the myth of a world wide anticolonial peasant revolt comparable to Marx's myth of the proletarian revolution.

Like Marx, Fanon was fond of using a peculiar tense which one might perhaps call the "revolutionary present." Just as Marx writes, for instance, of the revolution to come—"The knell of capitalist private property sounds. The expropriators are expropriated"[11]—Fanon writes of the popular uprising: "On every hill a government in miniature is formed and takes over power. Everywhere— in the valleys and in the forests, in the jungle and in the villages—we find a national authority."[12] The function of this tense is to make generalization easier, for although Fanon drew most of his material from Algeria, he never- theless wrote in general terms about *the* colonial situa- tion, *the* revolution and, of course, *the* people.

Being an alien, Fanon was even more of an outsider than the Russian populists who viewed "the people" from above. He was aware of differences and tensions among various groups within the colonial population in Algeria and elsewhere, and was concerned about the implications of such differences for the anticolonial struggle. How- ever, he explained these differences in terms of a dis- tinction between on the one hand, the urban classes, bourgeoisie, workers, and political leaders who had been corrupted by coming into contact with the colonizers and acquiring vested interests, and on the other hand, the country people about whom he wrote in lyrical terms:

> The militant nationalist who decides to throw in his lot
> with the country people instead of playing at hide-and-
> seek with the police in urban centers will lose nothing.

The peasant's cloak will wrap him around with a gentleness and firmness that he never suspected. . . . Their ears hear the true voice of the country, and their eyes take in the great and infinite poverty of their people. . . .

These men get used to talking to the peasants. They discover that the mass of the country people have never ceased to think of the problem of their liberation in terms of violence, in terms of taking back the land from the foreigners, in terms of national struggle and of armed insurrection. It is all very simple. These men discover a coherent people who go on living, as it were, statically, but who keep their moral values and their devotion to the nation intact. They discover a people that is generous, ready to sacrifice themselves completely, an impatient people, with a stony pride.[13]

As in the case of Russian populism, Fanon's attitude to the people reveals a certain ambivalence between enthusiasm for the qualities they already have, and belief in a revolutionary transformation of the people into a higher type of humanity. Fanon argued, in terms that earned him fame and notoriety, that the source of this new humanity was revolutionary violence, about which he managed to sound as high-minded as the terrorists of *Narodnaya Volya*: "Violence is a cleansing force. It frees the native from his inferiority complex and from his despair and inaction; it makes him fearless and restores his self-respect."[14]

One of his main concerns was to keep anticolonial revolutions from turning into mere changes of elite, with "nationalist" leaders stepping into the shoes of the colonizers. Instead, he hoped for a truly popular society, in which the party that had made the revolution would be a channel for direct popular self-government, and where the economy would be organized not by centralized, authoritarian state planning but on the basis of popular cooperatives in the countryside.

In some Third World countries, *narodnik*-style views have not remained at the level of romantic idealism, but have actually influenced policy. This has been noticeably the case, for instance, in Tanzania, where President Nyerere (echoing Russian dreams of agrarian socialism) has aimed at an "African Socialism" drawing on traditional tribal communalism. As Nyerere has put it: "We, in Africa, have no more need of being 'converted' to socialism than we have of being 'taught' democracy. Both are rooted in our own past—in the traditional society which produced us."[15] There is much in Nyerere's outlook that recalls the *narodniki*: for instance, his belief that, if capitalist individualism could be prevented from eroding communal values, the transition to socialism would be easier in Africa than elsewhere; or his high-minded attacks on luxurious living by the political elite and his reluctance to accept socialist elitism: "A people cannot be developed; they can only develop themselves."[16]

A hardheaded and successful politician, Nyerere has of course always displayed much greater political realism than the *narodniki*; nevertheless, his policies have been influenced by a kind of agrarian romanticism reminiscent of the Russians. Like them, he overestimated the communal instincts of the peasants, and made efforts to congregate the country people into village collectives—a move that turned out to be much less popular than expected.

This particular tendency to attribute collectivist attitudes to peasants seems, indeed, to be a recurrent weakness of populist intellectuals. When a revolutionary land reform was set under way in Bolivia in the 1950s, for instance, the M.N.R. leaders proposed to reserve 10 percent of the land for cooperative farming, which they believed to be in accordance with the communal traditions of the Indian villagers. To their surprise, the villagers opposed all collectivist schemes and opted for family farms.[17] Elsewhere, controversies very much in the *narodnik* manner over whether or not traditional village communities prefigure communism have raged among Peruvian and Vietnamese intellectuals.[18] Such cases indicate the typical lack of close rapport with the actual "people" characteristic of populist intelligentsias.

The similarities between the *narodniki* and contemporary versions of agrarian socialism current among Third World intellectuals are suggestive rather than precise. They are sufficient to indicate, however, that the Russian experience was not unique, and that similar problems and solutions tend to recur among the intelligentsias of developing countries. One problem in particular which the Russian populists never managed to solve successfully, and which we have seen coming to the surface again in the case of Fanon and Nyerere, is the problem of elite/mass relations. If the farmers' movements we have looked at seem to be capable of generating either charismatic demagogues or participatory democracy, intelligentsia populism has its own particular political dilemma: a tendency to oscillate between deference to the wishes of an idealized peasantry and stress on the leading role of the elite. Since populist intellectuals often misjudge popular attitudes, the relationship between the progressive minority and the reactionary populace presents peculiar difficulties for them—a subject to which we shall return.

## PEASANT POPULISM

So far, our evidence suggests that it may indeed be useful to regard U.S. Populism and *narodnichestvo* as paradigm cases of two sorts of recurrent rural radicalisms, characteristic in the one case of farmers dependent upon a commodity market and in the other of intellectuals in a developing country. On the face of it, however, there seems little to hold these two genres together, apart from the negative point that both are cases of radical movements based on or directed toward the country rather than the town, and the fact that both (in their different ways) idealize "the people."

Grass-roots farmers' movements and intellectuals romanticizing the peasantry—what have these in common? If we are to make any headway toward a more general notion of agrarian populism, we can do so only by seeing these two types as opposite ends of a spectrum, the center of which remains as yet unfilled. For between grass-roots farmers' movements on the one hand and intellectual dreams of the transformation of society by the peasantry on the other, there surely lies another vast and significant category of rural radicalisms: actual grass-roots peasant movements. Such movements, from the Zapatistas in Mexico to the Agrarian Union in Bulgaria, are also frequently given the title of "populist,"[19] and we must now grapple with the thorny question whether there is a characteristic "peasant populism" that will link together our two existing types.

General discussion of peasant movements involves venturing into an academic minefield. What, to begin with, is a "peasant"? What are the distinguishing marks of the species, and who counts as belonging to it? Indian villagers in the High Andes, the French rural population in the nineteenth century, Russian *muzhiks* before and after emancipation, workers in Chinese rural communes: all these, and many other diverse categories of people, receive the designation of "peasant," so that the enormous range of variation within the term is obvious. There is a large and controversial scholarly literature on the subject, some of it stressing that peasants as cultivators are primarily geared to subsistence rather than the market; some emphasizing their subordinate and exploited status; some the role of the family farm; and some the dependence of the peasant "part-society" upon a wider social organization.[20] It is clear that, whatever definition one adopts, there are many differences among the people generally so designated. Some are personally free and others not; some much more geared to commercial markets than others; some are well-off, others miserably poor; while some have strong communal traditions and others do not.

If we are to say anything to the purpose about such a diffuse subject, it is clear that we must find a concrete case of a peasant movement to set alongside our American and Russian examples. The difficulty here is that while those two have classic status in the field, there is no comparable example of a peasant uprising which all commentators would acknowledge as the classic case of peasant populism.

Our choice must inevitably be somewhat arbitrary; it

will perhaps help to reduce the centrifugal tendencies of our subject matter, however, if we fix upon an example that has direct links with the Russian movement we have already discussed: namely, the "Green Uprising" in Eastern Europe after World War I. This peasant movement—or rather, this collection of related but different peasant movements in Poland, Czechoslovakia, Yugoslavia, Bulgaria, and Rumania—had numerous links with *narodnichestvo*. Many of the East European peasant leaders were influenced by *narodnik* ideas, although their movements were grass-roots affairs as Russian populism never was.

The Green Uprising has the further advantage for our purpose of being, like U.S. Populism, not only a grass-roots movement but a fairly self-conscious and articulate one. Unlike the innumerable peasants who have risen in revolt throughout history and been repressed without leaving any clear program behind, the East European peasants after World War I took advantage of their sudden (and short-lived) acquisition of democratic rights to establish organized movements expressing a specifically "peasant" point of view which was formulated in conscious opposition to both modern capitalism and socialism. Faced with alternatives which struck them as equally unattractive, the peasants' leaders put forward a third possibility, the vision of a democratic society based on small family property, widespread cooperation, and respect for traditional rural values. This agrarian outlook appeared with variations in many different countries and even led to the formation of a short-lived Green International.

In discussing this sample of grass-roots peasant movements, we must of course recognize two caveats. In the first place, although the peasant leaders in the various Eastern European countries did cooperate to some extent and did think of themselves as members of a common movement, there were very large variations between (and indeed, within) the different countries. Ethnic hostilities, for instance, between Slavs and non-Slavs, or between Croats and Serbs, were often divisive. Second, even if, for the sake of clarity, we may be allowed to treat the Green Uprising as more of a unity than it really was, and to play down some of the significant national differences, it may still be the case that the peasants involved were untypical of peasants in other times and places. This latter, however, is a problem that we must postpone until after we have looked (however cursorily) at the brief invasion of politics by the East European grass roots.

Eastern Europe is an area in which ethnic groups have for centuries been intermingled, and in which a state's boundaries have generally had little to do with the nationality of its inhabitants and a great deal to do with the fortunes of war. At the beginning of this century, most of the population of the area had a history of being governed by alien and distant emperors, the Hapsburgs, the Turks, or the Tsars. Of the three, Hapsburg rule was the most enlightened: generally speaking, however, in the eyes of the rural population in all areas, the state was an alien organization for extracting taxes and conscripting soldiers—a negative evaluation that survived the breakup of the empires after World War I and the creation of what were supposed to be national states.[21]

Peasants made up the bulk of the population in these states—80 percent in Bulgaria, 78 percent in Rumania; 75 percent in Yugoslavia; 63 percent in Poland[22]—and the vast majority of these had long lived in poverty and squalor, dominated locally by an elite caste of landlords. While in most areas the formal bonds of legal serfdom had been removed in the nineteeth century, various forms of economic neoserfdom persisted. In Rumania, for instance, the countryside had become divided between vast latifundia and peasant plots so tiny that most peasants had to lease extra land and pasture from the landlords, who took care to insist that their rents should be paid in the form of labor on the lords' estate. By the early twentieth century, land hunger among the peasants and the competition faced by grain-exporting landlords on the world market had combined to drive up the rents to a point where the population of one of the major granaries of Europe was chronically overworked and undernourished. Peasants often had to get in the lord's crop while their own rotted in the fields, and the effects of bad and insufficient food showed themselves in an alarming increase in disease. Rural misery and discontent burst out eventually in the terrible Rumanian peasant revolt of 1907, suppressed only with the loss of at least ten thousand lives.[23]

Neighboring Bulgaria, which had gained independence from the Turks in 1879, had fewer large landowners since the former Turkish landlords had been expropriated, and rural society there was exceptionally egalitarian and homogeneous.[24] But even here the peasants were not much better off. They were burdened with a top-heavy government apparatus: an expensive army and bureaucracy that provided the urban upper class with prestigious jobs, but had to be paid for by the peasants. Under the Turks, they had had to pay the tithe, a much-hated tax payable in agricultural produce. This was abolished to celebrate independence, but the relief did not last long. The Bulgarian government chose 1899, a year of famine, to restore the tithe, a singularly insensitive decision that caused great unrest and led to the founding of what became one of the most radical of peasant organizations, the Bulgarian Agrarian Union.

Besides the specific grievances peculiar to each country, the people of Eastern Europe in the early twentieth century were subject to all the evils endemic to peasant life: famine, shortage of land, the subdivision of plots into parcels so small that effective farming was impossible, and the ever-present curse of usury.

Into this wretched countryside came the cataclysmic upheaval of World War I. Peasants were conscripted by hundreds of thousands, livestock was requisitioned, and cultivation languished, while empires fell and boundaries were redrawn wholesale. But from the point of view of many peasants, one of the most striking effects of the war was the land reform that followed it. Uncertain governments, shocked out of their complacency by the spectacle of the Russian Revolution, suddenly realized that their own peasants had weapons in their hands and no reason to feel loyal to their betters. Government after government hastily promised redistribution of the land, and although more was promised than performed, in most Eastern European countries substantial amounts of land were distributed to the peasants.

The usual pattern was for legislation to fix a maximum

that any particular proprietor could hold, and to break up the surplus into small holdings for distribution.[25] These reforms did not solve the peasants' problems: in fact, by stimulating a general increase in population they rapidly increased land hunger and subdivision of farms. What they did do, however, was to make Eastern European society even more overwhelmingly peasant in composition and outlook than previously.

As another result of the postwar settlement, most of the East European countries were presented with formally democratic constitutions. The corrupt and self-serving regimes that followed may have had little connection with the principle of rule by the people, but since "the people" were, without question, the peasants, there was a rapid blossoming of peasant political parties.[26] Many of the organizations which now acquired mass followings had been founded well before the war, often by men who had felt the influence of Russian populism. The founder of the Polish Peasant Party, for instance, Boleslaw Wyslouch, was a member of the gentry who had been at the university in St. Petersburg in the 1870s and picked up *narodnik* ideas there. Until World War I, Poland was partitioned and it was impossible to engage openly in politics in the Russian-controlled section, but in the Austrian-ruled province of Galicia peasants actually possessed votes, although they were in the habit of using them at the direction of their social superiors. When the Polish Peasant Party was founded in 1895, one of its slogans, provided by Wyslouch, was "Peasants, elect a peasant!"[27]

This revolutionary suggestion that peasants themselves

might participate in politics was altogether too radical for the liberal democrats of the time, who protested, "No civilised country has ever entrusted ploughmen with seats in parliament."[28] It is not surprising, therefore, that when genuinely homespun peasant leaders did emerge, they made a point of demonstrating their authenticity to their peasant constituents. One of the most influential Polish populist leaders was Wincenty Witos, whose introduction to responsibility had been grazing the family cow when he was five years old.[29] When Witos became a politician he made no attempt to disguise his origins. On the contrary, he refused to wear a collar and tie, spat on the floor at official gatherings, and claimed that when the call to form a government after World War I came, he was out plowing the fields like Cincinnatus.

Such deliberate flaunting of the symbols of peasant life was a natural response to centuries of contempt. Another of the Polish peasant activists, Jakub Bojko, published a book in 1904 called *Two Souls*, in which he urged peasants to cast off the domination of the lords over their minds and spirits and realize that they could be their own masters. He claimed that "there is a struggle going on within every peasant: a soul shaped by the past—humble, shy and frightened—is struggling against the soul of a man who is free, modern, equal to his former masters."[30]

This new sense of the peasant's worth found its most militant expression in the Bulgarian Agrarian National Union under the leadership of Alexander Stamboliski. Stamboliski had been born into a peasant family, although (like most peasant leaders) he was not himself a working peasant, but had gained an education and become a schoolteacher. In the years before World War I he worked out his own theory of the Agrarian movement, which he put forward in *Political Parties or Estatist Organisations?*, published in 1909.[31] Political parties of the traditional type, liberal or conservative, had had their day, he said. In the modern world, politics was increasingly preoccupied with economic questions, and the natural political groups were those based on socioeconomic interests. Political parties which purported to appeal to members of all economic groups in fact served only the selfish interests of the politicians themselves. They should be replaced by organizations openly serving the interests of the various "estates" or socioeconomic groups, who could then bargain among themselves and adjust their conflicting interests. The largest of these estates was of course the peasantry, and Stamboliski set out to turn BANU into an effective peasant organization, standing for the interests of the small family farm, seeking to aid it by providing cooperatives and education, and aiming to reduce its burden of taxation by cutting down military and bureaucratic expenditure.

When Stamboliski came to power in Bulgaria in 1919 he did his best to implement this program. Land reform redistributed holdings to small or landless peasants, and the introduction of a progressive income tax reduced the tax burden of the average peasant family to about half its prewar level.[32] The government introduced cooperative marketing of grain, so that small peasants would not be forced to sell at low prices to the first buyer. Funds for university education were cut to pay for a thousand village schools, and special rural courts were created in which peasants could plead their own case without recourse to lawyers. But the most controversial of all Stamboliski's radical measures was his scheme for Compulsory Labor Service. In order to exalt the dignity of labor, to reduce social parasitism, and to weld together people of all classes, every male over twenty and every female over sixteen were to be subject to conscription, men for a year and women for six months. According to the original scheme, there were to be no exemptions or substitutes. The conscripts were to live in camps and work on road building and other public services. Not surprisingly, this high-handed scheme met with violent opposition and was never fully implemented.[33]

Another of Stamboliski's cherished projects was the Green International, an organization for peaceful cooperation between the agrarian parties of different countries. In pursuit of this aim he traveled around Europe and made contact particularly with the leaders of peasant parties in Poland and Czechoslovakia. Stamboliski did not have long, however, to put his dreams into practice. Having thoroughly antagonized the entire urban elite in Bulgaria, he was overthrown by a right-wing coup in 1923 and tortured to death. Given the violence of Bulgarian politics, this was not altogether surprising. He had himself been quite prepared to use strong-arm methods against his opponents, suppressing communist teachers and recruiting a paramilitary Orange Guard to break strikes by force. Even his large electoral majority in 1923 was achieved partly by altering the electoral system.[34]

Stamboliski's radical program undoubtedly enjoyed a good deal of support among the peasants themselves, and after his death he was honored as a martyr. Some European peasant parties, however, were not radical at all, and it would be unwise to take the various peasant leaders entirely at their face value as spokesmen for their massive electorates. In the nature of things, peasant parties were often led or influenced by intellectuals rather than working peasants; while those among them who, like Witos in Poland, really did on occasion work a plow, were inclined to treat politics as a ladder to personal advantage. Corruption was a perpetual weakness in the peasant movements, and so was infirmity of purpose. Olga Narkiewicz, who remarks of Witos that "his personality was strong, but his ideology was weak,"[35] suggests that the slipperiness of some peasant leaders may have been derived from traditional peasant tactics in tight corners.[36] Faced with opposition or domination, the peasant had learned over the centuries that it is wiser not to stand and fight except as a last resort. Instead, like his epitome, the Good Soldier Schweik, he retreats, apparently acquiesces, and conceals behind an appearance of stupidity a craftiness that can, in politics, become indistinguishable from lack of principle. In the case of Polish populism, deficiencies of leadership were aggravated by disputes between the parties that had grown up in the different partitioned areas of the country. It was not until 1931 that all the various peasant groups united—too late—into a single party, to oppose the dictatorship of Pilsudski.

The Versailles treaties that ended World War I had provided for "national self-determination," but given the chaotic mixture of ethnic groups in Eastern Europe this was not possible. Since each state contained minorities who considered themselves oppressed, it was perhaps unavoidable that some peasant parties, particularly those representing the smaller linguistic groups, should have become diverted into representing ethnic interests rather than specifically peasant ones. The Croatian Peasant Party, for instance, had been founded before World War I by the two Radic brothers, intellectuals from a poor peasant family, who mobilized the peasantry in support of a program of land reform, direct democracy, and national self-determination. After the war, in a new Yugoslav state dominated by Serbs, the party became in effect the spokesman of the entire Croatian community, and was consequently deflected from its overriding concern with the interests of the peasants.[37]

The heyday of the peasant movement was the 1920s, when the Green International—the International Agrarian Bureau originally set up on Stamboliski's initiative—seemed to many observers to represent the wave of the future. Comintern leaders in particular were sufficiently alarmed to set up a rival, the Red Peasant International, in an attempt to woo the peasants away from populism.[38] The Green International's official organ plunged in its first issue into agrarian romanticism, claiming that all virtue sprang from the mystical tie between man and the soil.[39] Mysticism apart, however, the movement did have a fairly coherent platform of support for private property coupled with land reform and cooperatives, social insurance, technical education, and low tariffs. A General Assembly of the Green International, called in May 1929, attracted representatives from seventeen European peasant parties, and looked at the time like a serious political force.[40]

Nevertheless, the peasant parties succumbed one after

another to the right-wing coups that spread over Eastern Europe. The only one to survive intact until it was suppressed by foreign invasion was the Czech Agrarian Party, which was in some ways anomalous. For Czechoslovakia was much more industrially developed and less of a peasant society than the other East European countries. The Czech Agrarian Party did not attempt to cater exclusively for peasant interests, but instead formed the nucleus of successive coalition governments, cooperating with a variety of other parties further to the right to provide the country with stable government right up to the time of Hitler's invasion.

Peasant parties sprang up again after World War II, only to be suppressed or absorbed by the new Communist regimes. Their political record, therefore, is one of almost unmitigated failure. Nevertheless, they did succeed in expressing a distinctive political and social standpoint. Let us now look in more detail at this peasant ideology.

## THE GREEN UPRISING

In the nature of things, it is not to be expected that a peasant movement should have a very sophisticated ideology. Ideology is the stock-in-trade of urban intellectuals, and the peasant leaders could on occasion pride themselves on their *lack* of anything so inauthentic.[41] Many of the theoretical formulations of the peasants' position were in fact put forward by intellectuals speaking for the peasants from above as the *narodniki* had tried to do. One of the most persuasive Rumanian theorists, for instance, Constantin Stere, was a Bessarabian boyar who had associated with the *narodniki* to the extent of being banished to Siberia for his activities.[42]

Generally speaking, however, even the intellectuals of the East European movements had more experience of real peasant life than their Russian predecessors. Many of them had been born into peasant households, like Stamboliski in Bulgaria, or like the Radic brothers in Croatia, who bore the physical marks of their poor childhood diet of cornmeal mush, dried beans, and noodles.[43] There seems little reason to doubt that the ideology which these various ex-peasants formulated did correspond in its main outlines to the interests and aspirations of many of the peasants themselves.

The cornerstone of peasant ideology was a stress upon the sacredness of family property. This was given enormous impetus by the Russian Revolution. "Socialism" rapidly became a label for the disastrous requisitioning of supplies the Russian peasants had suffered in the early years of the Soviet regime and the forcible collectivization which was inflicted upon them later. After this, socialists were branded in many rural eyes as urban doctrinaires whose chief aim was to deprive the peasant of his land, his crops, and his cattle.

Although the agrarians were enthusiastic defenders of peasant family property, they were by no means in favor of all property rights. Their views on the idle rich, landowners, plutocrats, and usurers were similar to those of the U.S. Populists, and peasant programs often supported nationalization of industries such as mining which were too large-scale to be broken down into small enterprises.[44] Their point was that property is justified not by legal title alone but by *work*. This view found its most dramatic expression in Stamboliski's compulsory labor scheme, but the principle was universal.

What the agrarians had in mind was a society of independent producers, linked together not by forcible, bureaucratic state collectivism but by voluntary cooperation. As Stere put it, what was needed was "a vigorous peasantry, master of the land on which it works, and for which—through the organisation of a perfected system of cooperative societies—the advantages of small properties are united with all the technical advantages today available only to large property."[45] This stress on cooperation is entirely typical. Throughout Eastern European populism, cooperative organization became the panacea that nationalization has at times been for socialists. When Stamboliski was in power, for instance, he fostered cooperative banks to provide peasants with cheap credit, cooperative storing and marketing for grain, and cooperatives among fishermen and lumbermen to exploit Bulgaria's waters and forests. Some of the most successful experiments in cooperation took place in Czechoslovakia, where there were cases of direct exchanges between agricultural cooperatives in the countryside and consumer cooperatives in the towns.[46] The agrarians found inspiration in the example of Denmark, which seemed to have succeeded, partly through the widespread use of cooperative methods, in creating a prosperous society of small producers, achieving modernity while remaining rural and avoiding both large-scale capitalism and socialism.

This notion of a third path which was neither capitalist nor socialist but superior to both was a constant theme. It seemed to them that a society of prosperous peasants linked by voluntary arrangements was not only more appropriate to agrarian states, but also more attractive

and humane than either of the alternatives with their
stress on large-scale enterprise, urbanization, and bureaucratic organization. Attitudes to industrial development
within the populist movement varied from hostility to
qualified approval. At one extreme there was a tendency
to idealize rural life and to regard towns as parasitic
excrescences. To quote Stamboliski:

> The village and the town are inhabited by two peoples,
> different in their appearances and needs. . . . In the
> villages live a people who work, fight and earn their
> living at the caprice of nature. In the towns live a people
> who earn their living not by exploiting nature, but by
> exploiting the labour of others. This is a rule to which
> there is no exception. . . . The city people live by deceit,
> by idleness, by parasitism, by perversion.[47]

This judgment on the towns, though harsh, was not unreasonable, considering the circumstances of East European society.[48] It was often accompanied, however, by
large claims about the moral superiority of rural life.
These were characteristic, for instance, of the Polish
youth organization, *Wici*, which was influential during
the 1930s. *Wici* laid great stress on the wholesomeness
of agricultural life, and established people's universities
in the countryside where young peasants could gain an
education that would link them more closely with nature
and the land, instead of going off to be socialized into
the ways of the town.[49] Populists liked to exalt the practical common sense of the "ignorant" peasant above the
slick cleverness of town dwellers.

Particularly after the peasant parties had succumbed
to dictators and political activity was no longer possible,

it was tempting to find solace in romantic pictures of rural life. All the same, most populists were not opposed to industrialization as such, provided that it was promoted in a way that would benefit the mass of the rural population. What they wished to see was light industry scattered throughout the countryside on the pattern of Switzerland or southern Germany, employing surplus peasant labor and producing goods that would be useful to the local people.[50] One of the most cogent defenders of this kind of small-scale industrialism was the Rumanian economist Virgil Madgearu, who was in favor, for instance, of developing the production of agricultural machines and tools which could be made available through cooperatives to raise the productivity of the peasant farm.[51]

The political counterpart of this stress on independent peasant property was a commitment to democracy. Serenely conscious that peasants were the vast majority of the population in most of the countries concerned— that, as one commentator put it, "the interest of the peasants is the general, the national interest"[52]—they had no reason to be attracted by theories of elite rule or vanguard dictatorship. Although the case of Stamboliski showed that they could resort to strong-arm tactics in situations where political violence was universal (while their politicians were rarely above the corruption habitual in East European politics), at the level of doctrine the peasant parties favored all the techniques of direct democracy, the initiative, the referendum, and the recall. Suspicious of urban domination, they wanted decentralized administration which the peasants themselves could control. Their respect for work and their hostility to parasites

made their creed egalitarian, while their massive constituency encouraged them to avoid hasty revolutionary
methods and to stress the virtues of constitutional modes
of reform.

In contrast to the militaristic regimes of the right to
which they succumbed, the peasant movements were not
notably chauvinistic. Stamboliski was not untypical in
taking a stand (denounced at the time as unpatriotic)
against the various disastrous wars in which the Bulgarian monarchy involved itself.[53] His efforts to establish
a Green International for peaceful cooperation between
peasant parties in neighboring countries met with an
encouraging response, particularly in the other Slav
states. The International Agrarian Bureau was set up,
with its headquarters in Prague, and various attempts at
international cooperation followed. One of the enthusi-
asts declared: "We know that agrarian democracy . . .
is a strong bond which will bring the peoples together
in an international unity . . . against which all attacks
whether from the imperialist Right or the Bolshevik Left
will shatter themselves."[54]

The main blot on the image of the peasant movement
was anti-Semitism, which was as widespread among the
populists as it was among the rural population in countries such as Poland and Rumania. In Poland, most of
the inns and the local trade were in Jewish hands, and
since the Jews practiced something analogous to the
Protestant Ethic, living modest and sober lives and growing rich at the expense of the drunken peasantry, they
were much resented.[55] One of the main drawbacks Social
Democratic parties encountered, indeed, when they tried

to appeal to peasant electorates, was that socialism was associated in the popular mind with Jews. It is typical of the general pattern that Rumania's most notable Marxist theorist, Gherea, was Jewish, while his populist antagonist, Stere, was anti-Semitic.[56] Rumania later became the scene of a fascist and violently anti-Semitic movement with populist overtones and a good deal of peasant support: Codreanu's League of the Archangel Michael.

It must be recognized that Eastern European peasant populism had a serious ideological fault. Just as socialism has often alienated peasants because it tends to have no place for the privately owned family farm, so agrarianism, with its exclusive stress on family property and rural life, made little allowance for the rural proletariat. Where there were still large estates to be split up, populists might cherish the illusion that land reform would solve the problem of the rural poor, and establish each family upon its own substantial plot. The fact was, however, that land reform merely gave a stimulus to population increase, with the result that peasant holdings were divided and subdivided into ever smaller plots, leaving a growing number of people landless or with so little land that they were effectively proletarians. Only massive industrialization, upon which peasant populists tended to look with suspicion, could solve this problem. As Hugh Seton-Watson put it in 1946: "The brutal truth is that the Peasant States can only become prosperous and healthy when they cease to be Peasant States."[57]

## TYPES OF AGRARIAN POPULISM

Even a brief glance at the Green Uprising is perhaps enough to indicate that this type of peasant movement does in a sense provide the missing link between Russian and American populisms. There was on the one hand a direct historical link with *narodnichestvo* via such leaders as Wyslouch and Stere, while such notions as the possibility of noncapitalist development for peasant countries and the stress on saving the independent peasant from proletarianization, both clearly derived from Russia. The socialism and the emphasis on violent revolution that were characteristic of Russian populism tended to be dropped, however, as *narodnik* ideas moved west. Instead, the peasant parties showed considerable similarities to U.S. Populism, notably stress on the virtues of the producer, the family farm, and the cooperative; hostility to plutocrats; and emphasis on grass-roots democracy.

The differences from American populism are significant, however. The participants in the Green Uprising were much more traditionally minded than their American counterparts, more hostile to towns, more inclined to romanticize rural life, and more suspicious of government intervention—differences obviously related to the fact that they were still peasants rather than farmers. Although subsistence agriculture was increasingly affected by commercial considerations, the average East European peasant in the 1920s was much less geared to the market, much less of a businessman, than the average settler in the American West.

If we wish to characterize the outlook of the East European peasant movements, perhaps we should return to the definition of populism that we rejected when discussing the Russians: Walicki's claim that populism represents "the class standpoint of the small producer."[58] For the Green movements were indeed petty-bourgeois in outlook, anxious to escape from the anxieties and oppressions of the feudal past but to avoid the large-scale capitalism or socialism of the future.[59] They were also, on the whole, fairly staid, cautious movements, not revolutionary, and radical only where land reform was concerned—a disappointment to those populist intellectuals who longed for the peasants to rise with axes in their hands and create a new social order.

There have, of course, been plenty of examples of much more revolutionary peasant movements.[60] One need only think of the Zapatistas in Mexico, the Bolivian Revolution of 1952, or indeed the Russian peasants in 1917. These have tended to find more favor with radical populist intellectuals than peasantism of the Eastern European kind. It seems clear, however, that such violent outbreaks have generally not aimed at any radical reconstruction of society, but at getting back land which the peasants considered rightfully theirs and at throwing off landlord domination. Once they have succeeded in getting land and liberty, their radicalism disappears abruptly, leaving them with an outlook akin to that of the Green International.[61]

What, then, of those revolutionary movements which *have* mobilized peasants for a socialist transformation of society? Is Maoism, for example, a variety of populism and a vindication of *narodnik* hopes of founding socialism upon the traditional egalitarianism of the peasantry? There were certainly some points of similarity between Mao and the *narodniki*, as Mao's Soviet detractors lost no time in pointing out.[62] His stress on the essential role of the peasantry in revolution went beyond Lenin's tactical concessions into something like populism, while his gesture during the Cultural Revolution of sending

young intellectuals into the countryside recalls the movement "to the people." There is a *narodnik* air about Mao's
directive, which read: "It is very necessary for educated
young people to go to the countryside to be re-educated
by the poor and the lower-middle peasants."[63] The exaltation of the masses at the expense of elites and specialists,
which was so marked at the time of the Cultural Revolution, was also reminiscent of some aspects of Russian
populism.

Just how significant these populist elements are in the
total composition of Maoism, however, is another question, and a highly controversial one.[64] Mao was, after all,
chairman of a Marxist-Leninist Communist party, blessed
(or burdened) with a large body of theoretical doctrine
hostile to most peasant institutions and traditions. The
ambiguities of his position, disguised by the convenient
terminology of Marxist dialectics, can be discerned in
his formulation of the "mass line":

> In all the practical work of our party, all correct leader-
> ship is necessarily from the masses, to the masses. This
> means: take the ideas of the masses (scattered and un-
> systematic ideas) and concentrate them (through study
> turn them into concentrated and systematic ideas), then
> go to the masses and propagate and explain these ideas
> until the masses embrace them as their own, hold fast to
> them and translate them into action, and test the cor-
> rectness of these ideas in such action. Then once again
> concentrate ideas from the masses and once again take
> them to the masses.[65]

Similar ambiguities can of course be found in *narodni-*
*chestvo*, which involved a balancing act between stress
on the leading role of the revolutionary intelligentsia

and uncritical worship of the instincts of the *narod*. There is no doubt, however, that Marxism-Leninism acts as a stiffening agent, providing a legitimation for overriding popular wishes that populism itself cannot provide. It seems reasonable, therefore, to note the continuities and overlaps between populism (particularly of the intellectual kind) and Maoism and its imitators, but to recognize that the nonpopulist elements in the latter have contributed greatly to its effectiveness as an agency of social change.

To sum up: we have found certain continuities between the various agrarian populisms considered. They can perhaps be viewed in terms of a spectrum, one end of which is occupied by radical intellectuals (most often in developing countries) who are liable to idealize the peasantry, exaggerate their communal traditions, and dream of indigenous socialism to be created by a peasant revolution. One step further along the spectrum, those peasants may indeed rise in revolt, but—unless they are mobilized and dominated by Communist intellectuals— strictly in pursuit of "land and liberty." Having achieved these, they tend to settle into a peasantist outlook of the type expressed by the Green Uprising, stressing family property and cooperatives. Emancipated peasants are well on their way to becoming commercial farmers, involved in commercial markets and interested in currency questions. If they reach such a position, then in times of crisis radical populist interventionism of the type desired by the U.S. farmers may appeal to them.[66] "Socialism" of a sort could be said to appear at each end of our agrarian populist spectrum, but in fact there is a world of difference and of agrarian experience between the communal ideals of the *narodniki* and the interventionist program of the People's Party.

The continuities between our different forms of agrarian radicalism make intelligible the use of a single term, "populism," to describe such a wide range of movements. What they do not enable us to do, however, is to unite all these movements into a single political phenomenon with a single ideology, program, or socioeconomic base. Although there are considerable overlaps (a marked preference for cooperative modes of economic organization, for instance), it seems clear that intellectuals, peasants of various types, and commercial farmers characteristically have produced different types of populism, intelligibly related to their social and economic situations but not reducible to a common core.

It is not surprising, therefore, that attempts to define "populism" as such or to identify specific socioeconomic circumstances that give rise to it should have tended either to invite counterexamples or to remain at an unhelpfully high level of generality. J. B. Allcock has suggested, for example, that populism can be understood by reference to the distinction (developed by anthropologists to describe peasants) between "part-societies" and the "wholes" to which they are uneasily related.[67] Populists are people who are on the periphery—not fully integrated into the "whole," yet unable to remain independent within the "part."

Like many such explanations, this seems persuasive at first sight. Surely the relation of American farmers to the Eastern commercial community, of East European peasants to their national governments, or of intellectuals in developing countries to the West, is accurately described by this image of a part which is different from but not independent of a larger whole. The difficulties only become apparent when we recognize that the "whole" is defined differently in each case, whereupon we realize that this is a conceptual schema that could be applied to virtually any situation. The working class in an industrial society forms a "part" of the whole: are labor movements therefore populist, too? Is any minority nationalism, from Scottish Nationalism to Zionism or to the Jurassien separatist movement, to count as populist? Since all countries, however economically advanced, are now dependent parts of the international economic system, is all modern politics populist? If not, which elements are and which are not? The defect of the scheme is that it does not explain why certain movements qualify as populist, nor account for the variations in outlook and program between the various movements caught in its net.

Similar objections apply to attempts to identify populism by its "social roots." If we define populism as "a response to the problems posed by modernization and its consequences,"[68] then, given the all-pervasiveness in the contemporary world of these problems, all political movements appear to qualify, and there is no means of distinguishing what is populist from what is not, let alone of accounting intelligibly for the variations within populism. In other words, explanations which are general enough to cover all the cases fail because they are *too* general: they contain no criteria to enable us to identify our subject matter.

What conclusions may we draw from our discussion

so far? It seems that if we employ a predominantly socioeconomic focus we can identify a range of rural radicalisms, from intellectuals' via peasants' to farmers' populisms, which have a certain continuity but no fundamental unity of outlook. This rather deflating conclusion that there is no *one* populism must, however, be qualified with a significant exception. All the movements we have considered share a tendency to idealize the people and to regard elites with hostility. As we have seen, this outlook creates problems where it is an intellectual elite that is itself antielitist and inclined to idealize the people; it creates problems of a more practical kind, too, within a grass-roots movement, for every movement needs leadership, while populist movements have produced charismatic leaders as often as participatory democracy.

Once we begin to consider these questions, however, our focus is no longer limited to agrarian populism. For the antielitism and idealization of the grass roots which our various agrarian populisms have in common is by no means limited to rural radicalisms like these. Similar impulses occur in other forms and situations. It is time, then, to change our focus and turn from populism identified in socioeconomic terms—populism as rural radicalism—to populism in its political and cultural sense.

# 4. *Populist Dictatorship*

The more a populistic mass democracy advances, the more important the role of a charismatic leader in moulding public opinion becomes.—*Giovanni Sartori*[1]

A man is not a dictator when he is given a commission from the people and carries it out.—*Huey Long*[2]

## AGRARIAN AND POLITICAL APPROACHES TO POPULISM

An agrarian focus on populism has been much favored by scholars, particularly by sociologically minded analysts who have sought the causes of populism in socioeconomic conditions such as the response of backward regions to modernization. If we limit ourselves to the agrarian perspective, however, it becomes difficult to cater for many ordinary senses of "populism" which have little connection with rural radicalism. Instead, the stress in these uses of the term is upon political matters, often related to the tensions between populace and elite. There are, roughly speaking, four categories of phenomena often called populist in which the focus is political and cultural rather than agrarian.

1. Populist dictatorship: Caesarism, Bonapartism, Peronism; the familiar phenomenon of a charismatic leader who builds a dictatorship by appealing past the established elite and political system to "the people."

2. Populist democracy: populism as a practical political ideology, attempting to give substance to the democratic ideal of "government by the people" by means of some form of direct democracy, often by the use of referendums, popular initiatives, and recall procedures.

3. Reactionary populism: the mobilization of popular conservatism, ignorance, and prejudice in opposition to the progressive and enlightened views of the more educated and liberal elite. The most obvious danger areas for populism of this kind in modern Western democracies are ethnic hostilities and the demand for law and order.

4. Politicians' populism: a style of political mobilization that endeavors to enlist as wide a constituency as possible, and that appeals to "the people" in order to avoid divisive questions of ideology and class. Sometimes regarded as characteristic of Third World political parties, this kind of "catch-all People's Party" is not unknown in the West.[3]

These categories are not, of course, mutually exclusive, although it will make for greater clarity if we look at them separately. Neither do they exclude the more socioeconomic focus of agrarian populism. It may be the case, for instance, that certain types of *political* populism are characteristic of the socioeconomic circumstances that produce certain types of *agrarian* populism. There is much to be said, however, for the Hegelian procedure of using analysis as a stage on the way to synthesis. Attempts to lump as many as possible of the phenomena of populism into one barrel and to label them all "responses to modernization" tend to confuse the issues instead of clarifying them.

The need for distinctions, especially for the basic one between agrarian and political perspectives on populism, will become evident if we look for a moment at some uses of the term in connection with Latin American politics. Latin American countries, with their large and often exploited rural populations, might seem an obvious setting for agrarian populist movements of the peasant type. In fact, however, although there have been some striking examples of that genre, above all the rising of Zapata's followers for land and liberty during the Mexican Revolution, the term "populist" as used in connection with Latin American politics refers less often to agrarian movements than to urban political parties which are either headed by a charismatic leader or are catch-all in their support, and which therefore fall into one or both of the categories we have labeled "Populist dictatorship" and "Politicians' populism."[4]

One recent writer in the field maintains that populist movements in Latin America share three main characteristics.[5] These are a personalistic, demagogic style on the part of the leader; a following which includes the working class, but sections of higher classes as well; and an eclectic collection of policies aimed at modernization, national integration, and a limited degree of redistribution to the lower classes. Elsewhere, the picture of the populist party which emerges from studies of Latin American politics is of a vaguely radical but nonideological organization led by disaffected members of the higher classes, often with a charismatic personality at their head, but based upon the urban masses, particularly those newly enfranchised or previously left out of politics. According to much of the literature on the subject, the hallmark of such a party is the subservience of its popular following to the leadership. The people may on occasion gain tangible rewards for their support, such as the welfare and labor legislation granted by Peron in Argentina and Vargas in Brazil, but the relationship between leader and masses is essentially manipulative. The people, in other words, have no control over the party they support.

Populist politics is regarded by some writers as a stage on the way from pure subjection to democratic citizenship, but it is not itself democratic.[6] Rather, it results from the meeting between disaffected elites and "disposable masses." Torcuato di Tella has remarked of populism:

> The term is slightly derogatory, implying something distasteful, disorderly and brutish. . . . Populism also smacks of improvisation and irresponsibility, and by its nature, is not regarded as functional or efficient. . . . It may be defined as a political movement which enjoys the support of the mass of the urban working class and/or peasantry but which does not result from the autonomous organisational power of either of these two sectors.[7]

Di Tella provides an elaborate classification of the "assortment of political movements which, for lack of a better word, have been often grouped under the omnibus concept of populism."[8] He distinguishes between different types of populist movement in Latin America and elsewhere according to the nature of the elite which is undertaking the mobilization of the masses. How radical or moderate a movement becomes, he suggests, depends on the class origin of this disaffected elite, and the degree to which it has become cut off from its own background.

A somewhat different account of populism in Latin America has been provided by Gino Germani with particular reference to Peronism in Argentina.[9] Germani calls Peronism "national populism," in contrast to the "liberal populism" of earlier Argentine radical coalitions in which the middle classes enlisted lower-class support, and the "oligarchic populism" of "caudillo politics" manifested in the nineteenth century by bands of gauchos, each headed by a personal leader. He emphasizes that populist movements are multiclass affairs and do not fit into a Right-Left spectrum.

Mobilization of the lower classes into populist movements of this kind seems to Germani an alternative possibility to the kind of left-wing working-class movements that were the norm during early industrialization in nineteenth-century Europe. He isolates a variety of factors that will tend to make an emergent working class take to populism rather than socialism, and argues that this is particularly likely where rapid social change has produced a new proletariat who have not had time to acquire a distinctive working-class consciousness.[10] Like most writers on the subject, he points out that internal migrants, newly uprooted from a rural setting, are particularly prominent in populist movements.

The list of Latin American parties that count as "populist" varies somewhat from writer to writer, according to the emphasis given to different elements of the syndrome.

Some, like Germani, stress charismatic leadership and mobilization of the urban masses, and regard Peronism as the classic case.[11] Others treat as the hallmark of populism the union of different groups and classes into an amorphous coalition,[12] and regard Peronism as an atypical case because of its reliance on Argentine Labor.[13] What almost all seem to be agreed upon, however, is that a populist movement is one that does not emanate from the common people, but mobilizes and manipulates them. One student of Latin American politics even insists that populism has flourished in that region *because* "the political culture of Latin America was an elitist one."[14]

What comments can we make upon populism in its Latin American sense? Uses of the term in this area are not altogether clear or consistent, but a number of points stand out. In the first place, although there are connections here with rural radicalism, they do not seem close enough for us to subsume Latin American populism under the heading of agrarian populism. Some of these multi-class parties and movements have taken up the peasants' cause of land reform,[15] and others, notably Peronism in Argentina, found much support among ex-peasants recently migrated to the towns; but on the whole they have tended to be urban movements with urban preoccupations.

Second, two separate subcategories of our general category of political populism seem to be involved here. "Populism" has been attributed to Latin American movements both in the sense of populist dictatorship and in the sense of the politicians' catch-all party. The two may coincide, where a catch-all party is headed by a charismatic dictator; in many cases, however, they do not do

so, which explains the different lists of populist movements given by different scholars.

Third, throughout the literature there is heavy emphasis upon the mobilization of the people from above.
There is no sign, in accounts of Latin American populism, of "populist democracy"—populism in the sense of
vigorous grass-roots activity; on the contrary, it seems to
be assumed by scholars and politicians alike that the
masses are clay in the hands of the elite. While this may
be the case in Latin America, it is clear that in many
instances scholarly interpretations of events have been
strongly colored by intellectual assumptions about the
nature of the populace, and particularly by theories of
mass society.

At this point we run up once more against the link
between "populism" and the intellectuals. Since the relation between the populace and the elite is a recurrent
theme in all forms of populism (while the scholars who
conduct discussions of populism are themselves usually
closer to the elite), it is almost unavoidable that "populism" should be a heavily value-laden word, and that its
connotations should vary according to fashions in intellectual circles. Hence the bewildering fact that "populism" can sometimes signify the irresponsible unleashing
of dark popular passions, and at other times democratic
appeals to plain common sense.

The most derogatory sense of populism is one that has
had a good deal of currency in Latin American politics,
though it is also commonly employed elsewhere. This is
the view of populism which sees the populace as an
ignorant mass, easily manipulated by the appeals of

charismatic dictators. Given the nature of the masses, particularly in developing countries, popular mobilization cannot be expected to lead to democracy. On the contrary, domination of the people by politicians, or in the extreme case by a parasitic dictator, is the natural form for popular politics to take.

In this chapter we shall look at some of the phenomena of populist dictatorship, and at the implications for its interpretation of changing assumptions in intellectual circles.[16] Let us begin, however, by looking briefly at a concrete example, one of the most vivid cases on record of populist dictatorship. This is the movement led by Juan Domingo Peron, who—in the picturesque phrase of one scholar—"perceived the masses of barely literate but recently uprooted poor on the doorstep of the political system and invited them in."[17]

## PERONISM

The Argentina over which Peron established hegemony just as World War II ended was by Latin American standards an unusually rich and developed country, but it had a troubled history of social cleavage and political instability. Its traditional elite was a landowning oligarchy which had never shrunk from the use of force and corruption in politics, but there was a substantial middle class which, like the skilled working class, was largely of immigrant origin and heavily concentrated in the region around Buenos Aires. Massive immigration had left a cultural gap between the cities and the poor gaucho interior, creating an explosive potential when, from 1930 on, foreign immigration was replaced by internal migration which brought hosts of poor rural people into the cities.[18]

In 1943 the conservative government of Argentina (it-self the product of illegal violence) was overthrown by a group of army officers, one of whom was Colonel Juan Domingo Peron. Peron, the son of a small landowner, was an ambitious officer who had had the opportunity, on a mission to Italy, to observe and admire Mussolini's politi-cal methods. Most of the officers involved in the coup had fascist sympathies, but Peron was the only one to draw the practical conclusion that the way to get power was to mobilize a mass following. He got himself appointed Min-ister of Labor and used this position to build up support through the trade unions. He backed friendly unions in their disputes with employers and rewarded their mem-bers with high wages, paid holidays, and other tangible benefits.

Meanwhile his efforts to capture a more diverse popu-lar following were being greatly aided by the demagogic talents of his partner in power-seeking, Maria Eva Duarte. "Evita" was a poor illegitimate girl who had used her beauty as a lever to raise herself in society. Smarting from her own social inferiority to the haughty ladies of the landed oligarchy, she found it congenial to articulate the resentment of the *descamisados*—the "shirtless ones," Argentina's equivalent of the *sans culottes*—against the rich and established. Her own way of describing her re-cruitment to the cause was suitably idealistic: "When I saw Peron take the flag of the workers to carry it to victory . . . and when I saw that the people had decided to fight with Peron . . . I, a humble woman of the people, un-derstood that it was my duty to take my place with the workers, with the *descamisados*, to help Peron realize our hopes so that all could see the great Argentina of which I had dreamed."[19]

Although Peron's initial rise to prominence had been based on force alone, he owed his personal dictatorship to massive popular support. Between 1943 and 1945 opposition to the military government built up to a point where the military leaders wavered, and Peron himself was arrested to satisfy the liberal opposition. At this point, however, a new political force appeared on the scene. Gino Germani has described the events of October 1945:

> A general strike paralyzed the country and the *descamisados*, converging from the immense industrial belt of Buenos Aires, gathered in Plaza de Mayo demanding and obtaining the release of their leader. During the next three months the elections were organized and they took place freely for the first time in sixteen years. Contrary to all expectations, the results gave the presidency to Peron with about 55 per cent of the votes.[20]

Once in power, Peron did not hesitate to use repression, but his style of politics was unmistakably populistic. He addressed his audiences with his sleeves rolled up to show his solidarity with the *descamisados*; he delivered verbal attacks on the landowning oligarchy and on collaborators with U.S. imperialism, and proclaimed himself the servant of the people: "If my government is to have merit it must interpret completely the wishes of my people. I am no more than the servant. My virtue lies in carrying out honestly and correctly the popular will."[21] He rewarded his popular following with a massive program of social security, including old age pensions, sick pay, minimum wages, child labor laws, and cheap housing; and if the main result of the high wage rates he sanctioned was runaway inflation, nevertheless the workers were better off in real terms as a result of his rule.[22]

Meanwhile, Evita played a vital role in maintaining contact between the leadership and the ordinary people. She acquired a monopoly of charitable funds, and pressured industrialists and government employees to contribute to her Social Aid Foundation. No accounts were ever rendered of the money spent, and no doubt a good deal of it went into the diamonds and furs in which Evita delighted to display herself. But it also enabled her to play the part of lady protector of the poor. She held open court for those in trouble, handing out cash, redressing grievances, and earning the undying devotion of those she helped. On occasion she sent charitable aid to other countries: it must have been particularly satisfying to be able to embarrass the government of the United States by sending a gift of clothing for the poor children of Washington, D.C., as she did in 1949.[23] Within Argentina, though hated by the upper classes who had formerly snubbed her, she was regarded by many in the lower classes as a kind of patron saint.

Her death in 1952 weakened Peron's rule, while economic troubles made it harder for him to go on sanctioning the wage rises his followers had been led to expect. He had already alienated the upper classes and the army, and when he quarreled with the Church as well, his enemies managed to depose him in 1955. His influence continued, however, and loyalty to Peronism continued to flourish, to form the basis for subsequent revivals. A survey carried out in 1965 showed that between one-fifth and one-third of all adult Argentines were still Peronist supporters (the precise figure depending on how stringently "support" was defined).[24]

Peron's rise to power on the shoulders of the workers generated considerable shock among liberals and socialists at the time, and has engendered a great deal of scholarly debate ever since. There are, in particular, two problems to which it gives rise, one a problem of classification, the other of explanation. The first problem is that of deciding what *kind* of movement Peronism was. Into what category does it fit? Peron himself was certainly influenced by fascist and Nazi models; is one therefore to conclude that his regime was of the same type as fascism or Nazism? Or is his type of populism something fundamentally different from these? The second problem is that of understanding why Peronist workers supported the authoritarian regime so enthusiastically. In particular, are we to regard this support as what may be expected from ordinary people, in view of the characteristics of modern masses, or should we explain it in terms of particular extenuating circumstances?

Let us look first at the problem of classification, though it is not one that we can hope to resolve. The most decisive answer is provided by Gino Germani, as part of a theory of mobilization that includes both fascism and Communism. Germani maintains that in spite of the fascist trappings which Peron adopted in imitation of Mussolini, his movement drew on a quite different constituency and had a quite different historical function from fascism. Fascist movements are fundamentally attempts by middle classes,

who feel themselves threatened by working-class movements, to push their social inferiors back out of the political arena. National populism of the type led by Peron is,
on the contrary, a way of mobilizing the lower classes and
bringing them into politics for the first time. In spite of its
confusingly authoritarian ambience and lack of resemblance to European socialist movements, therefore, it is,
according to Germani, the exact opposite of fascism.[25]
Germani concedes that Italian fascism and Nazism contained some populist elements in their early days, but he
considers that these disappeared rapidly once the movements gained power.

Clearly, whether or not populist dictatorship is regarded as something distinct from fascism depends on
one's analysis of the latter—a desperately controversial
matter in which it would be unwise to involve ourselves.[26]
One thing which makes for difficulty in identifying populist dictatorship as a distinct genre, however, is the
simple fact that, since the advent of mass political mobilization, virtually *any* modern regime, however repressive,
needs to have some populist elements, even if these do
not go beyond rhetoric. The point can be brought home
by recalling a case of premodern autocracy. In the early
nineteenth century, when Tsar Nicholas was Autocrat of
all the Russias, the Tsar could claim his throne by royal
birth and divine right and make no attempt whatever to
elicit the support of his subjects. So exclusive, indeed,
was his conception of autocracy that on one occasion he
reprimanded a journalist for having had the impertinence
to comment *favorably* upon one of his government's measures.[27] By contrast, no modern ruler can afford not to

play to the gallery to some extent, with the result that modern authoritarianisms often contain a curious mixture of populism and elitism.

Both Mussolini and Hitler made much of the fact that they were men of the people, born outside the social elite and able to articulate the interests and values of ordinary people. Their techniques of mass rallies and balcony speeches gave many a sense of having political influence, while the leaders claimed to be representatives of the people. To quote Hitler on the subject: "I have come from the people. In the course of fifteen years I have slowly worked my way up from the people, together with this movement. No-one has set me to be above this people. I have grown from the people, I have remained in the people, and to the people I shall return. It is my ambition not to know a single statesman in the world who has a better right than I to say that he is a representative of his people."[28]

Alongside this populist strand in Nazism and fascism, however, there was also a strongly antipopulist element. One of the main sources of fascist theory, after all, was late nineteenth-century elitism. According to the sociological version purveyed by Pareto, Mosca, Gumplowitz, Weber, and Michels, the masses are clay in the hands of tiny elites which contain the only real political actors; while ethical versions of elitism (notably Nietzsche's) insisted that heroes are the only source of noble values, and inculcated contempt for the herd. As Mussolini put it on one occasion: "Left to their own devices, the masses gravitate toward the meanest mediocrity, driven by passion, suggestibility, and egotism."[29] In accordance with this elitist theory, fascism was explicitly antidemocratic, and denounced popular sovereignty in favor of the leadership principle. In practice, fascist leaders tended not to tell their followers to their faces that they were a contemptible herd fit only to be trodden under the feet of supermen. The elitist strand in fascist theory, however, fostered a consciously cynical and Machiavellian attitude toward manipulation of the masses.

If rhetorical appeals to "the people" are to be regarded as sufficient evidence of populism, virtually all modern regimes qualify. It seems wise, therefore, to restrict our examination of populist dictatorship to cases, like that of Peron, where the populist rhetoric was vindicated by a good deal of genuine popular support. How easily one is persuaded of the existence of popular support for a dictator, however, is likely to have a good deal to do with the way in which one answers the other question we posed in connection with Peronism: why did the populace follow Peron and Evita? Why, in general, should the lower classes disappoint the expectations of nineteenth-century radicals and support *any* dictator? How are we to interpret such support? Does it indicate merely that the people, anxious to participate in politics and to gain the benefits it offers, are willing to follow a leader if that is the only possibility available? Or, as disillusioned liberals have so often argued, does it indicate something much more sinister: namely, that the masses positively *like* dictators, so that the more they are allowed to participate in politics, the less liberal and democratic politics will become.

The rise of Peron was one of the prime exhibits used by

theorists of mass authoritarianism in the 1950s and 1960s to illustrate the dangers of widespread participation in politics. In some ways, however, it was not an ideal example. Grounds could be found for dismissing it with the argument that although Peron's regime was initiated by a comparatively free election, it was sustained by force, and was in any case supported by people who were unused to political participation and whose political culture was undemocratic. To sharpen the issue of why populist dictators are possible, let us add to Peronism another case of personal rule, this time based squarely upon the popular vote, employing much less direct repression than Peron, and established in a country whose voters could not plead the excuse of being unused to democracy. Let us look at the career of the ultimate in Southern demagogues: the "Kingfish" of Louisiana, Huey P. Long.

## HUEY LONG

Huey Long was born in Winn parish, Louisiana, in 1893, just at the time when the People's Party was making headway among the impoverished farmers of the district.[30] Most of the locals were far from prosperous, for the soil of Winn was thin and hungry, but the Longs were well-off by local standards. (Although Huey was born in a log cabin, the family moved shortly afterward to a house with less political resonance but fewer draughts.) He was a restless, hyperactive boy, notorious locally for his effrontery. At seventeen, seeking employment, he hit by chance upon a job as a traveling salesman and discovered that he had the ability to sell anything to anybody. He set his sights forthwith upon a career in politics.

One of the natural ways into politics for a backwoods boy was via the law. After a crash course at Tulane University, Long got himself admitted to the Louisiana bar at the age of twenty-one and rapidly built up a practice. He specialized in defending the interests of lowly citizens against large corporations, for instance, by winning suits for compensation on behalf of injured workmen. At twenty-three, making the most of his experience as a salesman, he won his first public office, a seat on the state Railroad Commission, soon to be given greater powers as the Public Service Commission. He was an enormously energetic commissioner, and soon got himself a name for redressing grievances and standing up to the corporations. His favorite opponent was the Standard Oil Company. As he later explained, "Corporations are the finest political enemies in the world."[31]

Having built up a reputation as the champion of the common man, Long set out to become governor of Louisiana. State politics there was habitually corrupt, and was dominated by an oligarchy of established planters and new industrialists. In New Orleans in particular there was a highly organized political machine which kept the voters under strict control.[32] The consequence of this oligarchic political monopoly was a profound gulf between the interests and outlook of the ruling class and those of the farmers in the poor country districts, for whom the state provided very little in the way of services.

Long chose to play upon rural grievances, such as the lack of good roads in the country districts. One handicap was that his potential constituency was divided between poor Protestant farmers in the north of the state, among

whom the Ku Klux Klan was strong, and poor Catholic
farmers in the south, where the Klan was anathema. According to one story, his way of evading the divisive religious issue was masterly:

> The first time that Huey P. Long campaigned in rural,
> Latin, Catholic south Louisiana, the local boss who had
> him in charge said at the beginning of the tour: "Huey,
> you ought to remember one thing in your speeches today
> . . . we got a lot of Catholic voters down here." "I know,"
> Huey answered. And throughout the day in every small
> town Long would begin by saying: "When I was a boy, I
> would get up at six o'clock in the morning on Sunday,
> and I would hitch our old horse up to the buggy and I
> would take my Catholic grandparents to mass. I would
> bring them home, and at ten o'clock I would hitch the
> old horse up again, and I would take my Baptist grand-
> parents to church." The effect of the anecdote on the
> audiences was obvious, and on the way back to Baton
> Rouge that night the local leader said admiringly: "Why,
> Huey, you've been holding out on us. I didn't know you
> had any Catholic grandparents." "Don't be a damn fool,"
> replied Huey. "We didn't even have a horse."[33]

Thus Long avoided divisive issues and concentrated instead on the interests that united ordinary rural people
against the oligarchs. One of his tactics was to attack the
local big man in each parish he campaigned in: "I don't
want the bosses. I want the people on my side."[34] He
campaigned with immense energy and ingenuity, promising the country people solid benefits in the shape of
better roads, lower taxes, and free schoolbooks. (The
last was an important issue because the state Department
of Education, in collusion with the bookselling firm

which held a monopoly on distribution, kept changing its list of approved texts, forcing parents to buy new ones instead of handing them down from child to child.)

This first attempt on the governorship was unsuccessful, but in 1928 Long was elected, with a vast majority in the country districts. He had campaigned as the people's champion, under a slogan borrowed from the populist Democrat William Jennings Bryan: "Every man a king, but no one wears a crown." Having reached office, he did not make his peace with the local oligarchy or lose his radicalism. Instead, he set out to put his electoral promises into practice. To do so he needed support in the state legislature, so he systematically used the patronage at his disposal to provide himself with what he sometimes called "the best legislature money can buy." He proposed to finance free schoolbooks from taxes on the oil and gas companies, and to raise loans to cover his grandiose road-building program. At first he could not find the money for more than a fraction of the roads he proposed to build, but instead of concentrating what he had on one superhighway, he insisted that each parish should have a few miles of good road, even though it changed abruptly back to the traditional dirt track, so as to demonstrate to his followers that he was sincere and whet their appetite for more.[35]

The oligarchs fought back and tried to impeach Long, but he managed to muster just enough support in the legislature to avoid this, and continued to mobilize the rural people behind him. While still governor he ran for the office of U.S. senator, emphasizing his record and the attempts to sabotage his road and bridge-building program: "If you believe that Louisiana is to be ruled by the people, that the poor man is as good as the rich man, that the people have a right to pass on issues themselves; if you believe that this is a state where every man is a king but no man wears a crown, then I want you to vote for Huey Long for the U.S. Senate."[36]

Long won the campaign by a combination of skillful popular appeal and Machiavellian maneuvers, which included the kidnapping of a couple of key witnesses whom his opponents had intended to use in an action to blacken his name.[37] He did not take his Senate seat until 1932, when his term as governor ended. Ceasing to be official head of the state did nothing to diminish his influence in Louisiana politics. He had by now acquired a sufficiently reliable political organization to put in one of his followers as the next governor. Every so often Long himself would fly back from Washington, order his stand-in to call a special session of the state legislature, and force through a package of measures increasing still further the dictatorial hold he had on the administration of the state. When one of his measures was of a kind at which even his tame legislature might revolt, he resorted to ingenious modes of deception:

An innocuous bill would go through the routine of house and senate consideration and come up for final vote in the senate. Suddenly a Long leader would move an amendment changing completely the nature of the bill. The vote would then be called for, and the bill would be passed and rushed to the house, which was anxious to adjourn. The clerk of the house would mumble a few words of the title, a Long leader would call for the vote, and the bill

would be enacted before the opposition realised what was
happening. But for that matter, most of Huey's own followers did not know what was happening. . . . "You
just followed the leaders," one Long legislator recalled
with resignation.[38]

Long's achievements as ruler of Louisiana cannot be
denied. He built 5,000 miles of surfaced roads and 111
bridges, and in the process provided jobs for thousands
during the Depression. He increased the number of
hospitals, and made the state penitentiary and the insane
asylums less inhuman places, for instance, by introducing
dental care for the inmates. He did a great deal to make
education more readily available to country children like
those of his home parish. But if he gave the people of
Louisiana a higher standard of living, he also reduced
them to political impotence. His political organization,
with its representative in every parish, worked with such
precision that he could ensure, when he chose, that a
Long candidate who was getting "uppish" should win
his election only by the barest of majorities.[39] He concentrated an unprecedented amount of patronage in his own
hands and made quite sure that all jobs went to his
supporters. During election campaigns all state employees
were expected to contribute to the Long war chest.[40]
Disloyal employees did not last long.

In 1932 Long took his seat in the U.S. Senate and burst
upon national politics with a call for radical redistribution of the country's wealth. The threat he might
present to more conventional politicians was made dramatically clear a few months later when he went to
Arkansas to campaign on behalf of Mrs. Hattie Caraway,
who was running for senator. Until his advent, Mrs.

Caraway's candidature seemed hopeless. But Long spent one week touring the state with his entourage of loud-speaker trucks, proclaiming to vast crowds of poor farmers that the country's troubles were due to the concentration of wealth in Wall Street, and that the answer could be found in the Bible, where the Mosaic Law demanded periodic redistribution of wealth. Against all expectations, Mrs. Caraway was elected.

In his autobiography, *Every Man a King*, published in 1933, Long claimed that he had come to the Senate "with only one project in mind, which was that by every means of action and persuasion I might do something to spread the wealth of the land among all of the people."[41] His plans to achieve this included a capital levy to prevent anyone from owning more than a certain figure (which varied in different statements[42]). With the money raised he proposed to guarantee each family a $5,000 capital endowment, minimum wages, plus pensions, grants for higher education, limits on working hours, and govern-ment purchase of agricultural surpluses. In February 1934 he formed the Share Our Wealth Society to gain support for this program (which he insisted was not socialist). The popular response was vast. Letters flooded in, and by 1935 the Society had about five million members.

Originally a Roosevelt supporter, Long had turned against F.D.R. on the grounds that he was not radical enough, and he began laying plans for a third party to challenge the Democrats and Republicans in the Presi-dential election of 1936. He was in contact with other radicals, including Father Coughlin, the populist (later fascist) "radio priest,"[43] and he hoped to build a move-

ment with sufficient popular support to break through
the two-party stranglehold on American politics. Given
his charismatic appeal as well as his astuteness and
energy, it is impossible to be sure he would have failed,
had it not been that in September 1935, in his own capitol
at Baton Rouge, he was assassinated by the son of one of
his political enemies.[44]

How are we to sum up Huey Long? There can be no
doubt about his popular backing, his common touch, and
the real benefits he gave his supporters. At the same time
he was a cynical manipulator who used his popular
appeal to gain wealth and power for himself, who had no
respect for law or constitution, who would not brook
opposition, and who made himself virtual dictator in
Louisiana. In view of the times in which he was living,
comparisons with Hitler were inevitable, although he
himself violently rejected the suggestion that there was
any resemblance: "Don't liken me to that sonofabitch,"
he roared. "Anybody that lets his public policies be
mixed up with religious prejudice is a plain Goddamned
fool."[45]

Long was not, of course, a tyrant in the full sense of
the term: in spite of his entourage of bodyguards and his
subservient legislature, he never wielded the life-or-death
power over opponents which is the hallmark of the tyrant.
He came near enough to being a real dictator, however,
to cause considerable scandal in a country with supposedly liberal democratic institutions.

## POPULIST DICTATORSHIP AND MASS SOCIETY

Let us now return, bearing in mind the cases of Long
and Peron, to the problem of populist dictatorship. Why

are ordinary people often willing to support a dictator?
And is there an intrinsic connection between the political
mobilization of the masses and the rise of authoritarian
leadership?

The connection between democracy and dictatorship
is one of the oldest clichés in political science. Aristotle
remarks in his *Politics* that "most of the early tyrants
were men who had first been demagogues," and gives a
list of examples.[46] Plato's *Republic* includes a vivid
description of the process by which a popular leader
turns into despot. The demagogue, stirring up the people
against the rich, incurs the enmity of men of property
and acquires power for use against them. Having got
himself into a position of strength, however, the people's
champion quickly degenerates. "In the early days he has
a smile and a greeting for everyone he meets";[47] he
distributes land to the poor and cancels debts. But as
soon as he has got rid of his enemies he stirs up wars,
using them to distract the people's attention and to
dispose of any who are disloyal to him. As the more
independent-minded citizens grow discontented with his
rule, the tyrant strengthens his bodyguard and, having
spent the plundered wealth of the rich, turns upon his
own former supporters and plunders them, too. Then
at last, too late, "the people will learn what sort of a
creature it has bred and nursed to greatness."[48]

The bitter relish with which Plato observed the populace making a rod for their own backs echoes over the
centuries, via sardonic Roman observations on Caesars
who built their power on bread and circuses for the poor,
and connects with analyses of the sources of popular
tyranny in more recent times.

There can be no doubt that the phenomenon is a real one. While popular participation in politics does not necessarily give rise to dictatorship and not all tyrants are popular, there is certainly something of a connection between mass mobilization and populist dictatorship. What is in dispute is the reason for this. *Why* do ordinary people sometimes support dictatorial leaders? The speculation which has been devoted to this question since the time of the Greeks, but especially since the rise of totalitarian mass movements in this century, has produced, broadly speaking, two alternative diagnoses. The differences between the two are important, if only because the diagnosis adopted may determine the prescription.

According to the more venerable of these two accounts, popular support for demagogues and dictators, however deplorable, is a fundamentally rational strategy adopted by the people in situations where their interests are strongly opposed to those of the elite, and no other means of redressing their grievances is available. In other words, in order to have a champion strong enough to give them bread and circuses (or good roads and free school-books) ordinary people may be willing to run the risk of tyranny.

The other diagnosis of popular authoritarianism is quite different and more depressing. According to this view (which is embedded in the theory of mass society), popular support for dictators is basically irrational and proceeds from the cravings for authority, status, and excitement characteristic of uprooted and frightened masses. Let us look at these two diagnoses more closely.

The first view, according to which support for a

potential dictator is a rational action (though a risky one), is implicit in Plato's sour account. Its basic assumption is that the demagogue's supporters belong to a particular class (the poor) whose interests are clearly opposed to those of the rich. Under normal circumstances, the rich form a ruling oligarchy and use their power to defend their privileges. The poor resent this but lack the political muscle to prevent it, and are therefore available for mobilization by a demagogue who can articulate their interests, notably their desire to plunder the wealthy. Given this situation of open or concealed class war, a popular leader will need to be determined, ruthless, and charismatic to succeed. More moderate men who are willing to compromise will be eliminated at an early stage by the process of natural selection inherent in such a political structure. Those who survive to fight on will be men of enormous energy, magnetism, and ambition— Huey Longs, in fact. For the sake of revenge against the rich and material benefits for themselves, the poor people may be quite willing to allow their leader despotic powers, especially since these will be mainly exercised, initially at least, against the old oligarchy. The people may, of course, realize too late that power corrupts even their chosen leaders; but, according to this interpretation, the root of populist tyranny is the people's rational response to an objective opposition of interests between them and the rich, and it is quite likely that support for the tyrant will bring them solid benefits: redistributed land and canceled debts in the ancient world, public services and a redistribution of taxes in the modern.

It can be rational, then, for the people as a class to

support a dictator. An even more likely possibility, however, is that it may be rational for an *individual* to sell
his support to a ruler, even though the regime is contrary
to his own longer-term interest. Patron-client relationships are often of this kind.[49] Consider, for example, any
one of the many poor boys in Louisiana who got jobs as
a result of supporting Huey Long. It might be said that in
helping to maintain such a regime he was acting against
his own interests as a citizen; but as an individual and
the member of a poor family, he could hardly adopt a
more rational strategy than to trade his vote for something
of more urgent interest to him. Political relationships
of this sort are manipulative on both sides: the client
manipulates the patron as well as vice versa, and receives
benefits in return for his support. The snag is, of course,
that the relationship is unequal. The balance of advantage
will tend to favor the patron, while by selling his support
the client may be helping to maintain a system that is
contrary to his own ultimate advantage.

Whether one attributes to the people collective or
individualistic rationality, a rationalist diagnosis of populist dictatorship appears to entail a radical prescription:
if you wish to allow the people access to political influence
but at the same time to prevent the rise of demagogues
and potential dictators, you must ensure that the political
system caters to the interests of the poor as well as the
rich and is not used to bolster a privileged section of the
community. In a just society, demagogues will not be able
to find an audience. The causes of popular democracy and
social justice go hand in hand, and where they are both
achieved, the liberal democrat has no reason to fear that

the people themselves will betray democracy into the hands of a dictator.

The difficulty with this bland prescription is, of course, that the situations in which support for a demagogue seem most rational may be times of economic crisis, like the Depression of the 1930s, which even the most just and democratic society may not be able to avoid. All the same, the rationalist diagnosis of populist dictatorship allows scope for a certain cautious optimism among democrats. Not so the alternative diagnosis, which has been much more influential in this century, and which regards popular support for tyrants as fundamentally irrational and all the more dangerous for that. This view is part of the theory of mass society, which is not specifically directed toward populist movements but regards them as a subspecies of mass movements in general.

While there is no single "theory of mass society" to which all who write in those terms would subscribe, there is a body of ideas about masses and their political impact which has had enormous influence, particularly since the rise of totalitarianism.[50] According to the "mass" theorists, under certain conditions which are endemic in modern society, large numbers of people are turned into "masses." They are uprooted, split off from any stable community, alienated from their society's institutions, deprived of convictions and inner strength. They crave community, authority, and a focus for their diffuse resentments. As one of their observers has put it, "The essential characteristic of the mass . . . is its manipulability."[51]

Such a mass is essentially irrational in its actions and attachments, and can be easily led by demagogues (themselves often déclassé members of the elite) who play upon its fears and hostilities. When such demagogues acquire a mass following, what results is extremist politics, authoritarian in style and given to witch-hunting of one sort or another.[52]

The political phenomena which have been analyzed in these terms range from Nazism and Communism to Peronism and U.S. Populism, and the practical implication of the diagnosis for those who value freedom, law, and rationality is that politics must at all costs be kept out of the hands of the mass. The most favored recipe for achieving this is to reserve political influence to a plurality of parties, organizations, and pressure groups staffed mainly from the elite levels of society, and concerned with matters too mundane to have much appeal for members of the alienated mass.

Diagnosis and prescription are both present in William Kornhauser's *The Politics of Mass Society*, which is the most explicit application of mass theory to politics. A central aim of Kornhauser's study was, as he says "to distinguish between mass tendencies and pluralist tendencies in modern society, and to show how social pluralism, but not mass conditions, supports liberal democracy."[53] He emphasizes that the "masses" are not identical with any particular class, but are instead made up of isolated individuals. Their isolation is seen as the direct cause of the extremism and lack of realism of their politics, their irrational alternations between apathy and frenzy, their preference for grand cosmic ideologies over down-to-earth bread-and-butter politics, and their desire for direct action and charismatic leadership rather than boring constitutional politics. Since it is uninterrupted communication between the masses and the elite that makes mass politics likely, the best safeguard of liberal democracy is pluralism, which interposes autonomous groups and organizations between the two.

According to Kornhauser, "masses" are to be found at all social levels, and are not to be identified with the poor or the working class. However, he and others belonging to the same school of thought have pointed out that many of what are taken to be the characteristic features of mass men—extremism, authoritarianism, and lack of tolerance—become much more common as one descends the social scale. In the course of one of the most influential studies in this genre, S. M. Lipset claims that lower-class people rarely appreciate the norms of liberal democracy, and remarks upon the sad dilemma of liberal democratic intellectuals, who inherit a radical tradition which exalts "the people," but who have discovered by bitter experience that "the people" are not themselves liberal democrats.[54]

We can see now that a good deal hinges upon which diagnosis of populist dictatorship is adopted. If we adopt the first, which focuses upon rationality and genuine popular grievances, then a concern for democratic values will tend on the whole to make us radical, seeking to circumvent possible dictators by eliminating injustice and allowing ordinary people to have effective political influence via ordinary constitutional channels. But if we adopt the mass-society diagnosis, the very same concern for liberal democracy will make us conservative and rather elitist, seeking above all to exclude from the political arena those dangerous masses (to be found concentrated particularly in the lower classes) who are alienated from social institutions and are authoritarian in outlook.

There are fashions in theories as there are in clothes or domestic architecture. Mass-society theories of popular authoritarianism were particularly high in favor with Western intellectuals in the period that saw the rise of Nazi, fascist, and Communist totalitarianisms and Peronism, and received a strong boost from McCarthyism. Recently, however, a reaction has set in, for reasons which we shall discuss later. Full-scale critiques of mass-society theory have appeared,[55] and political scientists analyzing popular support for authoritarian leaders or extremist policies are less inclined than formerly to attribute such phenomena to alienation and irrational impulses, and more likely to look for the explanation in terms of rational choices and solid (preferably economic) interests.[56]

If, in the light of these rival diagnoses, we look back at Huey Long, the issue seems fairly clear. While he undoubtedly possessed personal magnetism, there is not really any need to invoke hypotheses about mass alienation and irrationality in order to explain his popular support.[57] He promised the poor farmers roads and free schoolbooks and he kept his promises: rational pursuit of their interests as a class is enough to explain their support for him.[58] Once he was in power, of course, and putting his followers on the state's ever expanding payroll, every potential employee had a good reason in terms of individual interest for becoming the client of so useful a patron. Rational explanation of Long's rise seems quite adequate—with the caveat that among the "benefits" he gave his supporters were the less rational satisfactions of theatricality and showmanship in politics. Politics in Long's Louisiana was certainly not boring.

What of Peronism? Are we to regard that as a rational class phenomenon or as an irrational mass one? Jeane Kirkpatrick's investigations are particularly interesting in this connection, for although her book on Peronism is titled *Leader and Vanguard in Mass Society*, her findings go a long way toward discrediting a mass-society inter- pretation. The first point that emerged from her survey (carried out in 1965) was that Peronism was perceived by supporters and observers alike as the party of the working class. Peronists themselves were no more exclu- sively working class than are supporters of the British Labour Party, but working-class Peronists were exception- ally class conscious and particularly concerned with economic objectives and the redistribution of wealth.[59]

Kirkpatrick explicitly considered whether Peronists conformed to Kornhauser's picture of the alienated mass men who are supposed to provide support for extremist politics and authoritarian leaders, but found that they did not.[60] Unlike Kornhauser's mass men, Peronists were not concerned with remote, cosmic questions: on the contrary, their political concerns were very concrete in- deed, a matter of specific economic demands. Neither were they volatile in their political allegiance: they showed remarkably enduring loyalty to Peronism in spite of Peron's fall and exile. They were, it is true, authori- tarian in outlook and favorable to unconstitutional direct action, but in view of the traditions of Argentine politics this did not single them out from the rest of the population. Nor were they socially alienated or atomized: on the contrary, they seemed to be well integrated into social groups.

Kirkpatrick admitted that times might have changed: "Perhaps the *descamisados* who flocked to Peron's banner in the 1940's were alienated and disoriented by the transition from a traditional rural to a modern urban society. But 25 years had passed, and these internal migrants appeared to have been assimilated."[61] She concluded, however, that

> there is no direct evidence that Peron's authoritarian style or behaviour was or is a factor in the attachment of Peronists to his leadership. Far more important, the evidence suggests, were the actual and apparent economic benefits he bestowed on workers. . . . Peron's mass following might be explained by the absence of other political leaders who combined a high level of personal political skill and political salience with a stated concern for the status, income and power of the lower classes.[62]

More recently, irrationalist explanations of support for Peron have been challenged by Germani, who maintains that the movement was much less manipulative than commonly supposed. According to his account,[63] Peron rose to power not by means of Machiavellian rent-a-crowd tactics, but on a wave of spontaneous popular support from the migrant workers. Having got their leader into power, he claims, they "succeeded in instilling a popular character in the movement" in defiance of the original fascist predilections of the leadership.[64] Germani denies that the masses remained passive objects to be manipulated. On the contrary, through participation in the movement they discovered their own strength, and forged a consciousness of their own political significance that outlasted Peron's tenure of power.[65] Since Peron gave them both economic benefits and a new status and sense of personal dignity, it was in no way irrational of them to follow him.[66] Germani considers the objection that it would have been even more rational of them to support a *democratic* reform movement, but rejects it: "At this point one should ask oneself: was the democratic mechanism feasible . . .?"[67] The answer, clearly, is that in the circumstances of Argentina in the 1940s, it was not. The Peronists therefore behaved quite rationally in choosing the only available path to political participation and real betterment of their condition.[68]

Our conclusion, therefore, is that support for populist dictators of the type symbolized by Peron and Long may often be interpreted as instrumental rationalism in a difficult situation rather than as an indication of the pathology of modern masses. At first sight, this seems a conclusion to cheer the hearts of populist democrats. If the political systems most vulnerable to charismatic dictators are not the *genuine* democracies in which ordinary people have effective access to politics, but rather the systems that have a pretence of democracy but retain real power in the hands of an oligarchy, then it seems to follow that the way to guard against populist dictators is not (as the mass-society theorists would have it) to keep the masses *out* of politics, but rather to bring them *in* in an effective way. Where the masses genuinely possess power, there will be no reason for them to respond to the lures of a demagogue.

This argument was put forward long ago, paradoxically,

by a writer whom mass-society theorists often quote as an honored ancestor of their own views: Alexis de Tocqueville. For in the course of his broodings on the dangers, in an increasingly egalitarian age, of the ancient phenomenon of popular tyranny, Tocqueville argued that the way to prevent the evils of a "democratic society" was to introduce fully democratic politics.[69] Tocqueville pointed out that in the United States democracy had not so far given rise to tyrants, simply because ordinary citizens were in effective possession of political rights and were used to acting politically to protect their own interests. It was in France, with no such political tradition, that he feared the spread of egalitarian ideas would provide a basis for despotism.

Liberal fears of populist authoritarianism are not quite so easily disposed of, however, for two reasons. The first is that one cannot give ordinary people control over their own destinies simply by giving them political rights. Insofar as these rights are effective, this may enable voters to fight for their own interests *within* the political system, but it does little to help them if—as is increasingly the case within an interdependent world economy—their standard of living is at the mercy of decisions taken outside their own state altogether. In situations of this kind, a democratic electorate may crave for a strong and even (if necessary) dictatorial leader, for the same sorts of reasons that made the poor farmers of Louisiana support Long as their champion against the local oligarchs.

Part of the attraction of Peron's regime lay in his anti-American rhetoric, and voters elsewhere have frequently been willing to support a strong leader in the hope that he would be able to stand up to external economic interests.[70] Given the ever increasing dependence of people even in advanced industrial countries upon outside markets and suppliers, a major economic crisis could presumably create pressures for populist dictatorship even in the most genuinely democratic polity, and even assuming voters to be rational economic men rather than irrational masses.

The other drawback to Tocqueville's prescription of political participation is one that Tocqueville himself pointed out. For if he believed that participatory democracy provided a barrier against Caesarist dictatorship, he feared a populist tyranny of a different kind. He dreaded the "tyranny of the majority," believing that effective rule by the common man would mean an illiberal society. His worries have lost none of their relevance in the past hundred years, and it is to an examination of populist democracy and its advantages and disadvantages that we must turn next.

# 5. *Populist Democracy in Theory and Practice*

The value of the initiative process is that it is people's legislation, written by the people, qualified for the ballot by petitions signed by the people, and voted into law by the people.[1]

Your people, sir—your people is a great beast.—*Attributed to Alexander Hamilton*[2]

Since we turned from agrarian movements to populist politics we have so far seen populism only as a *problem* for democrats—as a dangerous phenomenon, threatening to bring dictatorship and reaction, creating dilemmas even for those with most respect for the common man. Connotations of this sort are certainly well-established in the literature on populism, and (as we have seen) not altogether without reason.

It would be a mistake to suppose, however, that populism appears in politics only in this unappealing guise. For we must recognize that it can wear the opposite aspect. In some contexts, and for some of those who use the term, populism does not mean a *threat* to democracy but the true, radical ideal of democracy itself. For those who are populist in this sense, calling the political system of most modern Western states "democracy" is a sham, and reserving the term "populism" for demagoguery and dictatorship, a libel.

As we have constantly had occasion to notice, the meanings and value loads of the term are inextricably bound up with the attitudes of those who have used it, and notably with the attitudes of academics. Nowhere is this more obvious than in the career of "populist democracy." This ideal of radical democracy, which aims at the closest possible approach to direct popular self-government without the intervention of a political elite, and which characteristically recommends the use of the initiative, referendum, and recall to make representative government more democratic, is perhaps the one version of populism that has some claim to be regarded as a political ideology on a par with conservatism or liberalism. Its intellectual reputation, however, has had remarkably little to do with the arguments that could be soberly invoked for or against it, and a great deal to do with fluctuations of opinion in academic and political circles. Besides examining the plausibility of populist democracy as an ideal, therefore, we shall need also to chart and account for its shifts into and out of intellectual respectability.

"Populist democracy" sounds like a pleonasm. Since "democracy" is widely supposed to mean "government by the people," how could a genuine democracy be other than populist? But this minor linguistic oddity conceals an important point: for the ideals and devices of populist democracy arise precisely in political contexts where "democracy" in some sense is officially accepted as a norm, but where dissidents feel that democratic practice does not live up to the promise of the name. Populist democracy consists of attempts to realize that promise and to make "government by the people" a reality.

The history of populist democracy has two connected aspects, theoretical and practical. It is, on the one hand, the story of the vicissitudes of an ideal of direct popular government and of the ways in which the stock of that ideal has risen and fallen among vocal elements in democratic states, particularly the United States. On the other hand (though the interconnections are obvious), it is also the history of the characteristic institutions by means of which populist democrats (chiefly in the United States and in Switzerland) have attempted to translate their vision of popular government into practice. It is perhaps not altogether unexpected that the practical history of such controversial devices as the initiative, referendum, and recall should have turned out to be less dramatic than populist victories and reversals in the realms of theory. These populist devices have in fact been much less practiced than argued about. At any rate, we will find it convenient to look at the theoretical history of populist democracy before considering how it works in practice and what is to be said for and against it.

## THE CURIOUS CAREER OF AN IDEAL

### U.S. Campaigns for Populist Democracy

The distinction between "populist" democracy and other kinds is a quite recent one. "Democracy" in its original meaning allowed of no such refinements or ambiguities, for among the Greek citizens from whom we inherit the term democracy was sharply distinguished from other forms of government, and meant "rule by the people" in a literal sense: the taking of political and judicial decisions in a face-to-face assembly of citizens.

It was modern attempts (taken furthest in the United States) to extend the principle of popular sovereignty to much larger states which made the notion of democracy ambiguous and gave scope for arguments about how "popular" it should be. Most of the U.S. Founding Fathers were not notably democratic in outlook, and Alexander Hamilton's famous reference to "the people," quoted at the head of this chapter, was probably only an incautious expression of what many felt. They took care, at any rate, to build into their Constitution elaborate checks against excessive popular influence on government. Nevertheless, that constitution was adopted by the official sovereign, "We, the People" (a potent phrase), while much of American political experience led the citizens to expect their political system to be democratic in a stronger sense. Those who ran their own local affairs in town meetings or in the *ad hoc* gatherings of frontier communities were familiar with something akin to Athenian democracy, and expected the higher authorities also to act as their agents. The notion that ultimate sovereignty lay with ordinary men was alive from the start, and gained institutional recognition in the common practice whereby state constitutions and amendments to them were established by means of popular referendums.

American political practice, on the other hand, while considerably less elitist and authoritarian than in most other eighteenth- or nineteenth-century states, was never as democratic as the ideal of popular sovereignty led Americans to expect. The stage was thereby set for a battle which was first fought between Jeffersonians and Hamiltonians in the first generation of the Republic, but which has been joined and rejoined at intervals ever since.

In the years before the Civil War the most notable eruption of populist democracy came in the Jacksonian movement, which asserted the rights of ordinary citizens against the "gentlemen," the ruling classes of the Eastern seaboard. As one Jacksonian paper declared, "We have an abiding confidence in the virtue, intelligence and full capacity for self-government, of the great mass of the people, our industrious, honest, manly, intelligent, millions of freemen."[3]

Half a century later a similar impulse returned, and this time acquired the title of "Populism." As we have seen, the People's Party of the 1890s was not just a classic agrarian movement aimed at redressing farmers' grievances: it was also a revolt of "the plain people" against the political establishment. Distrusting professional politicians,[4] the Populists wanted to make government more responsible to the people, and they recommended institutional devices for doing so—the initiative and the referendum, already developed for this purpose in Switzerland.

The People's Party was defeated and farmers' radicalism subsided, but the ideals of populist democracy were taken further and with much more success by the next generation of reformers, collectively known as the Progressive Movement.[5] In this movement, a great deal of energy was devoted to campaigns for the initiative, which would give the people the right to legislate without going through their representatives; the referendum, which would allow them to veto their representatives' decisions; and the recall, by which they could remove elected officials before their terms expired.

Direct democracy of this kind was part of Robert La Follette's "Wisconsin Idea," the model of Progressive government which involved cleaning up state politics, eliminating corruption, and regulating the big monopolistic corporations such as railroads. Where, as often happened, state legislatures were in the pockets of these great vested interests, it seemed a natural tactic for reformers to appeal past the corrupt politicians to the people. The National Progressive Republican League, founded in January 1911, included in its program of legislation calls for direct election of U.S. senators, direct primaries, direct election of delegates to national party conventions, and the institution of initiative, referendum, and recall within states. La Follette even demanded a national referendum on whether or not America should intervene in World War I. When he ran for President in 1924, his program was, he announced, "to break the power of private monopoly and restore government to the people."[6]

Although it could hardly be said that the reformers succeeded in their objective of "giving the government back to the people," they did have a considerable impact upon American institutions, particularly in some Western states.[7] It is striking that the overwhelming majority of the states that adopted populist devices for direct democracy were in the West. There were various reasons for this. Most of these territories had only recently achieved statehood, so that their constitutions were more malleable than those of long-established states,[8] while distrust of the distant federal government and popular experience in grass-roots organization on the frontier no doubt strengthened populist tendencies. It would be a mistake to think of the populist provisions of Western constitutions as a spontaneous expression of frontier democracy, however, for in many cases they were adopted in reaction against oligopoly and political corruption of the most blatant kind. They represented an attempt by reformers and "Good Government" lobbies to counteract the political influence of big corporations and also of big unions. The California Progressives, for instance, fought a long vendetta against the political influence of the Southern Pacific Railroad on the one hand and of corrupt labor bosses (notably Abe Ruef of San Francisco) on the other. Against any such corporate monopoly they invoked "the people," the citizens, asking voters to choose among the three alternatives: "a government controlled by corporate interests, Socialism, or if we have the courage, unselfishness and determination, a government of individuals."[9]

It is clear that the Populist and Progressive campaigns for direct democracy rested upon a view of politics and society according to which "special interests" (particularly the big corporations and the corrupt politicians in their pay) tend constantly to dominate the political process to the detriment of "the people." Political systems should therefore be structured in such a way that the ordinary citizen (pictured as an honest, sensible man with no particular ax to grind) can join with his fellows in making laws that are in the public interest and in defending himself against monopolies.[10] The assumption, explicit or implicit, is that the ordinary voter is much more trustworthy than the average politician or lobbyist, so that the more popular participation in government the better.

## The Advent of Democratic Elitism

This view of populist democracy as a practical ideal and a remedy for the ills of representative government was widely shared in America in the early years of this century, not only at the grass-roots level but by educated liberals who thought of themselves as the "progressive" element in the country. The reverse side of their distrust of politicians and corporations was trust in the people— or at any rate, in native-born Americans of the right ethnic stock. Between about 1930 and 1950, however, a gradual but very striking change took place in the view of democracy entertained in educated and (especially) academic circles in America. The populist ideal of direct popular legislation faded out of sight, to be replaced by a much more guarded attitude to democracy which eventually crystalized into a distinctly antipopulist orthodoxy. By the 1950s, what has since been labeled the "elitist theory of democracy" or the "theory of democratic elitism" was firmly ensconced in the writings of political scientists and having its effect on educated opinion in general.[11] Reduced to caricature, it might be stated thus:

1. "Democracy" means the system of representative government that exists in the United States, Britain, and various other advanced industrial countries. It does not therefore mean direct popular self-government, which all political scientists know to be impossible.

2. The main difference between democratic states and nondemocratic mass-participatory systems lies in the free competition between political parties and other organizations characteristic of democracy. As Joseph Schumpeter phrased it: "The democratic method is that institutional arrangement for arriving at political decisions in which individuals acquire the power to decide by means of a competitive struggle for the people's vote."[12]

3. Most citizens in democratic countries are apathetic and do not participate much in politics. However, this is just as well, since the masses are ignorant, irrational, and authoritarian by temperament. Democracy is a system in which liberally minded elites rule, and the masses participate just enough to make it impossible for their rulers to ignore their interests.

This view of democracy, which became deeply entrenched in the literature of political science after World War II, was fed by three sources. One of these was behaviorism: the concern of political scientists to make their study truly scientific, and therefore to concentrate on describing as accurately as possible what *does* happen, without speculating about what might or ought to happen. If voting studies show that most voters know next to nothing about politics and care less, then that—and not dreams of the dedicated citizen—is the basis upon which democracy is built.[13]

This behaviorist concentration on the actual rather than the possible was reinforced by the very strongly elitist cast of many of the classics of political sociology. Pareto, Mosca, Michels, Weber, and others had taken for granted that democracy in the sense of "rule by the people" is and must be a sham, because one of the most fundamental laws of human nature decrees that the few able men must rule the mass of incompetents. Like the behaviorists, these elitist thinkers believed that in relegating traditional democratic aspirations to the realms of myth they were merely being realistic.[14]

Besides the behaviorists and the out-and-out elitists, there was a group of writers who also contributed to the elitist theory of democracy and whose attitude was less straightforward. These were liberals who were not so sure that elites always rule and that masses are incapable of political influence. Instead, warned by the findings of mass-society theory, they were afraid of the havoc the masses might wreak if they *did* participate in politics, in view of the leaders and policies they would be likely to support. Consequently, writers like these were grateful for a system in which most people did not exercise political influence, and they believed that the liberal values they cherished could best be preserved by insulating the political elite from the masses. The conception of democracy as something to be defended *against* the people is epitomized by S. M. Lipset's remark, in *Political Man*, that "acceptance of the norms of democracy requires a high level of sophistication"—higher, evidently, than can be expected from the common man.[15]

This conception of democracy as a political system above the level of the masses was not entirely paradoxical, in view of the enthusiastic mass support which many recent populist dictators had been able to command. Liberal fears become most intelligible when they are related to the traumatic events of the anticommunist crusade in the postwar United States, particularly the antics of Senator Joseph McCarthy. When we remember that action against Communists was massively popular—that according to a 1954 Gallup Poll, 50 percent of the American population held a favorable opinion of the egregious senator, and that Congressmen were afraid to oppose him for fear of losing their chance of reelection—it is in no way surprising that liberal American intellectuals who valued civil rights, freedom of thought and speech, and due process of law should have relived the nightmares of Tocqueville, and felt themselves besieged by an intolerant populace.

Alongside a theory of democracy that stressed elite rule, this experience engendered a theory of "populism" which presented it as a threat to democracy in the liberal sense. One of the most outspoken of those who sought to connect populist politics with the death of liberty was Edward Shils. In a book prompted by the McCarthyite witch-hunting, *The Torment of Secrecy*, Shils maintained that McCarthyism had been made possible by the populist quality of U.S. political culture. Populists trusted "the people" and distrusted politicians, and therefore favored universal publicity in affairs of state: they went in dread of secret conspiracies against the people, but were at the same time inclined to exaggerate the value of national secrets (such as scientific-military knowledge) which had to be kept from the enemy. Looking with envy at Great Britain, where official privacy was respected, secrecy accorded its proper place, and witch-hunting was not a danger, Shils explained the greater liberalism and decorum of British public life by pointing to the fact that "although democratic and pluralist, British society is not populist. Great Britain is a hierarchical country. . . . The mass of the politically interested citizenry does not regard itself as better than its rulers."[16]

In a chapter on "The Deeper Sources" of the anticommunist scare, Shils followed up accounts of American "hyperpatriotism," "xenophobia," "isolationism," "fundamentalism," and "fear of revolution" with an extremely hostile characterization of American "populism." According to Shils, "populism proclaims that the will of the people as such is supreme over every other standard, over the standards of traditional institutions, over the autonomy of institutions and over the will of other strata. Populism identifies the will of the people with justice and morality."[17] He agreed that populism in America (under which rubric he included the Progressives) had produced some great reformers, but the dangers seemed to him to outweigh the benefits. To his mind, Nazism and Bolshevism were forms of populism, and so, of course, was McCarthyism: "McCarthy is the heir of La Follette."[18]

One of the aspects of "populism" to which Shils drew attention was distrust of the educated. Populism existed, he maintained, "wherever there is an ideology of popular resentment against the order imposed on society by a long-established, differentiated ruling class." Rising against their betters, populists proclaim that whatever the people want must be right, and sweep aside bureaucratic professionalism, constitutional restrictions, and due process of law. The very type of populism, according to Shils, is the "people's justice" of a lynch mob, whereas the careful, restrained sifting of evidence at a formal trial demands an unpopulist respect for the authority of law and lawyers. While distrustful of experts, however, and inclined to regard politicians as mere errand boys whose job is to carry out the people's will, populists are notoriously given to following demagogues, from Huey Long to Senator McCarthy.[19]

Similar characterizations of McCarthyism as a natural offshoot of populism were a prominent feature of the influential collection of articles on *The New American Right* edited by Daniel Bell and published in 1955,[20] while one of the contributors to that volume, Richard Hofstadter, incorporated in his book, *The Age of Reform*, an account of the U.S. People's Party that was obviously influenced by a supposed parallel with McCarthy.

As we have already seen, these attempts to tar the Populists of the 1890s with the McCarthyite brush provoked a furious controversy among the historians which has led to further historiographical revision. Meanwhile, the thesis of McCarthy's "populism" was attacked from the other end, notably by Michael Paul Rogin. In *The Intellectuals and McCarthy: The Radical Specter*, Rogin set out to disprove the link between McCarthyism and populism proposed by many liberal intellectuals, and the moral of distrust for populist democracy which they drew from it: "Before they wrote, McCarthyism meant something like character assassination, and Populism was the name of a particular historical movement for social reform at the end of the nineteenth century. Through their influence Populism has become an example of and a general term for anomic movements of mass protest against existing institutions—the type of movement typified by McCarthyism."[21]

Rogin argued that the U.S. Populists were not the zenophobic reactionaries portrayed by Hofstadter, that there was no significant continuity between their supporters and McCarthy's constituency, and finally that McCarthyism was not in any case a truly demagogic phenomenon, but rather a movement among traditional Republicans, drawing on the anticommunist views of Catholics and those with East European connections, and strongly supported by large sections of the U.S. establishment. He admitted that McCarthy resorted to populist rhetoric, but argued that this was not particularly significant. Given the nature of American political culture, it is normal for virtually all American politicians to do so, however far from populist their policies and intentions may be.[22] The senator was powerful not because of his mass support but because the Republican Party found him useful, and when he attacked the political establishment he fell.

If the hostile characterizations of populism by Shils and others represented the crest of the antipopulist wave that swept educated circles in America and elsewhere around the time of World War II, the revised interpretation of McCarthyism and Populism put forward by Rogin and others was a sign that the tide was turning. There was in fact a change in the prevailing academic mood during the 1960s which sharply reversed the previous trend, and by the end of the 1970s brought educated views of populist democracy back to the point at which the Progressive reformers left off.

The sources of this curious change of mood can be traced to the "participatory" movement of the 1960s and early 1970s. This movement was in some ways very different from traditional democratic populism, but since it undoubtedly contributed a great deal to the current revival we cannot afford to neglect it.

## *"Participatory Democracy" and its Effects*

"Participation" as a slogan was inextricably bound up with the international student movement of the 1960s. In keeping with its European connections, this movement was more theoretical and revolutionary than most political movements in American experience, while at the same time, reflecting the youth of its adherents, it was extremely idealistic and utopian in tone.[23]

One prominent attribute of its supporters was a violent disgust with the so-called democracies and their (un)representative institutions. As one writer put it, a truly democratic system would be one in which "people are able to control their own lives,"[24] and by this criterion representative democratic institutions fell lamentably short. Another influential theorist, Robert J. Pranger, described representative democracy as a kind of spectator sport: "Citizens sit in the dark, encouraging with their occasional applause the prominent players." Pranger stressed that this was not a defect that could be cured by institutional tinkering: "The issue here is not *more* citizen access to a remote government along the lines, for instance, of progressivist programs for initiative, referendum and recall procedures, but an improved *quality* of citizen participation."[25] What this latter signified was a complete change from a politics of "power," based on hierarchical relationships and supported by an appropriate political culture, to a politics of "participation" in which citizens who were equal among themselves would collaborate to solve their own problems.

The implication was that small groups of citizens should take decisions in face-to-face interaction. Throughout the literature, participatory democracy was closely connected with the notion of devolution from centralized states and their bureaucracies to much smaller units. The student movement turned away from the nation-state and its wars (particularly Vietnam) toward small communities on the one hand and international brotherhood on the other. There was a strong element of romanticism in the movement, hostility to rationalization and *Gesellschaft*, longing for fellowship and *Gemeinschaft*. One of the features of this romanticism was emphasis on spontaneity versus organization, and unwillingness in many radical circles to devise institutional structures.[26]

While calling for the creation of smaller communities that could be genuinely self-governing, most of the participationists tended to be rather vague about the boundaries of these communities, their relations with one another, and the general problems of international relations when existing political units had been transcended.[27] Robert Pranger, for instance, appeared to believe that "questions as personal and spontaneous as population control, world peace, racial harmony, physical survival," which had resisted solution within existing states, would yield much more easily to participatory democracies.[28] The explanation for this perplexing optimism appears to have lain in the widespread belief that participation would change the citizen's consciousness in such a way that a new and better man would emerge from the experience of community life.

Within the United States, the participatory movement was very strongly oriented toward the conspicuous nonparticipants in the existing political system—the poor in general, and black and other ethnic groups in particular. Not only blacks themselves, but also upper-class white students agitated for the right of the inhabitants of ghettos to organize their own lives, instead of being passive objects for the activities of politicians, policemen, and welfare workers. There were pitfalls here reminiscent of those encountered by the Russian *narodniki* a hundred years before. To quote an acid commentary upon the movement by Lewis S. Feuer:

> The fate of the notion of "participatory democracy" is instructive. It began as the apparent expression of a strong populist identification, with the unstated assumption . . . that, the poor, when they find voice, will produce a truer, sounder radicalism than any which alienated intellectuals might prescribe." As the doctrine evolved, however, it became the ideological bearer of elitism . . . as the citizenry proved quiescent, or failed to follow the students' lead, the doctrine . . . metamorphosed into an apologetic for the "putschist" action of a small student elite . . . to impose its will upon the recalcitrant majority of the people.[29]

In contrast to the campaigns of earlier American Populists and Progressives, the participatory movement was utopian, romantic, given to *narodnik* idealization of the poor and to distaste for practical institutional devices. In the nature of things, such a movement rapidly burned itself out. Nevertheless, it generated two kinds of political spinoffs that have had profound implications for populism, one of them theoretical and the other practical. At the theoretical level it led to a reexamination of current academic views of democracy and to their revision in a populist direction. At the same time it led to the revival of calls for populist democracy in practice and to a renewed interest in the initiative and referendum.

For political scientists whose working life spanned the period between 1950 and 1970, the change in theoretical assumptions about democracy was very striking. Positions which had been regarded as firmly and objectively established were suddenly branded "elitist democracy" and subjected to criticism, while flaws which had previously escaped detection in orthodox theories suddenly became apparent to every student.

Many postwar writers on democracy had succumbed, for instance, to what Barry Holden calls "the definitional fallacy."[30] That is to say that, in their desire to get down to hard facts, they did not stop to consider what democracy *is*, before deciding whether or not existing politics measure up to its requirements. They simply assumed that democracy means the kind of political system that exists in Britain or the United States, and took it that all essential elements of these systems must be essential elements of democracy as well, even when these included elite rule and mass apathy.

As for this apathy itself, the radical critics suggested that in many cases the reason why the poor showed little interest in the political system was that they knew that joining in would not help them: they lacked the resources in money, education, status, and contacts to play the political game, while their experience of life in general, whether at work in a lowly capacity or subject to the tender mercies of welfare officials, was not of a kind to encourage a sense of political efficacy.[31]

Other writers questioned the conclusion of so many

voting studies that most voters are too ignorant and irrational to be safely allowed near political decisions.[32] Do
voters choose their party out of family custom and "brand
loyalty" instead of rationally considering the alternatives? This is not unreasonable, since they and their
families are likely to have the same basic interests over
long periods, and they know by experience which party
is likely to do most for them. Do they often support a
party in spite of disagreeing with much of its program?
Since they have to take or leave the whole platform, without being able to reject particular planks, there is nothing
irrational in this. Do they take very little notice of their
candidates' promises? So, when elected, do the candidates.
In short, whereas the literature of political science in the
1950s was full of unflattering characterizations of the
ordinary voter, many writers since about 1960 have made
great efforts to treat that bewildered citizen with greater
respect.

The net result of this swing of the political pendulum
was to make faith in the people and their potentialities as
fashionable as it had been unfashionable in the previous
generation. Analysts of the workings of democracy are
now prepared to credit the people with greater political
abilities, and to discount the fears of mass participation
expressed by the liberals of the postwar period.

While this neopopulist revolution was going on within
the academic haunts of political science, there was a
marked revival outside in campaigns for direct democracy. Much greater use was made in the 1970s of the
facilities for direct popular legislation that already existed in some American states,[33] while there were also

moves to extend the scope of such facilities. In 1977 bills were actually introduced in Congress, proposing the amendment of the U.S. Constitution to allow voters to initiate legislation at the federal level.[34]

As an illustration of the way in which the wheel has come full circle, let us look briefly at a recent book which emanates from the current reform movement and which strongly stresses continuities with the Progressives. *Direct Democracy*, by Laura Tallian, was published in 1977 by The People's Lobby, an active California pressure group which had utilized the direct legislation processes of that state to place initiatives on the ballot.

Tallian's book, while very much geared to present-day campaigns, is marked by a sense of continuity with populist democrats in America's history. She begins with a quotation from Tom Paine on popular sovereignty, and her outlook is very similar indeed to that of the Progressive reformers, whom she frequently quotes. In terms heavily reminiscent of a populist democrat from 1910 or thereabouts, she draws the lines of battle between the special interests (notably the corporations and corrupt politicians) and "the people"—the honest citizens. Like her predecessors, she makes much of her effect by means of muckraking exposures of corrupt practices, and like them she has great faith in direct popular legislation. Another respect in which she resembles her forebears is in her interest in the technical devices and institutional details which can give substance to the will of the people. She is strictly practical, providing suggestions for model legislation on direct democracy and giving advice on tactics when collecting signatures for an initiative petition, even down to such exhortations as "Dress neatly," "Never take a chair," "Never argue," etc.[35]

All this practical advice on the most efficient way to achieve short-term objectives is reminiscent of the Progressive generation who devised the initiative provisions of Western constitutions, but forms the strongest possible contrast to the "participationists" of the 1960s, most of whom were flamboyantly utopian, disdaining such tactical questions. Another striking difference is that where the participationists tended to be particularly interested in participation by poor people and ethnic minorities, Tallian's appeal to "the people" (again recalling that of the Progressives) is determinedly middle class.[36] All the same, it took the tremendous impact of the radicals of the 1960s to make the intellectual and political climate hospitable once more to pragmatic populist democracy.

## POPULIST DEMOCRACY IN PRACTICE

Controversies over the ideal of populist democracy in the United States seem, therefore, to be picking up again from where they left off in the 1920s, after a long interval in which "populism" was regarded merely as a threat to democracy. While these revolutions and counterrevolutions were taking place in the realms of theory, however, what has been the experience of populist democracy in practice? Reformers at the turn of the century called for the initiative, referendum, and recall, and managed on occasion to get such provisions written into constitutions. Since reformers now are calling for the same things, or for more of the same, what conclusions can we draw from practical experience of populist democracy?

The object of populist democracy is to make "government by the people" a reality. Since representation is inevitable in any political entity larger than a town meeting, populist democrats seek to reduce the independence of representatives from their constituents as much as possible, and recommend the devices of recall, initiative, and referendum for doing so. Let us therefore look more closely at these devices.

The recall is a means whereby an elected official can be removed before the end of his term of office through a special election called on the petition of a certain number of voters. Like the other devices of populist democracy, it originated in Switzerland, but thirteen U.S. states[37] have machinery for the recall at statewide level as well as at the level of local politics. The number of signatures required for the holding of a recall election is usually high: in California, for instance, it is 20 percent of the number of those who voted in the previous election for the office in question, with the result that it has rarely been used at state level.[38] The only U.S. state governor so far removed by this means was Governor Lynn Frazier of North Dakota in 1921.[39] When Ronald Reagan was governor of California, two attempts were made to recall him, but neither gained enough signatures. At the level of local government, however, Americans have made considerably more use of the procedure. Four mayors of Los Angeles, for instance, have been subjected to recall elections, and two have been removed by this means.[40]

The recall admirably symbolizes the distrust of politicians and trust in the ordinary voter upon which populist democracy rests.[41] Since it has been used infrequently, however,[42] arguments about the pros and cons of populist democracy tend to focus rather upon the vehicles of direct popular legislation, the referendum and initiative. The referendum (in its populist democratic sense) is a popular veto upon legislation. In California, for example, if voters object to a law passed by the state legislature, they may sign a petition for a popular vote on the issue. The signatures, which must be equal in number to 5 percent of the total vote in the previous gubernatorial election, must be submitted within ninety days after the legislature adjourns. If enough are submitted in time, the law cannot be enforced until it has been endorsed by a popular vote.[43]

This negative power to stop legislation is complemented in the populist armory by the initiative, which allows voters to put their own proposed legislation to direct popular vote without going through their representatives at all. In California, voters equivalent to 5 percent of the previous gubernatorial vote may put a proposed legislative measure on the ballot at the next election for the people to vote upon.[44] Constitutional amendments may also be proposed, but require more signatures.

Exceedingly few of the world's political systems possess these means of direct popular legislation.[45] Discussion of populist democracy has often been confused, however, by the fact that a great many modern political systems use *some* kind of popular voting on issues, often giving to such popular votes the title of referendums.[46] The fact that "populism" often has strong connotations of dictatorship and demagoguery has made it easier for events like Hitler's plebiscites to be lumped together with Californian or Swiss initiatives under the same general heading.

Consequently, the first point to be made about direct consultation of the people is that the term "referendum" (as generally used) covers a very wide range of political circumstances and devices. To lump together all forms of direct popular voting and try to draw from them conclusions about populist democracy is confusing rather than helpful. Where referendums are concerned, indeed, it is possible to construct a rough scale ranging from votes organized and manipulated from above to genuine grassroots phenomena. Although referendums of the former kind have given populism a bad name, it is obvious that no populist democrat would be satisfied with anything short of the latter.[47]

The extreme position at one end of the spectrum is occupied by the numerous referendums held by authoritarian regimes under conditions of intimidation, in an attempt to manufacture legitimacy for the government. Regimes of this sort are usually satisfied with a fictitious 99.9 percent majority, but in two referendums held in Haiti in 1964 and 1971, President Duvalier was authorized to be President for life and to choose his own successor by a resounding 100 percent of the vote.[48] Votes of this kind obviously have nothing to do with democracy or populism.

The next category along the spectrum is more problematic, however. This includes the cases where a popular leader makes use of votes of confidence which are honestly counted, but which are used as a manipulative tactic to outmaneuver possible opposition. De Gaulle's refer-

endums were cases of this kind.[49] One of their main functions was to appeal directly to the French people over the
heads of the political establishment, including the people's elected representatives. As de Gaulle put it in a
speech before the January 1961 referendum on Algeria,
"I turn to you, over the heads of the intermediaries . . .
the question is one between each man and woman amongst
you, and myself."[50]

While making a great parade of appealing to the people, de Gaulle's referendums left the electorate little
scope for exercising power. Whether or not to hold a
referendum and its subject matter, wording, and timing
were all controlled by the government, while by turning
each one into a vote of confidence de Gaulle was able for
a long time to exploit the electorate's fear of the political
instability that might follow his resignation. On the other
hand, it cannot be said that the General actually *controlled*
the outcome, for his last referendum, in 1969, led to the
rejection of the government's proposals for constitutional
change and his own resignation.

A referendum may, in the Gaullist manner, be used by
a government in order to strengthen its authority. But it
may also be used simply as a political convenience, a
means by which a government can avoid burning its
fingers on an awkward and divisive issue by tossing the
hot potato to the electorate. The most conspicuous recent
case of such a referendum was Britain's vote in 1975 on
whether or not to stay in the European Economic Community. As almost all members of the British political
establishment agreed, referendums were contrary to Britain's tradition of parliamentary democracy, while in any

case, if it were necessary to hold a referendum on E.E.C. membership, the logical time to do it would have been before joining, on the pattern of several other states. Considerations of consistency and logic, however, were somewhat beside the point, since, as David Butler has put it, "the prime purpose of the referendum was to save the Labour party from tearing itself asunder."[51]

So far we have considered only cases in which the decision to hold the referendum, and the issue on which it is to be held, are entirely up to the government, so that the people's role is limited to voting in answer to a set question. Another type, however, which hardly amounts to populist democracy but which does tilt the balance of power away from the government and toward the people, is the case where the constitution of a country requires that certain measures (usually constitutional amendments) cannot be passed into law without a popular vote.[52] In Ireland, for instance, the government could not join the E.E.C. without a referendum, because a constitutional amendment was necessary to enable community legislation to apply in Eire.[53] In such cases it is still the government which actually decides to put an issue to the popular vote, but if it is determined to avoid referendums, its policy choices are restricted.

Referendums only really become part of the arsenal of populist democracy, however, when it is the people rather than the government that has the right to demand them, as in Switzerland and some U.S. states.[54] Just how populist such provisions are depends on technical considerations such as the number of signatures required for an initiative or referendum, and the time allowed to collect them. As Laura Tallian points out, it makes a great deal of difference whether the signature requirement is laid down as a figure or as a percentage. The Swiss constitution specifies figures, so that population growth makes it easier to collect the required number of supporters, whereas the American populists made the mistake of being satisfied with percentages. When the initiative was first introduced in California in 1912, the 8 percent of the previous gubernatorial vote required to qualify a proposed constitutional amendment for the ballot amounted to about 30,000 signatures. By 1978, population growth had raised the figure to 500,000, making their collection a massive and enormously expensive undertaking.[55] In Switzerland, by contrast, the required number of signatures for an amendment to the federal constitution long stood at 50,000. This was revised to 100,000 in 1977 to take account of population growth, but this figure will itself tend to decrease in significance with the years.[56]

There can be no doubt that Switzerland is the prime case of populist democracy. The Swiss not only possess facilities for initiative and referendum in their federal and cantonal constitutions, but use these tools with remarkable regularity. Whereas in most modern states popular votes on issues are occasional incidents stage-managed by the authorities, in Switzerland they are, as the theorists of populist democracy wished, a regular part of the ordinary business of government. Another respect in which Swiss democracy is more populist than any of the American states is that there is no judicial review at federal level in Switzerland.[57] In America, measures passed on popular initiative have frequently been contested in the courts and disallowed either at state or at federal level.[58] In Switzerland, by contrast, it is quite easy to amend the federal constitution by popular initiative, and no court can reverse the majority decision.

Most remarkably of all, whereas in most states referendums (when they are used at all) are ordered by the government for its own purposes, in Switzerland the federal government and parliament have no discretionary authority to order a referendum. This means that flexibility, choice of issue, timing, and the rest are in the hands of the citizens, not of the central authority.[59] When we consider, furthermore, that it was the example of Switzerland that inspired the American Progressive reformers with their schemes for populist democracy, it is clear that we must look at the Swiss system in a little more detail.

### Swiss Democracy

Most modern "democracies," as Schumpeter and the other elitist theorists have pointed out, are in no sense governed by the people. They are governed by ruling elites, tempered by institutions which make them responsible to the people in a greater or lesser degree. The fascinating thing about the Swiss political system, therefore, is that although it is a mixture of direct and representative democracy, the balance is strongly weighted in the direction of popular power.[60]

The six million Swiss people have, it is true, an elected national parliament and a central government like other nations. The highest authority in the land is the Federal Council of seven ministers, elected by the Federal Assembly according to long-standing conventions which share appointments among the various parties and language groups. There is a Federal President, but he is simply the chairman of the Federal Councillors, who hold the office for a year at a time in rotation, and his position is not comparable with that of a U.S. President or British Prime Minister.

The Federal Council and Assembly represent the electorate, but their authority is limited by the sovereign power of the people. This is exercised through initiative and referendum at the federal level and through direct democracy in the twenty-six cantons and thousands of communes that are the nation's component parts. The activities of the federal authorities are subject to close supervision by the electorate. All amendments to the constitution must automatically be submitted to a referendum, and a group of 50,000 voters may demand a referendum on any other federal law. In addition, any 100,000 electors have the right of initiative, and may propose a constitutional amendment to be put to a referendum.[61] To pass into effect, a constitutional amendment needs both a majority of votes in the country, and also majorities in more than half the cantons.

Between 1848 and 1978 there were nearly 300 national referendums, 212 of them required by the constitution and others by popular demand. Popular initiatives for constitutional change number 125, only 7 of which were accepted by popular vote. At the present time, voters are asked to give their verdict on some federal referendum or other every three months, and there are usually several different issues to be decided.[62] Issues upon which the man in the street has recently thwarted the intentions of the federal government include plans to introduce a value-added tax in 1977 and a proposal to bring Switzerland into line with European daylight saving time in 1979.

Populist democracy at the federal level is only the top layer in Switzerland, however, and not necessarily the most important one. Very much of the country's government is carried on locally in cantons and communes. It is the cantons, for instance, which levy income tax, run the schools, and organize police and medical services. The constitutions and practices of cantons and communes vary a great deal, but all are more democratic than most British or American citizens would suppose possible in a modern state.

In some of the rural cantons, direct democracy in the literal, ancient sense still survives. Appenzell Inner-Rhoden, for instance, with a population of under 14,000, still holds its *Landsgemeinde* or assembly of all electors on the last Sunday in April: a kind of giant annual general meeting to which the citizens traditionally come, armed with daggers, to sing an opening hymn and then settle laws and financial arrangements, hear reports, and appoint the canton's administrators for the coming year. Glarus, with a population of 38,000, rules itself by the same direct method, and in 1978 the assembly attracted 7,000 citizens. This cantonal assembly has in recent years had to cope with some large financial decisions, and it is perhaps typical of the priorities that emerge from direct democracy that the citizens have agreed to spend large sums on a school, a hospital, and new roads, but have steadfastly refused to pay for the construction of a new cantonal administrative building.[63] Other cantons are too populous and urban for the citizens to meet in this way, but they approximate direct democracy by the constant use of referendums. Even in Zurich, the largest, all legislation and all substantial expenditures must be put to the vote, and the electors may also initiate legislation.

The peculiarity of Swiss history is that whereas most modern states were unified from the top down, by conquests and the heavy-handed action of monarchs, Switzerland was federated from the bottom up by the creation of leagues among sovereign communes in their mountain valleys. While Swiss history has by no means been a record of continuous democratic harmony, the unbroken tradition of self-government has led the Swiss to take it for granted that the people are sovereign in a direct and literal sense. We shall need, therefore, to bear Swiss experience constantly in mind while trying to assess the virtues and defects of populist democracy.

### The Pros and Cons of Populist Democracy

The arguments that raged over populist democracy at the time when Progressive reformers were struggling to establish it in the United States have recently acquired a new topicality. Let us therefore try to assess the main points of dispute in the light of what practical experience is available. We must stress at the outset, however, that experience of populist democracy in its fullness is very rare. It is confined to a few states of the United States and to Switzerland, and since institutional blocks like high signature requirements limit its use in the United States, Switzerland is perhaps the sole genuine example. Switzerland, however, with its unique history, intricate federal structure, highly plural society, traditional neutrality in foreign affairs, and long-standing prosperity, is not the best case from which to generalize.

It is true that populist devices of a sort are much more widely used: referendums have occurred in a great many political systems in the course of this century. Most of these, however, have been of the types we identified as least akin to populist democracy, with the result that they may not provide a secure basis for generalization either. Bearing in mind these cautionary remarks, let us look at the grounds upon which populist democracy has been commonly attacked and defended.

1. *Tyranny of the Majority*

One of the standard objections to populist democracy is that it is an invitation to majority tyranny. Where issues are settled by direct popular vote, it is argued, the will of the majority must prevail, and the sharp yes/no nature of direct voting on issues rules out compromise and conciliation, overriding the interests and rights of the minority.[64] Particularly in societies divided by sharp communal differences, whether ethnic or religious, moves toward more populist democracy may therefore strengthen the stranglehold of the larger community.

Some political scientists use the category of "Herrenvolk Democracy" to describe political systems in which, paradoxically but quite intelligibly, greater equality, political participation, and respect for the common man *within* the dominant ethnic group has gone along *pari passu* with the progressive denial of rights to those outside it. Kenneth Vickery observes of the American South during the Jacksonian period that "the extension of political democracy among whites . . . was accompanied by retrenchment in the status of blacks. The point to be emphasised here is that these two processes were part of the *same social dynamics.*"[65] Later, under the impact of Populism and Progressivism in the South, democratic reforms like initiative, referendum, recall, trust-busting, and railroad commissions were instituted by the very men who extended discriminatory segregation against blacks.[66] South Africa, Vickery maintains, represents the ultimate triumph of Herrenvolk Democracy. The egalitarianism inherited from old Boer traditions defended the interests of all whites and prevented the emergence of a poor white class—at the expense of the blacks.

It is illuminating in this connection to look at the effects of some popular referendums in American cities and states on laws aiming to open housing to ethnic minorities.[67] Between 1963 and 1968 there were referendums in ten U.S. cities and in the state of California on open-housing legislation. In all cases the elected authorities had passed legislation favoring minorities, while opponents of the open-housing legislation used the initiative and referendum to take the question back to the voters. In all cases except one, where the authorities won by a very narrow margin, open housing was soundly defeated at the polls. In one instance, the referendum held in Toledo in 1967, the legislation was supported by the local council, both political parties, the churches and the unions, but it was still defeated, albeit on a very low turnout. In cases such as this, the machinery for direct democracy and citizen participation in local government allowed a minority of voters from the strongest ethnic group to override the interests of the smaller community.

This kind of objection to populist democracy is clearly a serious one. The populist democrat may reply that there is nothing to stop such a democracy having a constitution and a bill of rights guaranteeing vital minority interests; but the rhetoric of popular sovereignty may make it hard to uphold such constitutional checks in the face of a clear majority decision. The standard answer to the possible danger of tyranny by the majority is the principle, given classic form by John C. Calhoun, of the "concurrent majority."[68] This means that major issues which affect different sections of the community need to be decided by consensus among all parties—for example, among all states in a federal system—and not by simple majority voting with its unqualified defeat of the minority. Defenders of parliamentary democracy often maintain that something like this is provided for by the horsetrading that goes on at elite level between representatives and lobbyists, so that representative government caters better to minority interests than do referendums and initiatives. According to this line of argument, therefore, populist democracy threatens minority rights.

Since this argument seems quite persuasive, it is ironical that the only fully-fledged case of populist democracy should be a counterexample to it. Switzerland has no judicial review to limit the sovereignty of the people, but it is nevertheless an example of Calhoun's "concurrent majority" in operation. An extremely plural society, divided between two historically opposed religions, Catholic and Protestant, and four different language groups (Swiss-

German, French, Italian, and Romansch), Switzerland would seem to be a dangerous place in which to encourage popular referendums. But the Swiss seem to have solved the problem of combining populism and pluralism by two associated methods. The first is their extremely elaborate federal structure, which leaves cantons and communes very considerable autonomy and ensures that no communal group is in a minority everywhere. A feature that recalls Calhoun is the requirement that amendments to the federal constitution must gain not only a numerical majority of all voters, but also carry a majority of cantons in order to pass.[69]

The second feature of Swiss politics which prevents the ravages of majority tyranny is a characteristic of the political culture, which one distinguished political scientist, Jurg Steiner, has called a habitual inclination toward "amicable agreement" rather than majority rule. Most democratic theorists, Steiner maintains, have assumed that rule by the people means majority rule in the sense that decision-making is a zero-sum game: the bigger group wins, the smaller loses. This is a model which favors rapid, clearcut policy changes, but which provokes resentment among the losers and carries the danger of tyranny by the victors. In Switzerland, by contrast, while majority voting is of course used as a formal procedure, there is a very strong tradition that all interests should be taken into account, and compromises reached which are acceptable to all parties. The multiparty Federal Council is one example, but Steiner points out that even at the cantonal level, where one party often has a clear majority, representatives of the other parties are normally taken into the government.[70]

Among the institutional devices which strengthen this tradition of willingness to consider all interests are the popular initiative and referendum, since a group that is too small to win a majority in an election may nevertheless mount a successful (or at least troublesome) initiative and referendum campaign. Consequently, the reactions of voters to potential referendums are constantly anticipated by politicians, so that it is only when an acceptable compromise between groups has *not* been reached that a referendum is actually held.

The Swiss case is particularly significant in view of the recent interest among political scientists in what has come to be called "consociational democracy": that is to say, in democratic political systems which manage to function reasonably harmoniously in spite of deep communal divisions.[71] Theorists of consociational democracy, notably Arend Lijphart, have suggested that one of the requirements for its success is that the *leaders* of the different segments in society should be prepared to work together, and that these elites should be relatively insulated from the (presumably less tolerant) demands of their constituents.[72] The assumption here appears to be the familiar liberal, antipopulist one that tolerance is to be found at elite levels in society but not at the grass roots. This theory, however, sits uneasily in the Swiss case, where the popular rights of referendum and initiative make it impossible for the leadership to ignore the views of the man in the street.

There has been one notable case in recent times of a Swiss minority feeling that its interests were being overridden; the Jura dispute, however, seems to have been solved characteristically by accommodating the discontented minority with its own niche in the federal system.[73] The example of Switzerland seems, in other words, to indicate that populist democracy *need* not mean majority tyranny: not, at any rate, if it is combined with a highly articulated political structure and a favorable political culture—admittedly, large qualifications.

2. *Oversimplification of Political Issues*

Another frequent objection to populist democracy is that where the electorate is directly involved in political decisions, the issues have to be oversimplified to the point of caricature, whereas if decisions are left to the elite they can appraise nuances and balance complex considerations. Populists have in fact always tended to maintain that most political issues *are* simple, or at any rate much simpler than politicians pretend. Political leaders, according to this view, wrap up their activities in a fog of complexities and technicalities in order to protect the mysteries of their trade from the public gaze.[74] In this respect the confrontation between Tom Paine and Edmund Burke at the time of the French Revolution is the classic case of populist versus elitist: Paine maintaining that there was nothing about good government too complicated for the ordinary man, whereas Burke claimed that political wisdom and political judgment were matters of the utmost complexity.[75]

Laura Tallian echoes generations of populist democrats when she remarks that one of the advantages of submitting legislation to the people is that its proposers are forced to make it "simple, direct and clear," allowing no scope for the kind of mystification in which corrupt politicians habitually indulge.[76] It is clear that the issue of simplicity versus complexity is inseparable from the profound distrust of professional politicians that so characterizes populist democracy. Whether or not politicians should be trusted is, needless to say, a question that people in different states are likely to answer in very different ways.

It should not be supposed, however, that the issues submitted to popular voting must of necessity be childishly simple. The Swiss habitually vote on complicated budget provisions in their cantons, while in 1957 voters in Sweden managed to cope with a choice among three different pension schemes backed by different organizations.[77]

### 3. Overdramatization of Issues

Does the holding of a popular vote tend to produce an overexcited, emotionally heated political atmosphere, unfavorable to wise decisions? This objection can certainly be raised against government-sponsored votes of confidence of the Gaullist type, and perhaps against some recent constitutional referendums, such as the Norwegian European Economic Community vote in 1972, which brought a great deal of political resentment into the open. In Switzerland, however, where popular voting is so common, politics is notorious for its dullness and lack of drama. Reference of issues to the general public there seems, if anything, to make the tone of political events less hectic than otherwise. One student of Swiss political history remarks that "the effect of introducing the referendum in the 1860's in Zurich was that an exciting political period suddenly passed into a calm one."[78]

Perhaps the key point here is the frequency of popular consultation. Where referendums are an everyday occurrence, they may tend to be undramatic unless the issue at stake is an inescapably emotive one; whereas if the electorate are given a rare chance to deliver a verdict upon the proposals of their betters, the actual issue they are asked to decide may become overlaid with other considerations, adding up to an excessively dramatic confrontation. In Norway's E.E.C. referendum, for example, generalized resentment of the political periphery against the center and of country people against the city seems to have played a significant part in the rejection of the government's proposal to join the Common Market.[79]

4. *Loss of Authority by the Elected Government*

Does direct voting on issues by the electorate undermine the authority of the government and render it less capable of governing effectively? In some cases, where a government itself chooses to hold a referendum on an issue, turns the referendum into a vote of confidence, and then loses—as de Gaulle did in 1969—this is inevitable; but since governments mostly win referendums that they have themselves set up,[80] popular voting seems to strengthen particular governments more often than weaken them. Opposition to referendums, however, and even more to popular initiatives, is often based on the more subtle argument that since direct popular voting seems to render representation redundant, it is bound to diminish the authority of the government whether or not the popular vote supports particular governmental policies.

The counterexample to this quite plausible argument is, as usual, provided by Switzerland. Although the Swiss continually bypass their elected representatives and vote directly on issues, this does not appear to diminish the government's authority. The people express confidence in their representatives by almost always reelecting those who wish to stand again, while survey evidence shows a very high level of trust in the federal government, which appears to possess considerably greater authority than its counterparts in states that do not use the devices of populistic democracy, such as Britain.[81] It is noteworthy that Swiss governments do not treat referendums as votes of confidence, or feel obligated to resign if their schemes are defeated.[82] In other words, where the system of democracy is thoroughly populist, and the government is regarded as a servant of the people, there may be less loss of face involved in a referendum defeat than would be the case in a more elitist system. As a matter of fact, government measures on which referendums are held in Switzerland usually *do* win—partly no doubt because, knowing that the weapons of direct democracy may be used against them, the authorities try to anticipate objections before they arise.[83]

The difficulty is to know whether we can generalize from Swiss experience. Do the people trust the government because they know that ultimately power lies in their own hands and that the government is constantly mindful of this? This was one of the arguments used by the American Progressives in seeking to emulate the Swiss system; but do governments in the U.S. states with direct legislation enjoy any greater authority and public trust than in those without? Would they be more or less highly regarded if direct legislation were more readily available? On the face of it, Swiss and American political culture seem too different for institutional changes to bring about much of a convergence, while the prosperity long enjoyed by the Swiss must have contributed a great deal to their relaxed and confident attitude to government.

## 5. *Lack of Competence among the Public*

One of the obvious objections to direct democracy is an updated version of Plato's ancient objection to democracy as such: that it means taking decisions away from the experts and giving them to the ignorant. Populists have several different answers to this charge. The first, which was the most characteristic response of the early twentieth-century Populists and Progressives, is to emphasize not expertise but *honesty*. The cleverest politician, after all, may be precisely the most dangerous, if he is corrupt. Voters may or may not be as ingenious and well-informed as professionals, but in the mass they have fewer vested interests in policies damaging to the public.

As government and legislation have come to deal with more technical questions, however, populists have varied their answer somewhat. They may point out, as Laura Tallian does, that the voters are no more incompetent than the politicians, who are not themselves experts on most of the subjects on which they legislate.[84] They can indeed claim that citizen groups like the People's Lobby are evidence of the vast reserve of available expertise in the public in general, so that direct legislation does *not* mean turning over the direction of affairs from the expert few to the ignorant mob.[85] The shortest answer to this kind of objection, however, is simply to point to Switzerland, for the most dedicated elitist would be hard put to argue that the Swiss were worse governed than less populist societies.

## 6. *Popular Apathy and Low Turnouts*

Do most people want to be bothered with taking political decisions? Will they take the trouble to vote, or will they leave the polls to unrepresentative minorities of activists?

The average turnout in Switzerland, where a conscientious voter could spend all his spare time either voting or informing himself on the issues, is low and dropping. Between 1914 and 1944, turnout on federal referendums averaged 61 percent, but by the 1970s the average had fallen to 42 percent.[86]

In California the turnout is generally both low and unrepresentative, being much lower among the young and the poor than among the middle-aged and the middle class.[87] Since initiative measures are usually added to the poll at a regular election, turnout is affected by the nature of the election, with the highest turnouts in Presidential contests. It follows that a skillful initiative campaign manager might be able to time his proposition in such a way that it could pass against the wishes of a majority of the electorate.[88] The unusually high turnout on the tax-cutting Proposition 13 in 1978 suggests, however, that when people care a great deal about an issue, normally apathetic citizens will come out to vote.[89]

Some populists have argued that low turnout is not in itself a disadvantage, since "there is automatic disfranchisement by their own neglect of ill-informed and indifferent individuals; therefore, issues are decided by responsible and serious voters."[90] The difficulty here is of course that certain sections of the community may be systematically underrepresented, perhaps more so than in representative government because of the absence of professional politicians with a personal interest in mobilizing their votes.

7. *Do Opinion Polls Make Direct Legislation Unnecessary?*

Governments in all democratic countries now keep their

eyes on their ratings in the opinion polls and try to avoid making themselves unpopular. Then why bother with expensive referendums? One answer is that governments do not necessarily trim their policies to fit the polls. In Britain, with its strikingly unpopulist political traditions, politicians tend to make a virtue of unpopularity, implying that their measures are in the people's interest though against their wishes.

But in any case, opinion polls and direct voting on issues are not equivalent. Giving a casual answer to a pollster is not the same as going along to the polls to register a formal verdict that may have a result, and voters often reconsider their opinions when they have to take a genuine decision. At the time of the unprecedented British European Economic Community referendum, indeed, the air was loud with the cries of agonized housewives trying desperately to make up their minds, and protesting bitterly that it was not fair of the government to present them with such a difficult decision.

What opinion polls undoubtedly do is to alter the tactical situation by making it easier to guess the result in advance. This means that if the government has a monopoly in the holding of referendums or elections, it can wait until the tide is flowing its way. Where citizens also have rights of referendum and initiative, shifts in public opinion will favor different groups at different times, thus making for a less monopolistic political system.

8. *Government by the People?*

Our discussion of populist democracy has so far concentrated upon the arguments against it and populist answers to those objections. As we have seen, although antipopulists have some persuasive arguments, such experience as exists does not amount to much of a case against populist democracy. How much of a case, however, is there *for* it?

The populist case rests heavily upon the assumption, putatively shared by all parties to the dispute, that democracy—"government by the people," in some sense— is the best form of government. Populist democrats add to this the claim that the methods of direct legislation enable "the people," composed of honest citizens with no ax to grind, to defend themselves against "special interests." In American populist traditions "special interests" are generally identified as corporations, and politicians are distrusted as being in their pay. Populist rhetoric in other countries often has a similar structure but different components. Conservative politicians in Britain, for instance—of whom Mrs. Thatcher is merely the latest— sometimes use the populist tactic of appealing to "the people" against the trade unions and *their* captive politicians in the Labour Party.

While the possible applications of this approach are wide, the populist assumption in all cases is that one can distinguish between "special interests" on the one hand, and ordinary citizens with the public interest at heart on the other. The object of the initiative, referendum, and recall is to strengthen the latter against the former. Unfortunately, as political scientists have pointed out, the devices of populist democracy do not necessarily work quite like that. The Progressives who introduced the initiative and referendum in California, for instance, expected that " 'The People' would circulate petitions and put measures on the ballot for the promotion of the welfare of the average man."[91] One study of the workings of these devices found, however, that the referendum and initiative, instead of being the voice of the people, had become part of the ordinary process of politics—just another device whereby the usual pressure groups might influence legislation. Given the financial resources required to mount a referendum campaign, indeed, the authors suggested that the system actually favored the special interests it had been designed to thwart. They came to the deflating conclusion that the interests of the ordinary citizen who was not a member of a powerful group might be better cared for through the familiar interest-aggregating mechanisms of political parties.[92]

This jaundiced view is perhaps borne out by recent initiatives in California, in which the role of "special interests" has been prominent. There have been cases, for instance, of a housing measure sponsored by real-estate interests; movie theaters opposing pay T.V.; agricultural growers opposing unionization among farm workers; public employees seeking higher salaries; etc.[93] In the nature of things, interest groups are likely to be best able to find the finance and organization to mount initiative and referendum campaigns, particularly in political systems with high signature requirements and large populations. In California, such campaigns have actually generated professional organizations that will manage a petition campaign and collect signatures at so much per head.[94] Although grass-roots organizations as well as interest groups do participate in direct legislation, the costs are a considerable deterrent.

Even in Switzerland, where the collection of sufficient signatures, particularly at cantonal level, is a much less massive undertaking, the initiative and referendum are chiefly used not by the disinterested citizen of populist dreams but as tools in the hands of pressure groups.[95] Furthermore, such special interests can often influence legislation simply by threatening an initiative or referendum, without having to go to the expense of actually holding one—a weapon that is less available to ad hoc groups of citizens. As Jean-François Aubert says, "the most successful referendums are those which do not take place."[96]

Use by special interests of the very tools that were supposed to defeat them raises the more fundamental question whether or not it is possible to make a political distinction (as populist democrats commonly do) between "special interests" and "the people." Is there such a thing as "the people," with a general "public interest"?

It was with the idea of the public interest, under the name of the General Will, that Rousseau (that wayward populist) struggled in *The Social Contract*. Rousseau was well aware that there is no natural unity of interest or outlook among any people. His claim was, however, that among the conflicting interests of persons and groups there are some which all share and which can be abstracted and stressed. Under certain favorable conditions, citizens will be prepared to put these public interests above their private ones. The General Will, in Rousseau's understanding of it, is not the natural, spontaneous expression of an organically united people: it is a severely abstract conception which stresses those interests that all citizens share while recognizing the innumerable conflicts that divide them.[97]

Perhaps the nearest modern equivalent to Rousseau's abstraction of man-as-citizen from the squabbling conglomeration of actual persons is the notion of the consumer, and current attempts to mobilize popular support for consumer interests. For the point about consumer interests is that, like the General Will, everyone shares them, if only in some aspects of his life. The consumer interest in safe cars or nonpolluted air may conflict with the interests of shareholders and employees of the automobile or chemical industries: but even the most grasping corporate monster of populist imagination is, after all, a consumer in his spare time. Like Rousseau's General Will, consumer interests may not be uppermost in many persons' minds, but they are in principle common to the entire people, and should therefore be a basis for union across existing political lines.[98]

This base for popular unity has in recent years found expression in the consumer movement, and above all in the activities of Ralph Nader in the United States.[99] Nader is in some way a perfect example of modern democratic populism. An ordinary private citizen with no political machine behind him, no interest group financing him, no ideological ax to grind, representing simply the consumer, emerges from obscurity to take on the elite—in the archetypal shape of General Motors—and wins. There is a Chaplinesque symbolism in the image of the little man triumphing over the great organization. Furthermore, Nader's efforts undoubtedly demonstrated the vulnerability of commercial corporations in a competitive economy to bad publicity: sales of the car on which he concentrated his attack slumped to the point where it was taken off the market.

There is, however, a certain ambiguity about Nader's success. For one thing, although it may be taken to illustrate the power one ordinary man can generate by mobilizing other consumers, it is clear that Nader never was an ordinary man. His energy and charismatic force of personality are exceptional, while his ascetic life style makes him strangely untypical of the average consumer. More seriously, if he is not representative of the common man, neither is he responsible to anyone. This is an objection that can be raised more generally against the claims of consumerism and environmentalism to represent the people. For although such movements do stand for common interests in the sense that no one wants to eat poisoned food, breathe poisoned air, or ride in unsafe vehicles, this common interest is not the only interest people have. No one wants to contract cancer or have a deformed child as a result of nuclear radiation, but just what level of risk people may accept depends upon their other interests and commitments. For many, it may be worth accepting a very low risk of these horrendous possibilities, in order to keep up the supply of energy or to save their jobs.

It seems, then, that even the defenders of consumer interests are not spokesmen for the General Will of the whole people but partisans like everyone else: a special lobby, even though they are defending universal interests. One problem that Rousseau did not recognize was that even if one can identify a General Will common to all, this General Will may itself become a special interest because it is a higher priority for some than for others. The notion that populist democracy enables "the people" to declare "the public interest," therefore, is not one that stands up to close examination. A much more plausible claim is that devices like the initiative enable all interests to find a voice, and prevent the powerful from "organizing out" of politics certain interests and opinions. The problem here (which carries us on to our next topic) is that there are certain opinions that even democrats would often prefer to see excluded from the political arena, because they are reactionary.

## 9. Is Direct Legislation Antiprogressive?

One of the most common objections to populist democracy, and a considerable stumbling block for radical populists, is the claim that populism implies reaction. It is certainly true that conservatives in many political systems have favored direct appeals to the people, because they believed that the mass of the people were profoundly conservative, and that liberal progressives, though a vocal minority, were isolated from the majority of the populace.[100] It was chiefly the Catholic Conservative Party that made use of the referendum in nineteenth-century Switzerland,[101] and conservatives elsewhere have often favored the device. In Britain, for example, although the E.E.C. referendum was sponsored by a Labour government, previous support for popular consultation had come generally from conservatives who saw it as a way of preventing change.[102]

Not that direct legislation is by any means exclusively a scheme of the Right. In America, as we have seen, it was enthusiastically promoted by Populist and Progressive reformers who saw it as a means of bringing about change for the better, while at the present time support for populist democracy comes predominantly from the Left. Notable American examples of contemporary populist democrats include Michael Harrington and Ralph Nader, while in Britain it is the hope of the Labour Left, Tony Benn, who has placed most emphasis on popular consultation.

Laura Tallian of the Californian People's Lobby admits that popular votes tend to be conservative, but argues that reformers need to be patient and must convince a majority of the population of the justice of their cause.[103] Populists often claim (on the lines of J. S. Mill's defense of universal suffrage) that direct legislation is profoundly educative, and tends over a period of time to produce the kind of informed electorate that it requires.[104]

Butler and Ranney, surveying referendums in general, conclude that voters practically everywhere tend to oppose change.[105] On the further question whether popular voting favors the Left or the Right, however, they conclude only that "the referendum is a politically neutral device that generally produces outcomes favoured by the current state of public opinion."[106] Public opinion is rarely consistently on the Left or Right, and varies a great deal over time. As far as America alone is concerned, Austin Ranney concluded from a survey of referendums there that the voters have tended to veer to the left on economic questions, to the right on capital punishment, abortion, and racial discrimination, and to be evenly divided on environmental issues.[107]

There can be no doubt that the net effect of populist democracy in Switzerland has been to slow down change. For instance, Switzerland was notoriously the last Western democratic country by many years to give women the vote. Although the Swiss have been conservative, on the other hand, they have not on the whole used their powers to be reactionary in the sense feared by liberals. Since one of the evils liberals commonly associate with populism is unbridled racism, it is interesting to look at Swiss handling of the touchy issue of immigrant workers.

By the early 1970s one-fifth of all employed persons in Switzerland were foreign.[108] The largest group were Italians, followed by Spaniards, French, Yugoslavs, and Germans. To add to the potential explosiveness of the situation, the birthrate for foreign women resident in Switzerland was twice that for Swiss women.[109] A very much lower level of foreign immigration was enough to make possible the rise of Enoch Powell in Britain, and members of the British political elite at the time of his ascendancy would have shuddered at the thought of his being able to initiate a referendum on immigration. But this tactic was of course available to his Swiss counterpart, a publisher named James Schwarzenbach.

Schwarzenbach's initiative led to a referendum in June 1970 on a proposed constitutional amendment which would limit the number of foreigners to 10 percent of the population in any canton—a measure that would have meant the expulsion of some 300,000 foreigners. The proposal was opposed by all the government authorities and political parties, and by business and commerce. Seventy-four percent of Swiss electors turned out to vote—a record number for recent times—and the proposal came near to success. Schwarzenbach's cause gained 46 percent of the vote and was carried in seven cantons, most of them rural areas with comparatively little immigration.[110]

In the wake of this vote, right-wing political parties opposed to foreigners sprang up, and in 1974 the issue was again put to a referendum, this time on a bill to reduce the total number of foreigners living in Switzerland to 500,000 by the end of 1977. But this time the anti-foreign vote dropped to 34 percent and the proposal failed to gain a majority in any one canton, while support in a third vote held in 1977 dropped even lower. In spite of its concern over the scale of social and ethnic change, the Swiss electorate was evidently not, upon due consideration, prepared to go to extreme lengths. The struggle had been close enough, however, to alarm liberals and to give some of them doubts about populist democracy.

For many years, throughout the heyday of "elitist democracy" and mass-society theories, populist democracy was written off by liberals as obviously reactionary. Devices like the referendum were associated with authoritarian leaders from Hitler to de Gaulle, and direct consultation of voters was dismissed in progressive circles on the grounds that it would favor reactionary legislation of all kinds, from capital punishment to racial discrimination.

Since populist democracy staged a comeback among radical intellectuals, however, these conservative aspects of direct legislation have been accorded less attention. And yet they do pose genuine problems, particularly since those who are campaigning once again for populist democracy usually hold views considerably more advanced than those of the general public. As we have already seen, most of the participationists of the 1960s were as far removed from their supposed constituency as were the *narodniki*. Populist democracy contains severe internal tensions, for what becomes of populism when a progressive radical committed to direct legislation faces a surge of grass-roots reaction among the sovereign people? The dilemmas engendered by this situation require more extended consideration, to which we shall devote the next chapter.

# 6. Reactionary Populism and the Dilemmas of Progress

The average opinion of mankind is in the long run superior to the dictates of the self-chosen.—*Franklin D. Roosevelt*[1]

Learning survives among us largely because the mob has not got news of it. If the notions it turns loose descended to the lowest levels, there would be an uprising against them, and efforts would be made to put them down by law.—*H. L. Mencken*[2]

## BACKLASH AT THE GRASS ROOTS

In the 1960s the mass-society theories that had been previously invoked to explain cases of populist dictatorship, and that were particularly fashionable in American academic circles since McCarthyism, became casualties of the new wave of academic populism and the respect for the common man which it produced. By a curious irony, however, just at the moment when this new faith in grassroots participation in politics was burgeoning in the universities, populist movements of another kind (complete with populist anti-intellectualism) were pitting the reactionary prejudices of the common man against the liberal commitments of the enlightened and widening up the gulf between the people and the elite. This rift was strikingly symbolized by the rise to prominence of two politicians, George Wallace in America and Enoch Powell in Britain.

Governor George Wallace of Alabama began his career as a politician in the Southern populist tradition. Himself by origin a poor farm boy who had seen the mortgage on his family's farm foreclosed during the Depression, he gained a reputation in Alabama politics as an economic populist very much in the style of Huey Long, favoring welfare legislation and increased government expenditure. As governor of Alabama he broke the state's record for money spent on social services, increasing workmen's compensation, old age pensions, medical aid, teachers' salaries, and educational budgets in general. Like Long, he introduced free textbooks in state schools.[3] Not initially noted for racism, he started to campaign on the racial issue after being beaten in an election by a Ku Klux Klan candidate. He is reported to have exclaimed when his defeat was announced, "They out-niggered me that time but they'll never do it again."

The 1960s were a favorable time for a politician to use racism as a ladder to fame. As a result of the Civil Rights movement, federal legislation was passed to outlaw segregation and secure voting rights for blacks, and Wallace became nationally famous as a particularly outspoken opponent of desegregation. A hero to many in the South, he rapidly discovered that he could attract extensive grassroots support in the North as well, particularly when he incorporated into his program of racism plus welfare liberalism virulent denunciations of the American elite. This was the time of the student movement, of anti-

Vietnam demonstrations and the burning of draft cards, of calls for revolution coming from the privileged sons and daughters of the upper middle class. While the students idealized "participation" by the people, Wallace appealed more directly to the grass roots. It was said of him: "He is talking about poor people, 'ordinary folks,' and if you strip him of the Southern accent . . . you might mistake him for a New Left advocate of the poverty program, urging the maximum feasible participation of the poor and the return of local government to the people, 'participatory democracy.' "[4]

By 1968 Wallace was enough of a national figure to stand as a third-party candidate in the Presidential election on a platform of welfare, law and order, racism, and antielitism. He inveighed against "the trend of pseudo-intellectual government, where a select, elite group have written guidelines in bureaus and court decisions . . . looking down their noses at the average man in the street, the glass worker, the steel worker, the auto worker and the textile worker, the farmer, the policeman, the beautician and the barber, and the little businessman."[5]

Wallace got ten million votes in the 1968 campaign, 13.5 percent of the total. He captured five states in the Deep South, but half his vote came from outside that region. Support for him was strong among blue-collar workers, especially policemen, and he went down well in general with those who were neither members of disadvantaged minority groups nor, in Wallace's picturesque phrase, "pointy-headed intellectuals born with silver spoons in their mouths." His platform of concern with racial issues, crime, traditional moral values, and antielitism was clearly one which had considerable appeal to the mass of American voters.[6]

While Wallace was demonstrating some of the implications of increasing grass-roots participation in American politics, Enoch Powell was rocking the British political establishment by articulating analogous feelings among the people of Britain. Unlike Wallace, Powell was not at all populist in background or style, and had virtually no popular influence until 1968. His parliamentary reputation was that of a rather remote, intellectual politician. But in 1968 he shot to fame by breaking the tacit convention whereby all major parties in Britain had avoided making immigration and race political issues. In a sensational speech, he hinted at dire prospects of racial conflict as a result of excessive immigration: "Like the Roman, I seem to see the River Tiber foaming with much blood."[7] The shock was tremendous, not the least because of the contrast between Powell's own political and social respectability and the hitherto disreputable aura of racism in Britain. As a student of Powell has put it, "one of the country's leading political figures, a man of cabinet rank and experience with a powerful aura of cerebral severity had made all his own the cause of the pubs and the clubs, the bingo halls and the football terraces."[8]

Powell was promptly sacked from the Shadow Cabinet by the leader of the Conservative Party. The entire political establishment was against him—but the people appeared to be massively for him. According to various opinion polls he was supported by between 60 and 75 percent of the electorate—far more than any party leader could command. Powell hastened to underline, in terms similar to those used by Wallace, the dangerous gap that existed between "the overwhelming majority of the people throughout the country on one side and, on the other side, a tiny minority with almost a monopoly hold upon the channels of communication."[9]

It is important to recognize what was involved when Wallace and Powell were accused (with strong overtones of indignation) of "populism." For populism in this sense does not mean *any* attempt to appeal to the people, to stir up grass-roots support. If that were so, all election manifestoes without exception could be regarded as populist. The kind of "populism" that Wallace and Powell engaged in so successfully was democratic mobilization of a particular kind. "Populism" of this sort is an appeal to the people which deliberately opens up the embarrassing gap between "the people" and their supposedly democratic and representative elite by stressing popular values that conflict with those of the elite: typically, it involves a clash between reactionary, authoritarian, racist, or chauvinist views at the grass roots, and the progressive, liberal, tolerant cosmopolitanism characteristic of the elite.

The strength of reactionary populism, and the reason why it creates so much heartburning among its analysts, is that the problems to which it gives rise in a democracy are not just practical ones of managing political dissent, but problems of legitimacy. For what are enlightened democrats to do if "the people" in whose rule they are supposed to believe, utterly fail to share their views?

Such democratic paradoxes occur in their most extreme form, of course, in cases like those of Peron or Hitler, where the populace votes to reject democratic processes altogether and endorses dictatorship, thus leaving liberal democrats without a leg to stand on. But similar problems arise quite frequently in democratic states where the electorate may not actually support a dictator, but may share reactionary sentiments which the elite attempts to organize out of ordinary democratic processes. In such a situation, a demagogue who mobilizes these suppressed views spotlights the gulf between the normal workings of democracy (supposedly representative of the majority, but in fact heavily influenced by the more progressive and liberal sections of the community) and popular feelings which may be quite different. The obvious solution for a democratic politician is, of course, to jump on the bandwagon and adopt popular causes, which to some extent happened as a result of the activities of Wallace and Powell. Sometimes, however, the popular prejudices thus exposed are too deeply repugnant to many of the elite for this to be an easy option.

Clearly, any discussion of reactionary populism cannot be limited to the actual phenomena of outbursts like the "white backlash." It is necessary to consider also the context which makes these outbursts problematic. We must look more generally, that is to say, at the relations between the elite and the people, and particularly at the problems which this relation tends to create in a culture with democratic norms of respect for majority decisions and popular sovereignty. We shall find, in particular, that special dilemmas are created for democrats by the liberal belief in progress, and the consciousness which liberal democratic elites often have of being a vanguard of enlightenment, dragging behind them an unwilling populace.

The more populistic in their sympathies intellectuals are, the more agonizing such dilemmas become. Reactionary prejudices among the masses may, of course, present practical problems for any elite, but if that elite is convinced of its own superiority, there is at least no moral or intellectual problem involved in overriding popular views. But when members of an elite are themselves anti-elitist—when intellectuals feel respect for the common man—then the conflict between their idealistic populism and the reactionary populism of the masses becomes a severe stumbling block. The dilemmas it presents have been faced by populist intellectuals at many different times, and given the current swing away from elitist and toward populist attitudes in universities today, they will have to be confronted once again. In this chapter we shall explore the difficulties of populist intellectuals faced with a reactionary populace, starting with cultural questions but proceeding to the moral dilemmas which are the crux of the problem.

## POPULISM AND CULTURE

The relationship between populism and culture has never been an easy one. Cultural traditions, whether artistic, literary, philosophical, scientific, or religious, have mostly been elitist: a natural situation in hierarchical societies where leisure and learning were the preserve of the few. Not only art and science, but civilized manners, "urbanity," had traditionally been the monopoly of the patrician, while even goodness has been more often attributed to the cloistered monk than to the common man. Age-old assumptions lie behind the cult of Genius developed by nineteenth-century romantic thinkers, and Nietzsche's view, that the existence of "the herd" was justified only as a backcloth for the glory of his cultural Superman, merely took the argument to its ultimate conclusion.

Such cultural elitism has not stood unchallenged, however. Reacting against the traditional view of civilization as the preserve of the few, populists of all varieties have retaliated with praise of the common man. It is perhaps in the sphere of the arts that cultural populism has been most strident and least problematic. Popular songs, dances, and crafts of all kinds have been exalted and preserved in opposition to the high culture of the elite, particularly in areas where populism was reinforced by opposition to foreign influence. An idiosyncratic version was preached by Tolstoy after he had in his later years rejected the art of the cultured classes as a parasitic excrescence.[10] While cultural populism has been most common in areas where "the people" were peasants and their culture was a traditional one, similar impulses have recently generated a movement for "community arts" in modern cities. In place of the nationalism which often fueled interest in peasant culture, this new movement is closely connected with the populistic Marxism of the 1960s and 1970s, and opposes the culture of the people to that of the bourgeoisie.[11]

Contentious though artistic populism may be, however, it is not this field that generates the really difficult problems—mainly, as we shall see, because this is a field in which notions of historical progress need not be invoked. Much thornier issues arise from the tendency of populists not only to admire popular art but also to revere folk wisdom, and to attribute to the ordinary man a sturdy common sense and simple virtue which compare favorably with the overrefined speculations and corrupt morals of the elite.

Examples of this kind of thing could be found in any populist movement, but nowhere has the populist attitude to culture, intellect, and morals been more influential than in America, where a democratic electorate, emancipated from feelings of deference toward their social and cultural superiors, was from the beginning a ready target for praise of the common man.[12] The first great flowering of populism in the United States was the Jacksonian movement, which was fueled not only by hostility to the established ruling classes of the seaboard states, but also by a conviction, widespread among the frontiersmen who supported Jackson, that the judgment of the ordinary man was more reliable than that of the highly educated. During Jackson's Presidential campaign, his followers stressed as a point in his favor that he had "escaped the training and dialectics of the schools" and had a "judgement unclouded by the visionary speculations of the academician," which might have impaired his practical common sense. The ultimate frontiersman, Congressman Davy Crockett, who spent part of his political career in the Jacksonian party, boasted in his autobiography how he had coped with the job of justice of the peace in Tennessee, in spite of his lack of education: "I gave my decisions on the principles of common justice and honesty between man and man, and relied on natural born sense, and not on law learning to guide me; for I had never read a page in a law book in all my life."[13]

The peculiar irony of American experience lay in the

fact that, besides being the most stridently populistic of nations, the United States was also the nation most dedicated to change and progress. For the fact is that the demands of progress and enlightenment are extremely liable to conflict with the judgment of the common man. H. L. Mencken, the scourge of American democracy, declared that "the whole progress of the world, even in the direction of ameliorating the lot of the masses, is always opposed by the masses. . . . It is a tragic but inescapable fact that most of the finest fruits of human progress, like all of the nobler virtues of man, are the exclusive possession of small minorities, chiefly unpopular and disreputable."[14] No better dramatization of Mencken's point could be found than the confrontation between science and popular religion which he followed with contemptuous fascination in 1925: the celebrated "Monkey Trial" at Dayton, Tennessee.

Throughout the latter half of the nineteenth century, a war had raged in intellectual circles in Europe and America between science and religion, and particularly between Biblical faith and evolutionary biology. By the 1920s the evolutionists might have been pardoned for assuming that their battle was won, and that the march of mind had far outstripped literal belief in the Book of Genesis. Such confidence would have been premature, however, for the issues which had rocked the universities half a century before were only just filtering down to the public schools, there to become a matter of serious public concern in states where most of the electors were fundamentalists. The first state of the union to ban the teaching of evolution in public schools was Oklahoma, in 1923,

but—appropriately enough—it was Davy Crockett's old
state of Tennessee that provided the cause célèbre.[15]

A Tennessee farmer, John Washington Butler, himself
a primitive Baptist, was moved to act against the teaching
of evolution by hearing of a local girl, once a faithful be-
liever, who had gone away to the university and come
home a Darwinian. Anxious to defend other young people
against similar threats to their faith, Butler stood for the
state legislature on a platform devoted solely to the banning of unbiblical teaching. He was duly elected, and
armed with this mandate from the people he proposed a
law making it illegal for any teacher employed by the
state "to teach any theory that denies the story of the
divine creation of man as taught in the Bible and to teach
instead that man has descended from a lower order of
animals."[16] The bill passed the House by a massive
majority, got through the Senate at the second attempt,
and was reluctantly signed by the governor.

The American Civil Liberties Union promptly offered
to support any Tennessee teacher who would challenge
the statute, and an inoffensive young biology instructor,
John T. Scopes, agreed to be the victim. One of his friends
formally denounced him to the public officials for teaching evolution, and Scopes was put on trial. The case
rapidly acquired nationwide notoriety, particularly when
it became known that William Jennings Bryan had offered
to assist the prosecution. Bryan, the Democrat who had
led the Populist and free-silver forces in 1896, had since
become celebrated as a champion of prohibition and
fundamentalist religion. (He preferred, as he liked to put
it, to concern himself with the Rock of Ages rather than

the age of rocks.[17]) Clarence Darrow, a prominent reformer who had himself been a supporter of Populism in
the 1890s, immediately volunteered to act for the defense,
and the stage was set for a notable duel. Its seriousness
was, admittedly, somewhat impaired by the enthusiasm
with which the businessmen of Dayton seized their commercial opportunities. The local stores stocked up with
miniature cotton apes and pins reading "Your Old Man's
a Monkey," while an enterprising shopkeeper named
J. R. Darwin decorated his clothing store with a gigantic
banner proclaiming, "DARWIN IS RIGHT—inside."[18]

For Darrow and the educated public in general, the
issue was whether science and enlightenment should be
allowed to spread, or whether progress should be stopped
by ignorant prejudice. Darrow signaled his commitment
to progress when he remarked in the course of the trial
that "every child ought to be more intelligent than his
parents." But the issue for Bryan and the local populace
was quite different. The people of Tennessee, or at any
rate an overwhelming majority of them, believed in the
Bible; they had elected a legislator to defend their faith;
their children were taught in public schools which they
paid for. Had they not a right to guard their children's
religion from attack in their own schools? As Bryan
pointed out, America's democratic political system was
built upon the doctrine of popular sovereignty. By what
right, then, could a minority force its ideas on children
through the schools? The matter at issue could hardly be
regarded as a remote and technical question of interest
only to experts. It was, for the fundamentalists of Tennessee, a matter of eternal life and death. Why, then,

should the people's religion be sacrificed to those whom Bryan stigmatized as a "little irresponsible oligarchy of self-styled intellectuals"?[19]

Amid a blaze of nationwide publicity, Scopes was tried in the little courthouse (underneath a banner exhorting, "Read Your Bible Daily") and duly found guilty. To add to the drama of the case, Bryan, who had been mercilessly harassed by Darrow in the closing stages of the trial, and who had proved unable to offer any coherent defense of his faith, dropped dead a few days after the verdict. The Tennessee Supreme Court, to which the case was referred on appeal, managed to find technical grounds for quashing Scopes's conviction, thus wriggling neatly out of a difficult situation. To the incredulous urban public of America, the whole affair seemed nothing short of farcical, but for all its sensationalism, the trial involved a perfectly serious issue, and a genuine dilemma for any populist democrat. For when expert consensus and popular conviction stand directly opposed to one another on a matter of profound popular concern, which ought to triumph?

## DEMOCRACY VERSUS PROGRESS

This dilemma of progress and enlightenment versus popular sentiment is one with which modern democracy has been saddled from birth, and with which intellectual populists have come to terms in a variety of ways. In earlier times, the immemorial distinction between elite knowledge and popular superstition caused little embarrassment to scholars, who took for granted their elevation above the vulgar. Just at the point, however, when the reformers of the eighteenth century embarked upon the democratic project of diffusing knowledge among the whole people, this same democratic project was rendered hopeless by the new conviction that knowledge is progressive, continually advancing and expanding.

In its implications for the status of ordinary people, the great liberal creed of science, progress, enlightenment, and reform was profoundly ambiguous. On the one hand, it meant a call for the liberation of all men from the bonds of ignorance and superstition: the spreading of knowledge to all equally. But at the same time, precisely because knowledge continues to progress, enlightenment implied that some men must be in the vanguard of progress, and that the majority must lag behind. In a metaphor that was to become increasingly influential in politics, society was envisaged as a school in which those who are most advanced in knowledge must be the leaders and teachers of the rest. The whole liberal-scientific-progressive package, in fact—in spite of its close historical links with movements for democratic reform—had an inescapably elitist and antipopulist slant. In the nature of things, if we are all progressing toward truth, some of us must be in front.[20]

Progressive democrats had little excuse for ignoring the inherent tension between the notion of popular self-government on the one hand and that of progress and enlightenment on the other,[21] for at the very moment when the liberal democratic package was being put together, its internal contradictions were eloquently exposed by Jean-Jacques Rousseau. Perceiving a conflict between populist values and the cause of progress and enlightenment, Rousseau caused a sensation by rejecting the latter.

Attempts to assign Rousseau to any political camp or philosophical tradition invariably present difficulties. There is nothing straightforward about the preacher of the simple life: his writings are full of paradoxes and con- tradictions, and he often seems to take away with one hand what he gives with the other. If we call him a popu- list, therefore, we must do so with reservations, re- membering the elitist elements in his writings, and his posthumous career as an inspirer of Jacobins and other vanguard groups who proposed to force the people to be free.[22] Nevertheless, it can hardly be denied that Rousseau's writings contain, among their legacies, a popu- list defense of equality, popular sovereignty, and respect for the common man, coupled with denunciations of progress and enlightenment, and hostility to civilization.

Rousseau himself was scarcely one of the common men. Had he remained in the station to which he was born, he might have become an honest watchmaker and citizen of Geneva. Instead, he fled from Swiss democracy and rusticity to the hierarchical civilization of France. There he acquired an education and clambered up the social ladder, to appear in Paris among the crowd of clever young men who sought their fortune in the salons where culture and snobbery flourished together. He be- came a devotee of the opera and the theater—the most expensive and sophisticated of the arts—and the friend of those who, like Diderot and d'Alembert, stood con- sciously in the forefront of progress. He even contributed to the Encyclopedia that was designed to spread the fruits of enlightenment to a wider public.

Then, in the summer of 1749, Rousseau experienced the "conversion" that turned him against all this acquired civilization and forced him back upon nature and the people. Walking to Vincennes one day to visit Diderot, who was imprisoned there on account of one of his provocative writings, he read in the *Mercure de France* that the Dijon Academy was holding an essay competition on the subject, "Has the progress of the sciences and arts done more to corrupt morals or to improve them?" All Rousseau's latent hostility to the social snobbery and cultural sophistication of French society poured into the *Discourse on the Moral Effects of the Arts and Sciences* which won him the prize and made him famous. In the essay he claimed that progress in science, learning, and art was useless, and indeed worse than useless, for it reinforced despotism and undermined morality: "luxury, profligacy, and slavery have been, in all ages, the scourge of the efforts of our pride to emerge from that happy state of ignorance, in which the wisdom of providence had placed us."[23]

Contrasting Sparta, "a city as famous for the happy ignorance of its inhabitants, as for the wisdom of its laws," with Athens, the seat of philosophy, Rousseau argued that even the most cultured of ancient societies was less accursed than modern nations, where the invention of printing had spread dangerous enlightenment more widely than ever before. He even went so far as to defend (in a footnote) the Caliph Omar's decision to burn the books in the famous library of Alexandria. Rousseau conceded that there were occasional geniuses whom nature had clearly destined for profound thought— Newton, for instance, or Descartes. They could follow their vocation, however, without any need for the academic institutions which fostered learning among the second-rate. As for the rest of mankind, he maintained that morality, not culture, was what they needed: "Virtue! Sublime science of simple minds, are such industry and preparation needed if we are to know you? Are not your principles graven on every heart?"[24]

Having caused a sensation by denouncing culture and setting it in opposition to morality and freedom, Rousseau went on in his *Discourse on the Origin of Inequality* to attack the notions of progress and civilization more comprehensively. Painting a seductive picture of the "natural man," ignorant, solitary, completely uncivilized, but nevertheless equal, free, and happy, Rousseau described the sad process of degeneration whereby, as a result of man's "perfectibility," he had been progressively entangled in society and enslaved by the more and more hierarchical system that civilization engendered.

In opposition to the doctrine of progress through enlightenment, Rousseau presented a theory of degeneration. Man is best when he is closest to nature in societies that are simple, unrefined, and egalitarian. He is worst where he has progressed furthest along the road to civilization and inequality. Against Paris, the center of the civilized world, Rousseau set rude societies like Corsica or Switzerland, where men were more natural and more equal. He stressed, in addition, that such happy people were also *wiser* than the sophisticated intellectuals who despised them, since Rousseau's attack on progress and civilization was not an attack on intellect in itself. His position was not that of an arch-reactionary like Joseph de Maistre, who could write that "man needs beliefs, not problems. His cradle should be surrounded by dogmas; and, when his reason awakes, all his opinions should be given, at least all those relating to his conduct."[25]

Instead, Rousseau contrasted with the sophisticated and useless learning of the elite a picture of ordinary men, living close to nature and using their wits in ways that were relevant to their own lives.[26] It was this vision of the natural life that inspired Rousseau's *Emile*. One of the many remarkable things about this treatise on education is its extreme hostility to academic learning and sophisticated culture. Rousseau's main advice, constantly repeated, is that children should not be taught. Instead of wasting their childhood learning geography, history, Latin, Greek, and the rest, they should be strengthening their bodies and acquiring practical skills through exercise. Rousseau interjects, "Remember, reader, that he who speaks to you is neither a scholar nor a philosopher but a plain man and a lover of truth," and he takes every opportunity to attack what passes for "enlightenment." He exclaims, "I hate books, they only teach us to talk about things we know nothing about."[27]

The main thing that Emile was to be systematically taught was a trade, by which he would be able to support himself, if necessary: not a glamorous and useless trade like those of the artist and jeweler who minister to the rich, but an honest, useful trade such as carpentry. For the rest, he was to be trained to work things out for himself and to solve his own problems, without cluttering up his mind with useless knowledge.

> Who can deny that a vast number of things are known to the learned, which the unlearned will never know?

Are the learned any nearer truth? Not so, the further they
go the further they get from truth, for their pride in
their judgement increases faster than their progress in
knowledge, so that for every truth they acquire they draw
a hundred mistaken conclusions. Everyone knows that the
learned societies of Europe are mere schools of falsehood,
and there are assuredly more mistaken notions in the
Academy of Sciences than in a whole tribe of American
Indians.[28]

When Rousseau translated his rejection of civilization,
progress, and inequality into political terms in *The
Social Contract*, the result was profoundly ambiguous.
The book is to a large extent a defense of popular
sovereignty, of an egalitarian state in which the ultimate
rule is the general will of ordinary citizens, and Rousseau
eloquently defends the capacity of common men to
manage their own affairs.[29] Elsewhere in the book, however, he asserts flatly that "a blind multitude" is *not*
capable of working out its own laws,[30] and to help them
he introduces the mysterious figure of the lawgiver, who
is presented as a superhuman leader, presiding over the
birth of the state as Lycurgus did over that of Sparta.
Commentators have struggled unsuccessfully to reconcile
Rousseau's confidence in the people on the one hand
with his distrust of them on the other: unpopulist as the
figure of the lawgiver may be, however, he is definitely
not an enlightened despot. His function is not, à la Peter
the Great, to represent a more advanced stage of enlightenment than his people and to draw them forward
along the track of progress. On the contrary, he is concerned only to arrange things so that the simple people
will be able to stay as they are, as secure from the

corruptions of time and civilization as is possible in this degenerate world.

Let us speculate for a moment on how Rousseau would have reacted, had he revisited the earth in 1925 and been asked for his opinion on the trial of Scopes at Dayton. He would surely have stood with Bryan against Darrow: for what, to him, was the value of science and progress compared with popular self-government and religion? He was prepared to concede that scientific speculations were appropriate for those whose minds were such that they could hardly stop themselves from thinking about recondite subjects, but he saw no value in the diffusion of their ideas among the many. Faced with the progressives' trump card, that science makes possible improvements in the standard of living, Rousseau would have been unmoved: material advances seemed to him merely to increase men's needs and to render them ever more dependent upon one another. From his point of view, the frontiersman in his log cabin was better off then the suburbanite with his houseful of electrical gadgets.

## INTELLECTUAL POPULISTS AND REACTIONARY POPULISM

Rousseau's typically extreme solution to the dilemma of populist values versus progress and enlightenment was made possible by his profoundly pessimistic view of history and his low opinion of the benefits of progress, whether material or intellectual. But this uncompromising choice, while it has parallels elsewhere, is unusual.[31] Faced with the problem of reconciling populist commitments with the benefits of progress, thinkers have more often sought an accommodation of some kind.

No group of intellectuals struggled more earnestly with this dilemma than the Russian populists. These dedicated revolutionaries were devoted to the service of the people, and they dreamed of a new socialist society based on the self-governing peasant commune. As they were acutely aware, however, they were themselves enlightened, cultured, sophisticated, separated by a vast gulf from the ignorant masses. It is not surprising that they agonized over the role of the intellectual and his relation to the people, and in doing so explored many ramifications of the dilemma of progress versus populism. It happened that in 1869 and 1870 three Russian intellectuals, each with a separate standpoint, were thinking and writing about the problems of progress, and it may be illuminating for us to look in turn at the views of Peter Lavrov, Peter Tkachev, and Nicolas Mikhailovsky.

We have already encountered Lavrov's *Historical Letters* (p. 59) and looked at the profound impression made upon a generation of the Russian intelligentsia by their insistence upon the debt owed by the cultured minority to the masses whose toil had made culture possible. While Lavrov's writings contributed to the sense of guilt which drove young intellectuals to the people, however, his own position was ambiguous: "Progress consists in the development of consciousness and in the incorporation of truth and justice in social institutions; it is a process which is being accomplished by means of the critical thought of individuals who aim at the transformation of their culture."[32]

In other words, while he emphasized the immense debt that intellectuals owed the people, and called on them to sacrifice everything in the service of the people, Lavrov maintained that the "developed man"—the "critically thinking individuals"—represented the vanguard of enlightenment, whose duty it was to raise others to a similar level of awareness.

During the debates in the 1870s over revolutionary strategy, Lavrov stressed that the revolution must be made by the people themselves, not by a dictatorial minority claiming to speak on behalf of the people. In opposition to Bakunin's followers, however, he maintained that the people would never be able to accomplish a socialist revolution on their own. The intellectuals had a vital role to play in preparing and enlightening the people.[33] In accordance with this stress on the leading role of the intelligentsia, Lavrov's followers were less involved than the Bakuninists in the movement to the people and less inclined to adopt attitudes of reverence toward the peasant. Lavrov himself tried to maintain a precarious balance between too much *narodnik* stress on the inherent wisdom of the peasantry and too much reliance on the intellectual elite. He was acutely aware that the intellectual's "critical consciousness" often went along with anarchic individualism, egocentricity, and neurosis, and as his biographer remarks, "by 1876 he was almost as anxious to guard the *narod* against the intelligentsia as he was to induce the intelligentsia to go to the *narod*."[34]

Lavrov's ideas on the vital importance of the progressive minority were attacked not only by those in the revolutionary camp who had a romantic faith in the communal instincts and revolutionary zeal of the Russian peasants. They also came under fire from the strange but consistent standpoint of Peter Tkachev. Tkachev is often

called the "Jacobin" of the Russian revolutionary movement, and he represents the opposite pole from the
*narodniki*. His outlook has certain resemblances to that
of Rousseau, by whom he may well have been influenced.[35]

In 1870 Tkachev wrote a critique of Lavrov's *Historical
Letters* entitled, *What is the Party of Progress?* His manu-
script (which was confiscated by the police before it
could be published) set out with particular clarity the
understanding of history that informed his works throughout his career.[36] Tkachev began by questioning the whole
notion of progress implicit in Lavrov's position. Should
the process by which a minority of intellectuals had
developed their capacities at the expense of the rest of
society be called "progress" at all? The proper purpose
of society is the happiness of all its members, a happiness
which can be found only by the achievement of a balance
between needs and resources. Insofar as this is achieved,
said Tkachev, one might speak of "progress." But the
situation of Lavrov's "critically thinking" individuals
did not fit this criterion. Lavrov himself admitted that
their development had taken place at the expense of the
masses, but he had not faced the implications of this
admission, because he looked on the intellectuals as a
vanguard destined to raise everyone to their level.

Any such optimistic view of the future seemed chimeri-
cal to Tkachev. Every time the elite had acquired new,
sophisticated needs and cultivated their delicate individuality, they had drawn off resources from the people,
who could never benefit from such "progress." The only
way to maximize happiness in society was therefore to
achieve a balance between man's needs and his resources

by cutting down artificial and sophisticated needs—to level society, sacrificing the individuality and cultivation of the exceptional few in order to make possible satisfaction for all:

> To establish the fullest possible equality of individuals (one must not confuse this equality with the so-called political, juridical or even economic equality—it should be an *organic, physiological equality*, an equality stemming from the same education and from identical conditions of life) and to harmonise the needs of all individuals with the means which are available to satisfy these needs— that is the final and the only possible end of human society, that is the supreme criterion of historical progress.[37]

What Tkachev had in mind was a socialist society based on the *obshchina,* in which the gulf between the privileged intelligentsia and the common people would be overcome by the simple device of making everyone alike. A system of compulsory child-rearing and education would give everyone the same needs, tastes, and outlook, so that no collision between the demands of "culture" and "the people" could arise. Even within the bounds of this totalitarian vision, however, contradictions reared their head, for having eliminated one form of elitism, Tkachev promptly saddled himself with another. The people themselves could not, after all, be expected to bring about the kind of revolution he had in mind. He had little faith in their political capacities, and remarked on one occasion that, "the idealisation of the uncivilised masses is one of the most widespread and dangerous illusions."[38] Instead, what was needed was a disciplined and ruthless revolutionary party which would concentrate its energies on seizing power and exercise a totalitarian dictatorship until everyone had been recast in an egalitarian mold. Tkachev, in other words, escaped one form of the conflict between progressive intellectuals and the interests of the people only to fall into another.

Meanwhile, one of the most subtle and inventive attempts to close the gap between progress and populism was being undertaken by Nicolas Mikhailovsky, who was influential in the Russian movement over a very long period.[39] In sharp contrast to Tkachev, Mikhailovsky was first and foremost an individualist. So profound was his concern for self-development and the dignity of free choice that, had he lived in a more fortunate environment, he would surely have been a liberal in the style of James Stuart Mill. As it was, he found himself having to reconcile his individualistic outlook with a commitment to socialism and an admiration for the life of the peasant commune. The measure of his intellectual subtlety is the ingenious theory of progress he devised to close the gap, while the ultimate weakness of his theory indicates how intractable the problem is.

Mikhailovsky's essay "What is Progress?" appeared in installments during 1869 and 1870. In this essay Mikhailovsky launched an attack on Herbert Spencer's principle (then enjoying a European vogue) that progress consists in ever increasing heterogeneity and division of labor. According to this view, complex natural organisms like mammals are superior to simple ones like amoebae, and societies also advance by becoming more complex and heterogeneous. Just as a higher animal contains a great many different types of specialized cells, an advanced society contains many more different kinds of people and occupations than a primitive one. The gulf between the intelligentsia and the peasant is itself, then, a sign of progress.

Mikhailovsky put his finger squarely on the flaw in this analogy. For while it may be true that an advanced, heterogeneous community is fuller and richer than a simple one *from the point of view of society as a whole*, a quite different conclusion follows when one looks at the question from the standpoint of real, individual men. No doubt the development of advanced civilizations built on ever increasing division of labor vastly increases the capacities of society as a whole. But society is composed of individuals. Increasing social heterogeneity does not mean the all-round development of the individuals involved: on the contrary, it means their ever increasing specialization and restriction. In a complex society, as Mikhailovsky put it, "the worker only works, the farmer only ploughs, the thinker only thinks."[40]

Such one-sided development did not seem to Mikhailovsky to deserve the name of "progress": "True progress is the gradual drawing to completion of the individual personality: the most complete and varied division of labour possible between men's organs, and the smallest possible division of labour between men."[41] It was this principle that formed the basis for Mikhailovsky's defense of the peasant commune. Like modern exponents of self-sufficiency, he argued that a peasant in a primitive society leads a more developed and well-rounded life than a specialized worker in a modern industrial town, simply because of the variety of skills he is obliged to master.

Within the peasant village there is little differentiation of tasks, and one peasant's life is much like another's. But self-development does not require that individuals be conspicuously different from one another—simply that each of them should develop all of his or her capacities.

Mikhailovsky did not push this argument to the point of idealizing the existing Russian village. After all, some aspects of human life were conspicuously absent from it, notably the intellectual life of which the intelligentsia were such one-sided specimens. He wished only to argue that a homogeneous society on the lines of the commune represented a higher *type* of human association than a society in which men's lives were fragmented and distorted by extensive division of labor. Having recognized what *type* of society was desirable, one could then freely admit that existing peasant villages represented only a low *level* of this type, only an embryonic foreshadowing of the future socialist society in which men would live equal and unfragmented lives like the peasants, but would include within themselves all the areas of human experience that had been developed one-sidedly in fragmented societies.

At times Mikhailovsky flirted with the idea, which would fit in well with his theory, that the common man or "layman" is wiser than the narrow-minded expert.[42] As *narodnichestvo* gathered strength in the 1870s, however, and some romantic intellectuals deferred uncritically to the peasant, Mikhailovsky was forced to realize that he could not really share such views. He redefined his own position as "critical *narodnichestvo*."[43] Like Lavrov, he believed that the intellectual and moral development which he and his like had achieved at the people's expense was a precious heritage, although it ought to be paid for. His ambivalence was apparent in 1873 when he wrote:

> We realized that the consciousness of an all-human truth and all-human ideals has been given to us only thanks to the eternal sufferings of the people. We are not guilty in these sufferings; we are not guilty even in that our up-bringing was at their expense, just as a rich and fragrant blossom is not guilty in absorbing the best sap from the plant. But, while recognising this role of a blossom from the past as something fated, we do not wish it in the future. . . .
>
> We have come to the conclusion that we are debtors of the people. We may quarrel over the extent of the debt, over the means of liquidating it, but the debt lies on our conscience and we long to discharge it.[44]

For all his sense of duty to the people, however, and in spite of his ingenious demonstration that peasant society belonged to a higher "type" than what was commonly thought of as progressive civilization, Mikhailovsky became increasingly aware that he had values and commitments which he could not give up, however contrary to the people's wishes they might be. He could not share the more extreme *narodnik* illusions about the idyllic selflessness and moral superiority of the people. "The peasant," he stated flatly, during controversy with Peter Chervinsky, "is beggarly, dirty, ignorant, crude."[45] Far from looking forward with Bakuninist enthusiasm to the prospect of the peasants rising with axes in hand to overthrow existing society, he admitted to Lavrov that he dreaded revolution even more than reaction, being able to imagine all too clearly what havoc it would cause.[46]

The dissonance between the populists' humanitarian ideals and the actual outlook and behavior of the people was dramatized by the anti-Jewish pogroms of the 1880s. To the chagrin of Jews within the radical movement, some populists were prepared to condone anti-Semitic violence rather than separate themselves from the people.[47] One member of *Narodnaya Volya* deliberately went to the Ukraine in the hope of witnessing a pogrom, and wrote in an egregious account of his experiences: "Personally, of course, I had no animosity against the Jews, but my thoughts and feelings have become one with those of the people, and I was counting hours, minutes till the pogrom started."[48] Nicholas Zlatovratskii, challenged on the question by Mikhailovsky, agreed that in principle the Jews ought to have equal rights with Russians, but evaded the issue by adopting a pose of humility: "Who has given me the guarantee that I am right and all the people wrong? Wouldn't that be intellectual pride?"[49]

Mikhailovsky, by contrast, refused to compromise his liberal ideals, whether they were popular or not. The best he could do by way of reconciliation was to argue in an essay on "The Heroes and the Mob," published in 1882, that popular susceptibility to demagoguery and mob violence was a result of the distortions of personality caused by excessive division of labor. Acutely aware of the conflict between his liberalism and his populism, he exclaimed on one occasion: "Oh, if I could drown in that grey rough mass of people, dissolve irrevocably, preserving only that spark of truth and idealism which I succeeded in acquiring at the cost of that same people."[50]

Ultimately then, Mikhailovsky failed to reconcile his sense of being part of the vanguard of progress with his dedication to the people. He was prepared to sacrifice such benefits as freedom of thought and political rights, if this was necessary to serve the people, but he was simply unable to give up his enlightened hatred of anti-Semitism in deference to the spontaneous feelings of the *narod*. And it is precisely this kind of issue which represents the crux for populistically minded intellectuals. They may find it easy to prefer popular art (particularly of the precommercial variety) to the productions of the avant-garde; they may be prepared to argue that it is not worth the people's while to be given scientific forms of agriculture at the price of being dictated to by experts,[51] or that it is more important for the people to have their children's religion protected than to have evolution taught in the schools. But when deferring to popular wishes means condoning things that any enlightened person regards as barbarous and inhumane, whether it be pogroms against Jews, lynching of blacks, witch-hunting, or female circumcision, what are they to do?

Some intellectuals, faced with such a dilemma, violate their own convictions and force themselves into approval of the popular will, like those *narodniki* who approved the pogroms. Some reconcile themselves to popular barbarism by adopting a pose of "realism," imagining themselves inside the harsh existence of the poor man, and making brutalities of all kinds seem permissible from this point of view.[52] The danger of this is that by implying that the standpoint of the poor man is more "realistic" than that of the pampered intellectual, it gives a spurious respectability to popular cruelty and makes civilized values seem merely shallow.

It is on account of the moral dilemmas involved in populism that so many liberal intellectuals have been antipopulist. Rousseau could take for granted that the populace were *more* humane than the establishment: given the daily practice by the authorities of the time of barbarities like breaking on the wheel, this was not an unreasonable position. In recent years, by contrast, it has become accepted as axiomatic that in the all-important area of moral sensitivity the higher classes, and particularly the more educated, are well in advance of the rest of the population. In consequence, populistic attitudes and institutions are often seen as a menace to humane and enlightened reform. Richard Crossman, the British Socialist, summed up a widespread attitude when he wrote in the *New Statesman*, "Better the liberal elitism of the statute book than the reactionary populism of the marketplace."[53] The confrontation between populism and progress becomes urgent and unmanageable when it is posed in terms of a conflict between enlightened humanity and popular barbarism.

If the question is posed in these terms, there is only one way of answering it. However, since this kind of formulation has become something of a cliché, it is perhaps worth pointing out that it is not unassailable. For the advanced minority are not always on the side of humanity, nor are the populace always on the side of barbarism. What we need here is caution: for while it is unquestionably true that most of the elements of modern humanitarianism, such as condemnation of torture, antiracism, the abolition of slavery, etc., were formulated and fought for by advanced minorities of educated people, the relationship is not reversible. That is to say, it is not safe to assume that the ideas for which advanced minorities are willing to fight against popular inertia are necessarily humane. The most "progressive" ideas of the day are, on occasion, more barbarous than mere popular prejudice.

This is a claim that could be documented from many areas of history. Take witch-hunting, for instance. The fear of witchcraft common to all peasantries exploded into mass witch-hunts only where, as in most European countries from the end of the Middle Ages on, elaborate *theories* about devil-worship at the witches' sabbat became fashionable in intellectual circles. Where these advanced theories did not seriously influence judicial practice, as in England, treatment of "witches" was relatively mild.[54] A salutary recent example is the history of the eugenics movement, an interesting case which indicates the dangers of a faith in "advanced" ideas. Eugenics, the project of improving the human race by controlled breeding on the analogy of scientific livestock farming, is now so strongly associated with Nazism that many people suppose it to have been always a disreputable and "reactionary" idea. It comes as something of a shock to realize how respectable eugenics once was in advanced and progressive circles not only in Germany but in Britain, America, and other countries. Yet there is really nothing surprising in this, for eugenics was part of the striving for scientific control over man's environment and destiny that stemmed from the Enlightenment itself.[55]

Several morals can be drawn from this. One is that there is nothing about science or higher education that necessarily makes people humane—after all, one quarter of the Nazi SS elite reputedly held Ph.D.'s.[56] Another is that enlightenment does not progress like an infinite escalator, carrying mankind smoothly ever upward. What is "progressive" at one time may be "reactionary" in the next, not because it has been left behind by the steady advancement of knowledge, but because it has gone out of fashion. Indeed, one of the best reasons for inclining toward a populist distrust of intellectual elites may be that, since intellectuals always go to extremes and reduce ideas *ad absurdum*, the prejudices of the common man may be more trustworthy.

There may be a tendency, furthermore, for liberal intellectuals—panicked by the threat that reactionary populism poses to their status as democrats—to write off popular views too easily as irrational outbursts, mere symptoms of social alienation not to be taken seriously. As we saw when looking at populist dictatorship, the disreputable forms of populism are not necessarily irrational. Just as the masses may in some situations support a dictator not just from irrational cravings for authority but because he seems the best of the bleak options open to them, so also they may take hard lines on law and order or racist issues not just to work off generalized spite but because, unlike their liberal mentors, they cannot avoid walking dangerous streets at night or sending their children to troubled schools. This point was of course one which Wallace and Powell stressed to great effect, but it is not an unreasonable one.

The moral dilemmas involved in this area of democracy are genuine and serious. Before the populistically inclined intellectual chooses sides, however, and decides whether to throw in his lot with the common people (however reactionary their views) or with the liberal progressives (even though they form an undemocratic elite), it would be as well for him to recognize that the choice is rarely quite as existentially stark as that. For populists and elitists habitually conspire to oversimplify the issue. Although their remarks have different overtones, both tend to talk as though there were *one* people (whether massively barbarous or united in simple common sense) and *one* elite (whether enlightened and heroic or snobbish and fraudulent).

Any actual confrontation is likely to be more complex than that. For one thing, in real life there are generally members of the elite on both sides: populist intellectuals[57] versus elitist/progressive intellectuals; Bryan versus Darrow; the extreme *narodniki* versus the more liberal-minded; the Right Honourable Enoch Powell (ex-professor of Classics) versus the supposed stranglehold of the liberal establishment on British politics.

Second, "the people"—so often visualized in the rhetoric as a solid block representing either humanity or barbarism—are generally even less homogeneous than the elite. Any actual "people," seen at close quarters, dissolve into individuals, families, and groups, each with their own idiosyncracies. It is natural enough for a reactionary populist politician like Wallace or Powell to claim to have "the people" solidly on his side, but that is no reason for others to be frightened into believing him. Significantly, the opinion polls that seem on occasion to indicate massive popular consensus on explosive issues like racism are rarely translated into long-term voting patterns, because of the intervention of a multiplicity of other interests, habitual loyalties, and even second thoughts. While Enoch Powell certainly voiced a genuine grievance among British voters in his original denunciations of immigration, very few of his supporters felt strongly enough about it to go on to vote for the only thoroughly racist party in Britain, the National Front.

We must recognize, therefore, that while the gulf between the people and the elite may sometimes be a real one which poses genuine problems, particularly where populistically minded intellectuals are faced with grassroots reaction, very often "the people" is merely a fiction, convenient for politicians but misleading to others. Let us now consider some of the other ways in which this fiction is employed in politics.

# 7. *Politicians' Populism*

> For us, peoples power is not a propaganda gimmick. It
> is a cardinal concept in political organisation. It proceeds
> logically from our view that, in the last analysis, the
> people are the motive power of history. The people are
> the salt of the earth—the workers, peasants, fishermen,
> craftsmen, youths, traders, small businessmen, self-em-
> ployed persons as well as professionals, academicians, big
> businessmen, and traditional rulers with a social con-
> science.—*Program of the People's Redemption Party,
> Nigeria*[1]

GENERAL MOTORS IS PEOPLE.[2]

We have so far looked at three types of political (as
distinct from agrarian) populism: first, at those comple-
mentary opposites, Caesarist dictatorship and direct democracy, and then at populism in the sense of grass-roots
reaction against elite progressiveness. There is, however,
yet another broad category of populism, which may be
linked with the others in various ways, but need not be.
The label "populist" is sometimes applied to certain
*styles* of politics that draw on the ambiguous resonances
of "the people"—to politicians who claim to speak for
the whole people rather than for any faction; to "catch-all

people's parties" short on ideology, eclectic in their policies, and prepared to accept all comers; to broad, amorphous, reformist coalitions crossing classes and interest groups.

From the point of view of the academic analyst, one of the most serious weaknesses of populism in all its forms is that the notion of "the people," while providing a fine rallying cry, is singularly lacking in precise meaning. Other group concepts may present difficulties (consider "middle class" or "nation") but "the people" surpasses them all in sheer vagueness. It is easy enough to demonstrate how lacking in definition the notion is, and to show that it is rarely possible to find a single "people" among the conglomeration of individuals and groups that inhabit political systems.

What is a weakness from an academic point of view, however, can be a political opportunity. It is precisely this combination of vagueness and emotional resonance that makes "the people" such an effective battle cry, and a particularly useful one for politicians who seek to blur established differences, to unite followers across former party lines, and to spread their appeal as widely as possible.

This is a technique that can be used in a very wide variety of circumstances. On occasion this vague, unifying "politicians' populism" has been raised to the status of an explicit ideology in claims that "the people" are a single entity, that supposed divisions among them are unreal, and that one leader or one party can stand above maliciously divisive politics and represent them all. While this kind of claim can be used by an established government to justify its monopoly of power, similar appeals are often used by outsiders in competitive political systems. Politicians (so the argument goes) squabble among themselves over unreal issues and create divisions where none need exist. What is therefore needed is a party that will set aside both doctrine and selfish interest and put *the people* first. The British Liberal Party, for instance, as part of its forlorn attempt to woo the electorate away from two-party politics, habitually argues that Labour and Conservatives between them perpetuate an unnecessary and damaging class conflict in Britain, whereas the Liberal Party stands for the people, not any particular class.

One of the main functions of appeals to "the people," indeed, is to cancel existing political divisions and to propose a realignment. Instead of allowing themselves to be mobilized by traditional parties, let the people stand together against the self-serving politicians; instead of dividing along class or sectional lines, let the whole people unite against the people's enemies. As Schattschneider has pointed out, politics involves "the mobilisation of bias."[3] The organized lines of conflict in any political system, whether between Democrats and Republicans in the United States, between Labour and Conservatives in Britain, or along more complex lines in multiparty systems, always exclude a host of alternative possible battle arrays. Conflict in America happened to crystalize along Democratic versus Republican lines, and once such a conflict is established, it is difficult to change. But there are innumerable potential conflicts which could form the basis for alternative alignments, and one of the most useful tactics available to those who seek such a realignment is to appeal past traditional loyalties to "the people." The U.S. Populists did so in the 1890s, when for a time they managed to shake the hold of sectional (and even racial) loyalties, and to induce substantial numbers in the West and South to see themselves as "the people" in opposition to "the plutocrats."

The kinds of unifying populism we are discussing may, then, take the form of explicit appeals to "the people" and explicit claims about popular unity. They need not do so, however. When the term "populist" is applied in this sense to parties and politicians, what is meant may not be that they proclaim an ideology of popular unity, but merely that certain assumptions are implicit in their political tactics. Such parties do not limit their appeal to a particular class or group, nor restrict their freedom of movement by tying themselves to a controversial ideology. Instead, they are coalitional in their nature, examples of the "catch-all 'people's' party" which tries to attract *all* voters and therefore plays down ideology and concentrates on issues that will not alienate any group.[4]

Since all-embracing vagueness is virtually the stock-in-trade of "politicians' populism," it is difficult to give a precise account of it. Let us look, however, at some examples which will provide a more concrete impression of the various forms this political style can take.

## ONE PEOPLE

One of the most venerable forms of politicians' populism consists in appealing away from politics altogether. Those who adopt this tactic denounce parties as factions and politicians as self-interested manipulators. As an alternative, they call upon some leader from outside the strife of parties to rally the people to him and put their interest first. A classic statement of this antipolitical populism can be found in a book published in England almost 250 years ago, *The Idea of a Patriot King* by Lord Bolingbroke, self-appointed theorist of the opposition to Sir Robert Walpole's regime. Denouncing Walpole's corruption of Parliament by the systematic use of patronage, Bolingbroke looked for salvation to a Patriot King who would end party strife: "he will put himself at the head of *his people* in order to govern, or more properly, to subdue *all parties*." The grand solution to political ills was to be "a Patriot King at the head of a united people."[5]

Although George III's attempt to live up to this ideal was not much of a recommendation for it, much the same kind of yearning for popular unity, coupled with distrust of factions and of the whole tribe of politicians, is a recurrent motif in states with competitive politics. Although its manifest content is antipolitical, it is itself, of course, a political position, and one that can be used to great political effect in times of crisis, particularly by those who seem in one way or another outside the ordinary political arena. The idea of sending the politicians packing, and of setting up a government of national unity that will put the people first, is one that continues to have great popular appeal, in prospect or in retrospect. Britain in 1940, with party differences submerged and the people mobilized behind Churchill, is one potent memory; another is the return of General de Gaulle to power in 1958, emerging from retirement as the savior of France on the grounds that he alone stood outside and above parties and so could speak for the nation and communicate directly with the people: "I am a man who belongs to nobody, and who belongs to everybody."[6]

The notion that "the people" are one; that divisions among them are not genuine conflicts of interest but are manufactured by a few men of ill will; that parties are merely self-serving factions; and that the people will be best looked after by a single unpolitical leadership that will put their interest first—these ideas are *anti*political, but they are nevertheless essential elements in a political strategy that has often been used to gain power. With only minor alterations, furthermore, this attack on parties in the name of the people can be turned into a justification for rule by *one* party that will represent the interest of the united people. This version of unifying, antipolitical "politicians' populism" has obvious attractions for leaders of one-party states, particularly if they lack the more sophisticated justifications for hegemony provided by full-blown Marxism-Leninism or fascism.

In his study of the Third World first published in 1964, Peter Worsley maintained that "populism" was the characteristic ideology of the ex-colonial one-party states of Africa and Asia, and although the sense in which he used the term was wide and imprecise, it was clear that unifying "politicians' populism" was a prominent element. According to Worsley, "the populist asserts that there are no divisions in the community, or that if they are discernable, they are 'non-antagonistic'. Thus class-divisions can then be dismissed as *external* ('imperialist') intrusions, alien to the society." This social harmony implies political unity: "Since the society is undifferentiated, organic, undivided, it needs only one single political organization to express its common interests, only one party. . . . The party does not represent a particular, narrow, sectional interest: it represents everyone."[7]

In his characterization of "populism" Worsley added to this emphasis on unity a stress on rural *Gemeinschaft*, small property, cooperation, and radical hostility to big business.[8] He cited as examples of populist leaders a great many Third World politicians, including Soekarno, Nkrumah, Nyerere, Senghor, Sekou Touré, and others.

Worsley's notion of populism was open to attack on two general counts. In the first place, it was loose and imprecise, since Worsley assumed not only that populism was common to all Third World countries, but also that it was the same thing as *narodnichestvo*, U.S. Populism, Social Credit in Alberta, Peronism, McCarthyism, and many other phenomena, all of which were assumed to share the same outlook and social base.[9] As we hope to have shown above, there are far too many significant differences between the movements in this list to make it helpful to cram them into a single category without a great many qualifications and distinctions. In the second place Worsley seemed surprisingly willing to take at their face value the claims of leaders like Soekarno that they represented a united people.[10] He defended the populist one-party state on the grounds that while a one-party state in a European country must involve the suppression of genuine differences of interest, this was not so in the Third World: "One-party states in the Old World are responses to long-developed and deep-rooted division in society. The one-party state in the new countries, however, expresses the opposite; the genuine unity of the country."[11]

Even at the time this seemed somewhat credulous, while the subsequent history of many Third World countries has shattered this vision of organic harmony, lending substance to the view that many "one-party" states were really "no-party" states with a very low degree of political mobilization and little defense against military coups.[12] In the course of an interesting and subtle discussion of the application of unanalyzed notions of populism to African politics by Worsley and others, John Saul remarked that populist stress on unity and solidarity might be politically useful without being true: " 'populism' is thus a creed most attractive to leaders. In very many cases the stress upon solidarity will represent neither the real situation of the mass of the people, nor their views of that situation. . . . Rather it will represent an aspiration to make a particular view as to the characteristics that unite people prevail over any continuing awareness of the elements that divide."[13]

In retrospect, therefore, the unifying populism which Worsley accepted as a description of reality in Third World countries seems more appropriately treated as a rhetorical device of great use to politicians. This is not to deny that there may be cases of communities with such uniform interests that the notion of one people, and of one leader or party to represent them, may have genuine substance, if only temporarily. Where a nation is under direct military threat this may well be the case, as we have already noted of Britain in 1940. Such a degree of unity is possible (though rare) in less drastic conditions. In his study of Social Credit and its predecessors in the Canadian province of Alberta, C. B. Macpherson attributed to the province a "quasi-party system" to describe the fact that politics had been dominated successively by two political movements, neither of them a conventional political party and each in its heyday receiving overwhelming support.[14] From 1921 to 1935 the province was ruled by the United Farmers of Alberta, and after 1935 by Social Credit, in each case with a massive majority. Both movements were distrustful of conventional party politics. According to Macpherson, what made possible this unusual situation of a united people choosing to be governed by a single movement was the relatively homogeneous social structure, while what made it necessary was Alberta's "quasi-colonial" status in relation to Eastern Canada.[15] Since the main function of the provincial government was to stand up to Eastern politicians and business interests on behalf of Albertan farmers, the notion of one organization representing one people could make political sense.

Spontaneous and lasting expressions of popular unity are rare, however. What is much more common is for a political leader to make use of populist rhetoric and, by playing upon the resonances of popular unity and distrust of faction, to ride to power on a fragile and temporary mood of popular harmony. Although this kind of appeal plays upon popular distrust of conventional politics, it is itself, of course, very much a political device. In the nature of things it is the political outsider, not himself stamped with the brand of faction, who is best placed to make such an appeal away from the squabbling politicians to the neglected people. If he is an imposing personality like de Gaulle, so much the better; but it is feasible in some circumstances to play the card of populist unification without possessing charisma, as the election of President Jimmy Carter in 1976 showed. It may help to clarify politicians' populism if we look briefly at the campaigning style that helped Carter to victory.

When campaigning for President and being badgered by interviewers who wanted to know whether he was a liberal or a conservative, Jimmy Carter avoided the question by describing himself as a "populist." His campaign was certainly populist in the sense with which we are concerned at present, aiming to appeal past factions and special interests to the people as a whole. However, Carter's reasons for using the term no doubt had much to do with his own background and birthplace, Georgia. Georgia was, after all, the home of the foremost Southern Populist, Tom Watson (after whom one of Carter's uncles was named)[16]; and the traditions of Southern Populism had not entirely died out by the time that Carter entered state politics. He was elected governor of Georgia in 1970 after a traditionally populist campaign in which he attacked his opponent as a member of the local elite, and promised to "return the control of all aspects of government to the people."[17] Unlike many Southern populists, however, Carter's style was not strikingly demagogic, nor did he carry on the tradition of open-handed government spending established by populist governors like Huey Long and George Wallace. Instead, he placed great stress on economy, reduction of waste in government, and a balanced budget.

Carter's unexpectedly successful bid for the Democratic Presidential nomination and his subsequent election campaign drew on themes that happened to be peculiarly appropriate to the political mood of the time.[18] Given popular distrust of Washington after Watergate, his situation as an outsider with no Washington experience was an advantage rather than a drawback. Not being a member of the national political establishment himself, he could attack it uninhibitedly and draw attention to the gap that had developed between the governing elite and the people. Over and over again, as the keynote of his campaign he proclaimed, "We must give our government back to the people." Governmental policies had gone wrong, he said, because they had been made in secret by a remote elite and had been of a kind that the people would never have endorsed: "Each time our nation has made a serious mistake the American people have been excluded from the process. The tragedy of Vietnam and Cambodia, the disgrace of Watergate, and the embarrassment of the CIA revelations could have been avoided if our government had simply reflected the sound judgement and good common sense and high moral character of the American People."[19] In place of secret elite rule, he called for truth, honesty, and openness in government, promising, "I will never lie to you." In an echo of Jacksonianism, he proclaimed that "the government must be well-organized, simple, efficient—so that the average person can understand what goes on there."[20]

Carter projected himself as a prospective President who would have a close relationship with the people. The existing political establishment was, he claimed, out of touch with the life and problems of the ordinary American. In his speech accepting the Democratic nomination, he said:

> Too many have had to suffer at the hands of a political and economic elite who have shaped decisions and never had to account for mistakes or to suffer from injustice. When unemployment prevails, they never stand in line looking for a job. When deprivation results from a confused and bewildering welfare system, they never do without food or clothing or a place to sleep. When the public schools are inferior or torn by strife, their children go to exclusive private schools. And when the bureaucracy is bloated and confused, the powerful always manage to discover and occupy niches of special influence and privilege.[21]

But Carter's attacks on the rich and privileged did not include any radical redistributive proposals. In fact, in its studious moderation and avoidance of commitment, his campaign style provided a good example of the technique of populist unification across as much as possible of the political spectrum. Political commentators found him difficult to label because he appeared to be liberal on such matters as the need for national health insurance, but conservative on the virtues of balancing the budget, claiming that the two could be reconciled by efficient management of government spending. He rejected all ideological labels except that of "populist," explaining that this last epithet indicated "that I derived my political support, my advice and my concern directly from people themselves, not from powerful intermediaries or representatives of special-interest groups."[22] This claim to represent the people rather than any particular section or group he voiced constantly.

Seeking to be viewed as the people's representative, Carter stressed his own ordinariness: "I am just an average human being."[23] He dwelt constantly upon his home and family, the small town he lived in, his experience as a small businessman, his family farm: "We haven't had a farmer in the White House since Thomas Jefferson."[24] Even his religion—that of a "born-again" Southern Baptist, which seemed so exotically archaic to the reporters—helped to confirm his image as an ordinary, decent American who was not too clever to believe in God.

It is interesting that Carter's version of a populist style was not at all the charismatic one associated with populist politicians like Huey Long or Peron. Rather, he gave the impression of being a representative American. This was, inevitably, an illusion: no one could have successfully played such a role without unusual political ambition. Once in power, there was a tendency for Carter's Presidency to fall between stools. On the one hand, it was not possible for him to "return the government to the people" and solve political problems in line with the simple decency of the American people; political problems remained as intractable as they had always been. On the other hand, however, the very inexperience of national politics that had been an asset during his campaign became a disadvantage when he had to get on with Congress and manage foreign affairs. His sheer ordinariness, formerly so refreshing, became boring and contributed to his bad press; while the fact that he had won his party's nomination as an outsider made him insecure, forced to worry about the next election but knowing that he would not be able to play the anti-Washington card a second time.

In what sense was Carter's original campaign style populist? It combined various elements. His rhetoric drew heavily upon the American tradition of populist antielitism, the Jacksonian insistence on giving the government back to the people. There were certain continuities with the Populism of the U.S. People's Party. Carter was, after all, a farmer, and there were traces in his rhetoric of the familiar radicalism of producers versus plutocrats. It is striking, however, that this rhetorical radicalism never extended to anything definite in the way of proposals for reform, and that he displayed remarkable agility in not committing himself on issues or policies: for the most fundamental sense in which his campaign was populist was his attempt to appeal to all the people at once and to avoid alienating anyone. Without going to the lengths of Worsley's Third World leaders and explicitly claiming that all the people have one interest, Carter implied this, thereby implying that there need be no real conflicts of interest or principle on which it was necessary to take sides.

## POPULIST PARTIES

Although Carter was unusual in describing himself as a "populist," and although his position as an outsider made it comparatively easy for him to project himself as an honest man who would rise above factions and represent the people, he was in no way unusual along American politicians (and particularly Presidential candidates) in trying to appeal to everybody at once. As has often been pointed out, the amorphousness of American political parties, their comparative lack of ideological commitments, has much to do with their "catch-all" nature. Parties of this kind are sometimes termed "populist" in contradistinction to those with definite commitments and limited constituencies. Whereas a Communist Party can have little appeal for a businessman, nor a Catholic party expect to attract a Protestant or atheist, a party that is populist in the present sense is in principle prepared to appeal to anyone, and to keep its commitments to a minimum for fear of alienating any potential group of voters. Many parties (a conspicuous example being the British Labour Party) are the scene of constant infighting between an ideological faction who wish to stiffen their commitment even if this will limit their appeal, and a populist group who wish to extend their appeal at the price of watering down their doctrine.

One thing we should note at this point, since it is a potential source of great confusion, is that many of the populist movements and parties considered in this book were *not* populist in this catch-all sense. The *narodniki*, the peasant parties of Eastern Europe, and the U.S. People's Party all claimed to speak for the people, but each in fact meant by that something more restricted and definite than "everyone," and each had definite commitments which could not be easily discarded to gain support. As we have seen, the U.S. People's Party tore itself apart in 1896 over the question whether or not to fuse with the Democrats, even though the latter had actually adopted much of the Populist platform. There was a degree of radicalism in American Populism inconsistent with the vote-gathering vagueness of politicians' populism. We must therefore beware of supposing that any party or movement that is populist in some other sense must be populist in this sense, too. As we have stressed throughout, there is so little essential unity to the concept that we must not be surprised to find some of its meanings coming into direct contradiction to others. Clearly, however, it is necessary to be sure which sense we mean when we use the term, and the habit of calling political parties "populist" because they are amorphous and coalitional is capable of producing a good deal of confusion.

We saw in Chapter 4 that one of the areas in which this sense of the term is best established is in Latin America. To quote Alistair Hennessy: "Populism in Latin America can be defined as an organizational weapon to synchronize divergent group interests and is applied to any movement not based in a specific social class."[25] In fact, as we saw when discussing Peronism, "populism" is also used in this context to mean cases of popular mobilization by a charismatic dictator. It has been possible for this double meaning to become established because Latin American radical parties have frequently been both coalitional and led by charismatic leaders. Since these two features need not always be united, however, it is as well to keep them separate for analytical purposes, if only to avoid sterile disputes about whether, for instance, Peronism ceased to be populist when Peron lost the middle-class support he had originally enjoyed and was left with a predominantly working-class following.

Parties that are populist in the coalitional sense, then, may or may not have charismatic leaders. Furthermore, they may vary a good deal in the degree to which they are radical and challenge the status quo. A priori, it would seem obvious that the more radical they are, the less they will be able to function as catch-all parties, while the more all-embracing their constituency, the less effectively radical they are likely to be. The difficulties of applying this a priori generalization to the real world can be illustrated, however, by the case of the Mexican governing party, the P.R.I.

The P.R.I. (*Partido Revolucionario Institucional*), which has held virtually undisputed power in Mexico for many years, is in some ways the classic example of the catch-all party, an all-embracing, nonideological organization that integrates many different and potentially conflicting groups and sections of the people.[26] Since it has inherited the glamor of a successful peasant revolution, however, this party is not only all things to all men, but continues to call itself "revolutionary"—a designation that may not carry much weight with radical students, but that does still seem to evoke some loyalty among other potentially discontented sections of the population.

It is unusual, however, for a party to combine this degree of cross-class appeal with a radical image. In most Latin American countries a party that is radical in the sense of seeking to redistribute wealth and power may gain support from more than one class, but could hardly be catch-all to the extent of the P.R.I., because there would be too many vested interests opposed to it. Most Latin American populist parties, therefore, have not exactly been populist in the sense of appealing to the *whole* people; rather, they have been coalitions of different groups among the *common* people—those not members of the elite.

We must stress at this point that (unfortunately for the cause of clarity) "the people" has two sets of connotations, one more inclusive than the other. It can mean either *the whole people*, everyone, or the *common people*, the nonelite. Naturally, populist politicians habitually blur the distinction in order to isolate their opponents,[27] with the result that the term "populist" is applied to parties sometimes because they appeal to *everyone*, sometimes because they mobilize the masses against the elite, and often because they try to do both at once, to attract the masses without actually alienating influential sections of the population. Many "populist" Latin American parties seem to fall into this ambiguous intermediate category. Commentators stress that while such parties have mobilized workers and peasants as well as the middle classes, they have tended not to be grass-roots affairs, but have usually been dominated (if not manipulated) from above by leaders who generally came from the elite themselves. Nevertheless, some such movements have been genuinely radical.[28]

Just which Latin American parties are counted as populist varies from one scholar to another. Let us look very briefly, however, at one case of a multiclass coalition that is usually given the title, and that had the distinction of bringing about a genuine revolution: the *Movimiento Nacionalista Revolucionario* in Bolivia. When it seized power in 1952, the M.N.R. was a radical party of middle-class origin. It commanded a great deal of middle-class support but was also strong among the militant miners of Bolivia's tin industry, and it became increasingly interested in mobilizing the Indian peasants who were subject to feudal exploitation on the haciendas. This broad coalition of interests united in a movement for reform that involved little in the way of ideology, but that centered on hostility to the great mining companies and landowners, the army, and the foreigners who were held to benefit most from the exploitation of Bolivia's resources. The new government nationalized the mines, enacted labor legislation, and in a sweeping land reform hastened by spontaneous peasant uprisings, transformed the system of land tenure, giving the Indians land and liberty as well as votes.

Although the revolutionary regime had achieved a remarkable unification of many sections of the people against the former elite, and changed the Bolivian social system for good, in the nature of things it was unlikely that this heterogeneous coalition could be held together indefinitely. The interests of the militant workers and the middle classes became more obviously opposed to one another, while the peasants rapidly ceased to be revolutionary once they had achieved their traditional aims. By 1964, when a military coup ousted the M.N.R., the way was open for a different kind of political alignment: a conservative coalition of middle class, peasants, and army against labor and the Left shattered the populist coalition that had made the revolution.[29]

When the M.N.R. is called "populist," the emphasis is not just upon its coalitional nature but particularly upon its being a coalition of classes—middle class, workers, and peasants—who might be expected, according to both sociological theory and European experience, to have opposed interests. The term not only has overtones of unification across the social spectrum, but also implies that such unification is unnatural and unstable.

For all the coalitional fragility and ideological vagueness of such populist parties, it has sometimes been suggested that they form a functional equivalent in the Third World to the liberal and socialist parties that brought about reform in Europe. The conditions under which such parties arise, and the various forms they can take, have been most thoroughly examined by Torcuato di Tella in an article on "Populism and Reform in Latin America."

According to di Tella, several characteristic features of underdeveloped societies give rise to populist parties. One is the existence of widespread discontent, owing to the "demonstration effect," the constant comparisons made between poverty and frustration at home and prosperity in more advanced countries. This generalized discontent produces not only a "disposable mass" of potential supporters for radical parties, but also a supply of "incongruent groups" to lead them: dissident intellectuals, businessmen snubbed by the aristocracy, professionals whose aspirations outrun their status. According to di Tella, "the incongruent groups (generally of above-average status) and the mobilized, disposable masses complement each other. Their social situations are different, but what they have in common is a passionate hatred of the *status quo*."[30]

Here, then, is a basis for radicalism which might by analogy with European history be expected to take the form of a liberal or labor movement. Such models, however, are tarred with the brush of imperialism, and therefore unacceptable. Instead, the leaders of populist parties concoct their own ideologies and programs out of socialism and other elements. The crucial feature of such parties is that while their rank and file belong to the lower classes, they are led by dissident members of the middle or upper middle class, driven into opposition by economic stagnation and political repression. Just how radical the movement becomes depends, according to di Tella, on two factors: does the populist leadership include only lower-middle-class elements, or are there also members of the upper levels of society, the army, the clergy? And second, have these reformers lost touch with their own class, or are they still socially accepted? The most conservative type of populist party will be one led by men of rather high social class who are still accepted by that class; the most radical will be headed by lower-middle-class leaders who are rejected by their class.

Armed with these variables, di Tella proposes a typology of Third World populist parties with four main varieties. The first and least revolutionary variety is the "multi-class integrative party," headed by leaders of high social status who have the support of their own class. Examples given by di Tella include the Mexican P.R.I. (in its more recent and less radical stages) and the Indian Congress Party. Such parties have strong organization and trade-union support; having a broad base which includes the middle class, they are moderate in their radicalism, avoiding demagoguery and ideology, and are capable of becoming very strong and stable political forces.

Di Tella's second type is the "Aprista" party, based on

the support of the working class and lower middle class, but without aid from the upper levels of society. Such parties, like the Peruvian *Alianza Popular Revolucionaria Americana*, which is the paradigm case, may have a strong and lasting power base, but are only moderately radical, for fear of antagonizing the military and losing their own middle-class support.

The third variety is the reforming party led by members of the upper class who have turned against their own social group—notably dissident military men. Di Tella calls these "Nasserite" parties, and notes that they try to mobilize the masses by means of charismatic leadership, that they stress authoritarianism and modernization, and tend to lose their radicalism as a new upper class emerges from within their own ranks.

The final category is "Social-Revolutionary Parties" à la Castro: parties based on working-class and peasant support and led by an elite of professional revolutionaries, drawn from the lower middle class but thoroughly alienated from it.

Di Tella stresses that populist parties are characteristic of underdeveloped countries rather than industrial societies, where the working and middle classes are self-conscious and organized. Peronism in Argentina seems to him an anomaly, a populist coalition which was possible in such a comparatively developed country only because certain upper- and middle-class groups had very strong grievances, and which changed quite rapidly into an essentially working-class party.

The sense in which di Tella calls parties "populist"— although it takes in such a wide range of examples—is

more limited than our general category of politicians'
populism because it is specifically tied to conditions of
underdevelopment in the modern world. As a matter of
fact, although he invokes underdevelopment to explain
discontent at popular and elite level, the link is not
altogether convincing. He defines populism as "a political
movement which enjoys the support of the mass of the
urban working class and/or peasantry but which does not
result from the autonomous organizational power of either
of these two sectors. It is also supported by non-working-
class sectors upholding an anti-*status quo* ideology."[31]
There is room for a good deal of debate about what
counts as "autonomous organizational power," but on the
face of it this definition could apply to a good many
political parties in developed countries—certainly the
British Liberal Party until about 1920, and perhaps the
U.S. Democratic Party, too. Similarly, di Tella stresses
the coalitional character, ideological vagueness, diffuse
antielitism, and manipulative leadership of populist parties—characteristics which, as we have already pointed
out, are not restricted to the Third World.

## THE TACTICAL USE OF POPULISM

If one of the most important characteristics of the notion
of "the people" is its sheer vagueness, one of the salient
features of politicians' populism is clearly a willingness
to make use of this vagueness in order to win support
and build coalitions. As we suggested earlier, this technique is particularly useful to those who wish to challenge
existing political boundaries and to redraw the lines of
battle in a new place. Third parties in two-party systems

are obvious examples, and those best placed to use this
tactic are perhaps sectional nationalists within existing
states, such as the Scottish National Party in Britain.
H. J. Hanham, writing in 1969, quoted an S.N.P. statement
that "the National Party stands for the nation, all sections, all people in it," and remarked that the party had
become "a populist party appealing to all those who feel
that the present system fails to offer them the sort of
opportunities they would like to have."[32] Hanham noted
that in its earlier days S.N.P. policies had shown similarities to North American agrarian populism, and had been
influenced, like the Alberta farmers' movement, by Social
Credit. Generally speaking, however, the obvious tactic
for the S.N.P. was to avoid definite ideologies and policy
commitments (including the more specific and doctrinal
forms of *populism*, too) and to concentrate its efforts on
politicians' populism, arguing that the Labour and Conservative Parties had achieved nothing except to foster
artificial divisions which drew attention away from the
real interests of the entire Scottish people.

In the 1970s the exploitation by multinational companies and the British government of oil off the Scottish
coast gave the S.N.P. a golden opportunity, and "It's
Scotland's Oil" provided a potent slogan. For a while,
with S.N.P. successes in the two British general elections
held in 1974 and the importance of the Nationalists in
the subsequent hung Parliament, it seemed that their
tactics had succeeded in redrawing the political boundaries in Scotland. Their hopes were dashed by the next
election, but victory had perhaps been close enough to
make some Nationalists aware of the problems they would

be faced with if they were to gain power as the party of the whole Scottish people, and be forced to choose among the divergent interests within that broad constituency.[33]

In a two-party system where the established divisions are along class lines, an obvious tactic for a third party is to appeal to the vision of a united people against the divisiveness of class strife. Similar tactical considerations may apply where the primary divisions are ideological or religious. But what are challengers to do in a two-party system where the main parties already are populist catch-all coalitions, as in the United States? The answer seems to be that even when what they are proposing is, in effect, a new political division along class lines, the challengers still feel obliged to talk in populist terms, exploiting the ambiguity of "the people" (which, as we have seen, means both "everyone" and "the underdogs").

The U.S. Populists of the 1890s used their appeal to the people to perform two functions. One of these was a unifying one: an appeal past the sectional division between North and South, and even the racial split between black and white, to the whole people of the United States. But the other function which the term performed simultaneously was to draw a new line of battle in place of the old, and along economic lines, pitting "the producing classes" against the "plutocrats." A recent example of the same double maneuver used in the interests of a class-based view of politics is provided by the *Populist Manifesto* published in 1972 by Jack Newfield and Jeff Greenfield.

The *Manifesto*'s thesis—put forward consciously in the tradition of the Populists of the 1890s—is that a small number of people in America, concentrated in the

large corporations, have too much wealth and power, and
that it is in the interest of all nonowners of large-scale
capital to unite against them. The authors stress that
"the real division in this country is not between generations or between races, but between the rich who have
power and those blacks and whites who have neither
power nor property."[34] Their claim is that everyone in
America below the corporate elite—black or white,
middle class, working class, or on welfare—shares a
common interest in the redistribution of wealth and
power. They advocated breaking up the great corporations;
treating the violators of antitrust laws as common crimi-
nals; control of banks, and public ownership of utilities;
revision of the tax laws so as to catch the rich; gun
control; a free health service for all; and a cautious,
unadventurous foreign policy, bearing in mind that, as
the authors put it, "the sons of Harvard and Yale sent
the sons of Watts and South Boston to die in Vietnam."[35]

This is a call for the realignment of parties along class
lines, but it is framed in populist terms, taking advantage
of the ambiguity of "the people." It is interesting to
contrast this kind of militant populism with Carter's
campaigning style. Both have in common a general antielitism, although this is directed against more specific
objects in the case of the *Manifesto*; but otherwise there
is a great deal of difference between the indefinite, all-
embracing "people" to whom Carter tried to appeal, and
the noncapitalist classes of the *Manifesto*. The great charm
of "the people" for a politician—and the fundamental
source of exasperation for a political scientist—is that the
term manages to be both empty of precise meaning and

full of rhetorical resonance. When used to mean "every-one," it is conveniently vague and yet *sounds* definite, conveying a sense of solidity and harmony. When used to mean a particular class or section of the population, it gains in definition but somehow manages to avoid losing its overtones of comprehensiveness and legitimacy.

What we have been examining in this chapter, there-fore, is a range of uses to which politicians put populist rhetoric and tactics. These types of politicians' populism shade into one another but are not identical, as we can see if we summarize them briefly:

1. Antipolitical populism, stressing the unity of the people against party squabbles and appealing to a Patriot King or some other political outsider.
2. A version of this which justifies the existence of only *one* party to mobilize and represent the people.
3. The catch-all pragmatism of nonideological parties which try to appeal to everyone at once, making use in doing so of the vagueness of "the people."
4. Cross-class radical coalitions of the "common people" against the elite.
5. Tactical use of populist rhetoric to bring about a political realignment, exploiting the ambiguity of "the people." This tactic can be used by many political parties, not just those that are catch-all in nature.

Politicians' populism is a matter of political style and tactics, not of particular policy commitments. It can on occasion be used to *avoid* being committed to any definite policies or doctrines at all, with the result that parties and politicians are sometimes called "populist" by com-mentators who mean to attribute to them nothing but sheer evasiveness. It is clear, however, that some of the kinds of politicians' populism that we have looked at can be combined with more definite policies, which may themselves belong to different points on the political spectrum. For although it may be of the essence of catch-all populist parties to find their base in the center of the political spectrum, populist coalitions are also to be found on the Left, while the notion of appealing past the politicians to the people has been frequently used by the Right. Similarly, the kinds of tactical populism examined here can be variously combined with some of the other populisms viewed in previous chapters. Let us briefly illustrate some of the possible combinations.

The Mexican P.R.I. is populist in being a catch-all party integrating many different groups into one governing organization; but it is also populist in harking back to a peasant populist revolution which gave it its commitment to agrarian reform, and in being influenced to some extent by *narodnik*-style romanticism about the Indian communal past.[36] To turn to a completely different case, de Gaulle has been called "populist" because of his appeal past the ineffectual politicians to the people as a whole, and also because he used referendums, those favorite devices of populist democracy, and because his rule leaned in the direction of populist dictatorship. Carter also, as we have seen, can be called "populist," partly on account of his outsider's catch-all appeal to the people against the Washington establishment in 1976, but also on account of the overtones of populist democracy and farmers' populism in his rhetoric.

In each of these three instances, politicians' populism

is combined with other populist elements to justify the attribution of the term. Since it is obvious, however, that these are different selections from the available populist ingredients, we should now consider the ways in which the different types of populisms are related to one another.

# Conclusion

We set out in this book to sample the range of political phenomena that are given the title of populism and to try to establish reasonably clear types in terms of which they can be analyzed. We have in fact suggested a typology with seven compartments, including three types of agrarian populism—farmers,' peasants,' and intellectuals'—and four of political populism: populist dictatorship, populist democracy, reactionary populism, and politicians' populism.

Now that we have taken populism apart in this way, can we put it together again into a coherent whole? If we look back over our discussion, two conclusions emerge. In the first place, there are a great many interconnections among our seven theoretical categories. Many actual populist phenomena—perhaps most—belong in more than one category, and we have often been able to invoke the same cases to illustrate different theoretical points.

Our second reflection must be, however, that there are severe limits to this overlapping. No movement has ever been populist in *all* the senses identified, and indeed— given the contradictions between some of our categories— none ever could satisfy all the conditions at once. What we seem to be left with, therefore, is the conclusion that populist traits do tend to cluster into certain highly characteristic syndromes, but that none of these exhausts the entire range.

The idea of looking at populism as "A Syndrome, Not a Doctrine" was put forward by Peter Wiles in an extremely suggestive paper of that title included in Ionescu and Gellner's symposium on *Populism*. According to Wiles, "populism is any creed or movement based on the following major premiss: *virtue resides in the simple people, who are the overwhelming majority, and in their collective traditions.* I hold that this premiss causes a political syndrome of surprising constancy. . . . Naturally no actual case is pure, i.e. contains every item on the list."[1]

Wiles's syndrome was made up of twenty-four points which can be summarized as follows: Populists stress a moral outlook rather than a definite program; they need leaders in mystical contact with the people, and expect these leaders to share the people's way of life. Populism is a movement rather than a party, anti-intellectual and with little precise ideology. It is antiestablishment, and arises among people who feel themselves outside the center of power; however, it does not encourage class war or glorify violence, and it is easily corrupted by success. It is sympathetic to small business, hostile to financiers, and favors monetary inflation and cooperative organization. It can favor state aid and equality, but only up to a point. Often rural, it can also be urban, though it is religious, hostile to science and technology, and nostalgic for the past. It is isolationist and antimilitarist, and while it inclines to mild racism, its general moral record is rather good. It varies "from the pre-industrial, anti-industrial 'peasant' strain to the affluent industry-tolerating 'farmer' strain."[2]

Wiles's approach represented a theoretical breakthrough by isolating populist elements that, forming a syndrome rather than a unity, could be combined in a variety of ways. As he himself admitted, however, his method was still not sufficiently flexible to accommodate all the recognized varieties of populism.[3] The exception he noted was *narodnichestvo*, but there are several others that cannot be fitted easily into his scheme, notably politicians' populism, the more manipulative forms of populist dictatorship, and much of populist democracy.

It is necessary, therefore, to extend Wiles's line of thought still further. The populist phenomena we have been exploring in the course of this study are too diverse to be collected into one category, even if that category is as loose and permissive as a syndrome. We can note, however, that they tend to cluster into a fairly small number of *different* populist syndromes, none of which exhausts the whole range of populism.

Perhaps the most common and wide-ranging populist syndrome is the one in which Wiles was interested: what one might call "the populism of the little man." This is the outlook of the small proprietor (peasant, farmer, small businessman, etc.) who believes in private property and looks with favor upon cooperation in some form, but fears big business, big unions, and big government. Not enthusiastic about "progress" and urbanization (especially the moral and artistic permissiveness they foster), and inclined to look back to the good old days, this kind of populist distrusts intellectuals and politicians, and is drawn either to direct popular democracy or to a strong leader who seems to understand the small proprietor's problems.

These characteristics add up to a fairly coherent and intelligible political outlook that is different from socialism, liberalism, and conservatism, and that can be found to a greater or lesser extent in many of the movements that are given the title of "populist." Examples would include the Eastern European peasant parties; Social Credit in Alberta; U.S. Populism (in some respects); the S.N.P. (up to a point); and other cases such as the nineteenth-century Norwegian Left.[4]

This is not the only populist syndrome we can construct, however. Consider, for instance, the familiar case of authoritarian populism: a charismatic leader, using the tactics of politicians' populism to go past the politicians and intellectual elite and appeal to the reactionary sentiments of the populace, often buttressing his claim to speak for the people by the use of referendums. When populism is attributed to right-wing figures—Hitler, de Gaulle, Codreanu, Father Coughlin—this is what the word conjures up.

Against this, of course, we must set revolutionary populism: romanticization of the people by intellectuals who turn against elitism and technological progress, who idealize the poor, particularly peasants and their traditions, assume that "the people" are united, reject ordinary politics in favor of spontaneous popular revolution, but are inclined to accept the claims of charismatic leaders that they represent the masses. This syndrome is very familiar from the romantic Maoism and Castroism that swept Western universities in the 1960s; most of it (though not, to be fair, the taste for charismatic leadership) was there in *narodnichestvo,* and it can be found in some of the less elitist of the intellectuals who sympathized with fascism in its early stages.[5]

The important point to note is that while our seven elements—farmers' populism, peasants' populism, intellectuals' populism, populist dictatorship, populist democracy, reactionary populism, and politicians' populism—can be combined in various ways, *they can also be detached from one another.* For instance, U.S. Populism combined farmers' radicalism and populist democracy, and the combination of the two is perfectly intelligible. However, there is no necessary connection between them: the Progressives took up populist democracy but not farmers' radicalism, while Huey Long carried on farmers' radicalism but dropped populist democracy in favor of charismatic leadership.

To give another example, it is notorious that reactionary populism at the grass roots can be united with support for charismatic dictatorship to give the kind of right-wing populism that makes liberal intellectuals shudder and reach for their theories of mass society: examples are legion. However, it is quite possible for these two objectionable elements to be separated: reactionary populism need not run to dictators, and populist dictators are not necessarily reactionary. The people of Dayton, Tennessee; the Swiss voters who delayed female suffrage for so long; the prohibitionist peasants of Norway—all these were reactionary and out of step with "enlightened" thinking without being in any way inclined to support dictatorship; on the other hand, populist dictators like Peron can be modernizing and progressive, and need not appeal to reactionary sentiment.

In particular, to try to label populism as either Right or Left is a lost cause. It can be either or neither, depending upon which variety or combination of varieties happens to be under discussion. Neither can one safely dismiss the matter by claiming that all populism is ideologically vague. Some varieties, certainly, are very evasive indeed: consider Peronism, or many instances of politicians' populism from President Carter to the P.R.I. However, as we have seen, many versions of populism carry definite ideological commitments, such as *narodnichestvo*, U.S. Populism, or populist democracy.

We can gather aspects of populism into syndromes, and we can note that our various types can all be detached from one another and recombined; but can we identify any elements common to the whole spectrum of populisms? Clearly, in the light of the evidence presented, it is no use trying to identify a definite ideology or a specific socioeconomic situation as characteristic of populism in all its forms. Nevertheless, two elements do seem to be universally present. All forms of populism without exception involve some kind of exaltation of and appeal to "the people," and all are in one sense or another antielitist.

Unfortunately these common characteristics do not go far toward proving the fundamental unity of populism, for they are themselves vague and ambiguous. To take first "exaltation of the people": "the people," as we know, is one of the slipperiest concepts in the political vocabulary, capable of meaning many different things in different circumstances. It can refer (as it did in *narodnichestvo* or in Peasant Party rhetoric) to the peasants; to the "producers" of U.S. Populist platforms; to Peron's *descamisados;* to the electorate (sometimes on a basis of universal suffrage, sometimes not, as in cases of *Herrenvolk* Democracy); to the nation; to everyone except one's political opponents[6]; or quite frequently (and often deliberately) to no determinate group at all.

Similarly, exaltation of this ambiguous "people" can take a variety of forms. Since it embraces everything from the cynical manipulations of Peronist rhetoric to the humble self-abasement of the *narodniki,* it does not give much definition to the concept of populism.

Antielitism, the other general populist characteristic, is perhaps marginally more precise because there are at least certain positions that it rules out. Nietzscheanism, for instance, or aristocratic disdain in its more traditional forms, could not by any stretch of the imagination be described as populist, and neither could the elitist demo-cratic theory of the post-World War II years. So charac-teristic of populism is antielitism, indeed, that "popu-lism" is sometimes used by political scientists and others to mean simply opposition to an elite, without any further connotations.[7]

One significant aspect of antielitism is distrust of pro-fessional politicians and their maneuvers, a distrust that is very widespread in populist movements although it takes a variety of forms. We can find this hostility to the politicians in calls for populist democracy; in the response which politicians' populism often evokes to its appeals away from faction; in preference for a charismatic dictator over ordinary politics; in peasant inclinations to anarchism; and perhaps even in the Russian populists' preference for terrorism rather than the struggle for a constitution.

Populism in at least some of its forms can therefore be connected with distrust of competitive politics and unwillingness to bother with elaborate constitutional structures. In so far as this is so, Edward Shils's strictures on the dangers posed for liberal political systems by "populism" (which we discussed in Chapter 5) must be justified. This tendency is by no means universal in populism, however. One need only think of the devotion to intricate constitutional mechanisms and regular political procedures shown by the American Progressives and the Swiss.

Similarly, antielitism and distrust of politicians can go along with conspiracy theories, often cited as one of the illusions to which populists are prone. The image of a few evil men conspiring in secret against the people can certainly be found in the thinking of the U.S. People's Party, Huey Long, McCarthy, and others. However, one should bear in mind that not all forms or cases of populism involve conspiracy theories, and that such theories are not always false. The railroad kings and Wall Street bankers hated by the U.S. Populists, the New Orleans Ring that Huey Long attacked, and the political bosses whom the Progressives sought to unseat—all these were indeed small groups of men wielding secret and irresponsible power.

One aspect of antielitism which is common to all types, and which is perhaps more important than political scientists may be professionally inclined to suppose, is populist imagery—the rhetoric of the underdog, the pathos of the "little man," his struggles, and his virtues. Populist movements are often accompanied by fictional representations of the common man which stress the quiet heroism, the unexpected resourcefulness, the solid common sense and gallant cheerfulness of ordinary people. Such images have the great advantage that—since fictional figures are simultaneously concrete individuals and symbolic representations of Everyman—they can evade the real-life difficulties of establishing *who* "the common man" is, and just what are the interests of "the people." Populist movements draw strength from the emotions tapped by stories about such everyday heroes, from David vanquishing Goliath, or the poor peasant who marries the princess in the fairy tales, to Schweik creating havoc in the imperial army or Chaplin's little man walking jauntily on beneath the hammer blows of fate.

Antielitist rhetoric, then, is typical of populism in all its forms, and the power of such symbols should not be underestimated. Once we look at the ways in which this general symbolism is utilized in different versions of populism, however, we must recognize that the similarities are rather superficial. Compare, for instance, the *narodnik* intellectuals' hostility to state and bureaucracy (echoed by the participationists of the 1960s) with Wallace's hostility to the intellectual elite, or Progressive distrust of politicians with Peron's accomplished mobilization of "the people" against the oligarchy. To say, that is, that all populists are for the people and against the elite is quite true, but not much more helpful than saying that all religious leaders are for holiness and against sin.

We must stress yet again, therefore, that while there are a great many overlaps and similarities between our different categories of populism, they are not reducible to a single core. And one important reason why the temptation to force all populist phenomena into one category should be resisted, is that the various populisms we have distinguished are not just different varieties of the same kind of thing: they are in many cases different *sorts* of things, and not directly comparable at all.[8] This is a point which needs elaboration, and it will be easiest for us to approach it by way of a question related to it.

It is sometimes asked whether populism is characteristically an ideology or a movement.[9] In the light of our evidence, the answer is that it depends upon which brand of populism one is talking about. Where our last category, politicians' populism, is concerned, ideology is clearly not an important characteristic, since most versions of this kind of unifying campaign take care to avoid anything as divisive as specific ideological commitments. Populist dictatorship in the style of Peron tends to be short on ideology for similar reasons. On the other hand, U.S. Populism, East European peasant populism, *narodnichestvo*, Social Credit in Alberta, and the C.C.F. in Saskatchewan were all of them undoubtedly movements, but also possessed ideologies to a greater or lesser degree. It should be pointed out, of course, that these ideologies were different and indeed mutually exclusive ones, and

did not therefore amount to a single all-embracing ideology of populism. The nearest that one can get to a
specifically populist ideology is probably populist democracy, which is primarily a matter of theory, although
there have at various times been movements to implement
it.

We cannot give a straight answer, then, to the question
whether populism is a movement or an ideology, and the
attempt to do so brings out an important and confusing
characteristic of our material. This is that the various
"populisms" that appear in the literature, and which we
have tried to disentangle from one another, are not readily
comparable. Many of them are quite different kinds of
things, reflecting not just empirical differences but also
the different approaches and interests of those who have
provided their names. In other words, the ways in which
the term "populism" is used in these different contexts
demand different kinds of analysis.

Let us illustrate this point by looking back over our
material. In both the cases from which we started, U.S.
Populism and Russian populism, "populism" is used as
an historical category to mark off a recognized cluster of
interrelated historical persons and events. Although the
substance of the two movements was different, there is a
parallel between the senses in which both are given their
names. When agrarian movements in general are discussed, however, "populism" is usually used in a different
way, as an explanatory category claiming to link certain
kinds of agrarian movements and outlooks to certain
socioeconomic conditions. "Populism" becomes a sociological category rather than an historical one. In gener-

alizing from American, Russian, and East European experience to talk about farmers' populism, peasant populism, or intellectual populism, we were, similarly, moving from historical categories to sociological ones.

When we turn to populist dictatorship or reactionary populism, we appear to be dealing once again with general sociological categories. But an extra element enters at this point, for these terms are far from being value-free. "Populism" in either of these senses is commonly used as the diagnosis of a malady: the word has strong overtones of condemnation, and describes not just a social phenomenon but a political and moral *problem*. Where populist democracy is concerned, the focus changes once again. What we have here is above all a theory of popular sovereignty and a set of specific proposals for reform, open to reasoned objection and capable of reasoned defense. Politicians' populism, by contrast, refers to a particular political style, and is an analytical category within the field of comparative politics. All these differences are complicated enough, but when our categories are combined into populist syndromes, the import of the term must vary once again.

In the course of this book we have tried to pay attention to these different functions of the term as well as to the different phenomena to which it can refer. This has meant attempting to give appropriate treatment to populism in its different guises—recognizing, for instance, that one cannot satisfactorily discuss a political theory in the same way as an historical movement, nor treat a moral problem along the same lines as a sociological explanation. Given that the same word is used in all these

different senses, however, it is inevitable that connotations rub off from one to another, helping to create the
prevailing confusion.

Finally, let us try to confront the question that the
reader may have been asking all along. If there are so
many different senses of the term, is "populism" a mean-
ingful concept? Or is it too confusing to mean anything
at all?

One thing is certain: if the notion of "populism" did
not exist, no social scientist would deliberately invent
it; the term is far too ambiguous for that. It would be far
preferable to invent different words to describe the different phenomena included within it. However, the term
*does* exist: there it is, firmly ensconced in a number of
languages, constantly used by scholars and journalists
alike. We cannot get rid of it, and this book has been
written in the belief that it need not be hopelessly
confusing, and can indeed help us to identify political
phenomena that are in need of study, provided that we
take the trouble to disentangle the various strands en-
twined in its use.

It is unlikely that the distinctions we have made are
sufficient to remove all the ambiguities surrounding the
term, and it is certain that others will wish to improve
upon the typology offered here. Our hope must be,
however, that this analysis will at least aid the process of
clarification required to turn one of the most confusing
words in the vocabulary of political science into a precise
and readily applicable concept.

# Notes

### Introduction

1. Andrzej Walicki, quoted in the report of a conference "To Define Populism," held at the London School of Economics in May 1967: *Government and Opposition*, 3, Part 2 (Spring 1968), 158.
2. Peter Worsley, *The Third World*, 2nd ed. (London: Weidenfeld and Nicholson, 1967), p. 167.
3. Peter Calvert, L.S.E. conference, p. 163.
4. Harry Lazer, "British Populism: The Labour Party and the Common Market Parliamentary Debate," *Political Science Quarterly*, 91, No. 2 (1976), 259.
5. Peter Wiles, "A Syndrome, Not a Doctrine: Some Elementary Theses on Populism," in Ghita Ionescu and Ernest Gellner, eds., *Populism: Its Meanings and National Characteristics* (London: Weidenfeld and Nicholson, 1969), p. 166.
6. Edward A. Shils, *The Torment of Secrecy* (London: William Heinemann, 1956), p. 98.
7. Torcuato S. di Tella: "Populism and Reform in Latin America," in C. Veliz, ed., *Obstacles to Change in Latin America* (London: Oxford University Press, 1965), p. 47.
8. See note 5.
9. On the changing uses of the term, see J. B. Allcock, " 'Populism': A Brief Biography," *Sociology*, September 1971.
10. Quoted ibid., p. 385.

11. For suggestions along these lines see the articles by Peter Wiles and Peter Worsley in Ionescu and Gellner, cited in note 5.

12. It may be appropriate here to declare a personal bias. The author (no doubt given a shove by the *Zeitgeist*) leans slightly in the populist direction: but this antielitist preference is countered (and balanced?) by a marked distrust of any form of romanticism, populist as well as elitist.

13. See Allcock, p. 372.

*1. Populism in the United States*

1. John D. Hicks, *The Populist Revolt* (Lincoln: University of Nebraska Press, 1961), p. 160.

2. Hicks, pp, 11–18.

3. Hicks, p. 61.

4. Hicks, p. 68.

5. Lawrence Goodwyn, *Democratic Promise: The Populist Moment in America* (New York: Oxford University Press, 1976), p. 204.

6. Quoted in Hicks, p. 27.

7. See George Brown Tindall, ed., *A Populist Reader* (New York: Harper & Row, 1966), pp. 42–51.

8. See William Ivy Hair, *Bourbonism and Agrarian Protest: Louisiana Politics 1877–1900* (Baton Rouge: Louisiana State University Press, 1969), p. 43.

9. Goodwyn, p. 26.

10. Ignatius Donnelly, *Caesar's Column*, ed. Walter B. Rideout (Cambridge, Mass.: Harvard University Press, 1960), p. 107.

11. On the money issue, see Irwin Unger, *The Greenback Era: A Social and Political History of American Finance, 1865–1879* (Princeton: Princeton University Press, 1964) ; Walter T. K. Nugent, *Money and American Society, 1865–80* (New York: The Free Press, 1968), Allen Weinstein, *Prelude to Populism: Origins of the Silver Issue, 1867–78* (New Haven: Yale University Press, 1970).

12. See two books by Solon J. Buck: *The Granger Movement* (Cambridge, Mass.: Harvard University Press, 1913) and *The Agrarian Crusade* (New Haven: Yale University Press, 1920).

13. Robert C. McMath, Jr., *Populist Vanguard: A History of the Southern Farmers' Alliance* (New York: W. W. Norton, 1975) ; Goodwyn, Part I.

14. Nelson A. Dunning, *The Farmers' Alliance History and Agricultural Digest,* 1891, quoted in Tindall, p. 103.

15. Goodwyn, p. 121.

16. McMath, Chapter 5.

17. Goodwyn, p. 145.

18. See, for example, Goodwyn, p. 131.

19. McMath, p. 51.

20. McMath, p. 151; Goodwyn, Chapter 5.

21. McMath, p. 27; Goodwyn, p. 83.

22. See Goodwyn, Chapter 10.

23. McMath, p. 24; Goodwyn, Chapter 3.

24. For details of the scheme, see Tindall, pp. 84–85.

25. Hicks, p. 194.

26. This is the main theme of Peter H. Argersinger, *Populism and Politics: William Alfred Peffer and the People's Party* (Lexington, Ky.: Kentucky University Press, 1974).

27. See William Warren Rogers, *The One-Gallused Rebellion: Agrarianism in Alabama, 1865–96* (Baton Rouge: Louisiana State University Press, 1970) ; W. I. Hair, *Bourbonism.*

28. Hicks, p. 32.

29. Goodwyn, p. 195.

30. Hicks, p. 155.

31. Argersinger, p. 35.

32. Hicks, p. 160.

33. Elizabeth N. Barr, quoted in Hicks, p. 159.

34. Argersinger, p. 43.

35. Goodwyn, p. 192.

36. C. Vann Woodward, *Origins of the New South, 1877–1913*

(Baton Rouge: Louisiana State University Press, 1951), p. 204.

37. Alex Mathews Arnett, *The Populist Movement in Georgia* (New York: AMS Press, 1967), p. 116.

38. McMath, p. 96.

39. Argersinger, p. 80.

40. McMath, p. 127.

41. Goodwyn, p. 290.

42. Hicks, p. 441.

43. Argersinger, pp. 122–50.

44. For Watson's account of this incident, see Norman Pollack, ed., *The Populist Mind* (Indianapolis: Bobbs-Merrill, 1967), pp. 381–84.

45. Hicks, p. 253.

46. Hair, p. 260.

47. Tindall, p. 161.

48. Tindall, p. 168.

49. Tindall, pp. 61–62.

50. Theodore Saloutos, ed., *Populism: Reaction or Reform?* (New York: Holt, Rinehart & Winston, 1968), p. 13.

51. For the views of Samuel Gompers, president of the American Federation of Labor, see Tindall, pp. 187–88. The nearest approach to a successful Populist-Labor coalition was that put together in Chicago by H. D. Lloyd, Eugene Debs, and others. See Goodwyn, pp. 411–21.

52. Tindall, p. 132.

53. Goodwyn, p. 427; Argersinger, p. 204.

54. Hicks, p. 346.

55. On the origins of the term in Kansas in 1892, see Argersinger, p. 126.

56. Paolo E. Coletta, *William Jennings Bryan*, Vol. I: *Political Evangelist, 1860–1908* (Lincoln: University of Nebraska Press, 1964), pp. 72–75.

57. Goodwyn, p. 523.

58. Robert F. Durden, *The Climax of Populism* (Lexington, Ky.: University of Kentucky Press, 1966), pp. 74–76.

59. Coletta, p. 201.

60. For opposing views, see Goodwyn and Durden.

61. Hicks, p. 389.

62. For useful surveys of the conflicting interpretations, al-
though they antedate the work of Lawrence Goodwyn, see
Saloutos, *Populism*, and Raymond J. Cunningham, ed.,
*The Populists in Historical Perspective* (Boston: D. C.
Heath, 1968). See also Part I of Walter T. K. Nugent, *The
Tolerant Populists: Kansas Populism and Nativism* (Chi-
cago, University of Chicago Press, 1963).

63. Minneapolis: University of Minnesota Press, 1931.

64. See C. Vann Woodward: "The Populist Heritage and the
Intellectual," *The American Scholar*, 59 (Winter 1959–60).

65. For a detailed account of this reinterpretation, see Part I of
Nugent, *Tolerant Populists*.

66. New York: Alfred A. Knopf, 1956. Hofstadter had contributed an essay, "The Pseudo-Conservative Revolt," to
Daniel Bell's collection of essays sparked off by the experience of McCarthyism, *The New American Right* (New
York: Criterion Books, 1955. On this book and the phase of
academic opinion it represented, see Chapter 5). Hofstadter
acknowledged in his Introduction to *The Age of Reform*
that his view of Populism was influenced by the prevailing
concerns of the time at which he wrote (pp. 12, 19). A
detailed account of the part played by *The Age of Reform*
in the reinterpretation of Populism as a forerunner of modern right-wing movements can be found in Nugent, *Tolerant
Populists*, pp. 16–26.

67. P. 62.

68. For example, Nugent, *Tolerant Populists*; Woodward,
"Populist Heritage."

69. In numerous works, but see especially *The Populist
Response to Industrial America* (Cambridge, Mass.: Harvard University Press, 1962).

70. Tindall, p. ix.

71. McMath, pp. 156–57.
72. Goodwyn, p. xviii.
73. Goodwyn, pp. 195–97.
74. Pollack, *Populist Mind*, p. 337.
75. Pollack, *Populist Mind*, p. 450.
76. Pollack, *Populist Mind*, p. 231.
77. Hicks, p. 81.
78. Pollack, *Populist Mind*, p. 13.
79. Pollack, *Populist Mind*, p. 213.
80. Pollack, *Populist Mind*, p. 46.
81. Argersinger, p. 62.
82. Stanley Parsons, *The Populist Context: Rural Versus Urban Power on a Great Plains Frontier* (Westport, Conn.: Greenwood Press, 1973), p. 130.
83. McMath, p. 66.
84. Goodwyn, p. 244.
85. Tindall, p. 187.
86. See Goodwyn, Chapters 3 and 13; Rogers, p. 215; Woodward, *Origins of the New South*, p. 253.
87. See C. Vann Woodward, *Tom Watson, Agrarian Rebel* (New York: Rinehart & Co., 1938).
88. Goodwyn, pp. 413–21.
89. *Wealth against Commonwealth* (New York: Harper, 1902).
90. Pollack, *Populist Mind*, p. 215.
91. There are other examples in North American history; see Chapter 3 below for further discussion of this point.

## 2. Russian Populism

1. F. A. Walker, "The Morality of Revolution in Pyotr Lavrovich Lavrov," *Slavonic and East European Review*, 41 (1962–63), 202.
2. Quoted in Franco Venturi, *The Roots of Revolution* (London: Weidenfeld and Nicholson, 1960), p. 368.
3. In an important article, "*Narodnichestvo*: A Semantic Inquiry," published in *The Slavic Review*, 23, No. 3 (Septem-

ber 1964), Richard Pipes drew attention to the contrast between the conventional use of the term in modern historiography and its meaning at the time when it was coined. Conventionally, he said, *narodnichestvo* denotes "an agrarian socialism of the second half of the nineteenth century, which upheld the proposition that Russia could by-pass the capitalist stage of development and proceed through the artel and peasant commune directly to socialism" (p. 441). Investigation of the sources revealed, however, that the term came into use about 1875 to indicate a particular attitude within the radical movement, namely a new humility toward the people, which prompted the *narodniki* to hold that "the intellectuals should not lead the people in the name of abstract, bookish, imported ideas but adapt themselves to the people as it was, promoting resistance to the government in the name of real, everyday needs" (p. 445). It was, according to Pipes, Marxist polemical writers of the early 1890s who took the term out of its context and pinned it on all those who thought it possible to avoid the capitalist development of Russia.

Other scholars, while accepting Pipes's evidence, have disputed his implication that there is no historical justification for using the term in a sense wider than its original meaning. Richard Wortman, in *The Crisis of Russian Populism* (Cambridge: Cambridge University Press, 1967), pp. viii–ix, maintains that a coherent ideological viewpoint centered on idealization of the peasantry and justifiably described as *narodnik* can be found in many nineteenth-century Russian writers. Andrzej Walicki, in *The Controversy over Capitalism* (Oxford: Oxford University Press, 1969), p. 12, adopts Lenin's position and argues that "populism was a broad current of Russian democratic thought which reflected the class standpoint of small producers," and which involved a particular view of historical development.

4. On the improvements achieved during the reign of Nicholas I in the condition of peasants belonging to the state rather than the nobles, see Basil Dmytryshyn, *A History of Russia* (Englewood Cliffs, N.J.: Prentice-Hall, 1977), pp. 347–48.

5. E. Lampert, *Sons Against Fathers: Studies in Russian Radicalism and Revolution* (Oxford: Oxford University Press, 1965), pp. 31–38.

6. On the formation and characteristics of this Russian intelligentsia, see Martin Malia, "What is the Intelligentsia?" in Richard Pipes, ed., *The Russian Intelligentsia* (New York: Columbia University Press, 1961).

7. James Billington, *Mikhailovsky and Russian Populism* (Oxford: Oxford University Press, 1958), p. v.

8. For a brief summary of the views of the Slavophiles, see Andrzej Walicki, "Russian Social Thought: An Introduction to the Intellectual History of Nineteenth-Century Russia," *The Russian Review*, 36, No. 1 (1977).

9. On the meanings of *obshchina* and *mir*, see Stephen A. Grant, *Obshchina and Mir*, *Slavic Review*, 35, No. 4 (December 1976).

10. On Herzen, see his autobiography, *My Past and Thoughts*, 4 vols. (London: Chatto and Windus, 1968); Martin Malia, *Alexander Herzen and the Birth of Russian Socialism* (Cambridge, Mass.: Harvard University Press, 1961); Venturi, Chapters 1, 4; Isaiah Berlin, *Russian Thinkers* (Hogarth Press, 1978).

11. See *From the Other Shore and the Russian People and Socialism* (London: Weidenfeld and Nicholson, 1956).

12. Quoted in Venturi, p. 35.

13. On Chernyshevsky, see William F. Woehrlin, *Chernyshevski: The Man and the Journalist* (Cambridge, Mass.: Harvard University Press, 1971); Venturi, Chapter 5.

14. Quoted by Adam B. Ulam, *Ideologies and Illusions: Revolutionary Thought from Herzen to Solzenitsyn* (Cambridge, Mass.: Harvard University Press, 1976), p. 24.

15. Woehrlin, p. 174.
16. Walicki, "Russian Social Thought," p. 21.
17. N. G. O. Pereira, "N. G. Chernyshevsky as Architect of the Politics of Anti-Liberalism in Russia," *The Russian Review*, 32 (1973), p. 273.
18. Rose Glickman, "An Alternative View of the Peasantry: The Raznochintsy Writers of the 1860's," *Slavic Review*, 32 (1973), p. 697.
19. Glickman, p. 698.
20. Wortman, p. 10.
21. Venturi, p. 152.
22. Woehrlin, p. 211.
23. Venturi, p. 450.
24. Quoted in Wortman, p. 16.
25. Walicki, *The Controversy over Capitalism*, p. 89.
26. Venturi, p. 502.
27. Vera Broido, *Apostles into Terrorists: Women and the Revolutionary Movement in the Russia of Alexander II* (New York: Viking Press, 1977), p. 85.
28. Adam B. Ulam, *In the Name of the People: Prophets and Conspirators in Prerevolutionary Russia* (New York: Viking Press, 1977), p. 220.
29. Ulam, *In the Name of the People*, p. 232.
30. Wortman, p. 19.
31. Quoted in Pipes, "*Narodnichestvo*," p. 445.
32. Wortman, p. 39.
33. Wortman, Chapter 2.
34. Wortman, p. 52.
35. Venturi, p. 582.
36. Venturi, p. 573.
37. Wortman, p. 26.
38. Wortman, pp. 73–75.
39. Wortman, p. 58.
40. Ulam, *In the Name of the People*, p. 248.
41. Venturi, p. 657.
42. Venturi, p. 719.

43. Venturi, p. 714.

44. The distinction made here between populism and Marxism, though in accordance with much of the literature on the subject, is a considerable oversimplification of a complex situation. For an illuminating discussion, see the first section of Michael Kitch's article, "Constantin Stere and Rumanian Populism," *Slavonic and East European Review*, 53 (1975).

45. Arthur P. Mendel, *Dilemmas of Progress in Tsarist Russia: Legal Marxism and Legal Populism* (Cambridge, Mass.: Harvard University Press, 1961), p. 104.

46. On the whole controversy, see Mendel; Walicki, *Controversy over Capitalism;* and Wortman.

47. On Chernov and the Socialist Revolutionaries, see Maureen Perrie, *The Agrarian Policy of the Russian Socialist-Revolutionary Party* (Cambridge: Cambridge University Press, 1976); Oliver H. Radkey, *The Agrarian Foes of Bolshevism* (New York: Columbia University Press, 1958); Oliver H. Radkey, *The Sickle under the Hammer* (New York: Columbia University Press, 1963); Oliver H. Radkey, "Chernov and Agrarian Socialism before 1918," in Ernest J. Simmons, ed., *Continuity and Change in Russian and Soviet Thought* (New York: Russell and Russell, 1955).

48. Perrie, p. 73.

49. Radkey, *Agrarian Foes of Bolshevism*, p. 20.

50. On the peasants before, during, and after the 1917 Revolution, see Launcelot A. Owen, *The Russian Peasant Movement, 1906–1917* (London: P. S. King, 1937); Teodor Shanin, *The Awkward Class: Political Sociology of Peasantry in a Developing Society: Russia 1910–1925* (Oxford: Oxford University Press, 1972); D. J. Male, *Russian Peasant Organisation before Collectivization, 1925–30* (Cambridge: Cambridge University Press, 1971); M. Lewin, *Russian Peasants and Soviet Power: A Study of Collectivization* (London: Allen and Unwin, 1968).

51. Radkey, *Agrarian Foes of Bolshevism* and *The Sickle under*

*the Hammer;* Adam Ulam, *Lenin and the Bolsheviks* (London: Secker and Warburg, 1966).

52. Walicki, *The Controversy over Capitalism,* p. 12.

53. P. 26.

54. See the works by Male and Lewin already cited.

55. V. I. Lenin, *What is to be Done?* (London: Martin Lawrence, 1932), p. 32. It was originally published in 1902.

56. See the contribution by Hugh Seton-Watson to the symposium "To Define Populism," *Government and Opposition,* 3, Part 2 (Spring 1968), 140.

57. Wortman, p. 6.

58. Quoted in Walicki, "Russia," in Ionescu and Gellner, eds., *Populism,* p. 72.

59. For sympathetic views on this point, see Mendel, passim; Isaiah Berlin, "Introduction" to Venturi.

## 3. *Agrarian Populism in Perspective*

1. John D. Bell, *Peasants in Power* (Princeton: Princeton University Press, 1977), p. 162.

2. Eric R. Wolf, *Peasant Wars of the Twentieth Century* (London: Faber and Faber, 1973), p. 31.

3. See J. B. Allcock, "Populism: A Brief Biography," *Sociology,* 5, No. 3 (Sept. 1971), 372.

4. S. M. Lipset, *Agrarian Socialism: The Cooperative Commonwealth Federation in Saskatchewan* (Berkeley: University of California Press, 1950), p. 94.

5. Lipset, p. xv.

6. For a brief account of the doctrines of Social Credit, see John A. Irving, *The Social Credit Movement in Alberta* (Toronto: University of Toronto Press, 1959), which describes the rise of the movement. A more general context for the rise of Aberhard is provided in C. B. Macpherson, *Democracy in Alberta* (Toronto: University of Toronto Press, 1953).

7. See Robert L. Morlan, *Political Prairie Fire: The Nonparti-*

*san League, 1915–1922* (Minneapolis: University of Minnesota Press, 1955).

8. Kenneth Barkin, "A Case Study in Comparative History: Populism in Germany and America," in Herbert J. Bass, *The State of American History* (Chicago: Quadrangle Books, 1970).

9. In the German context, the rhetorical equivalent was perhaps the anti-Semitic demand to regain control by the *Volk.*

10. Frantz Fanon, *The Wretched of the Earth*, trans. by C. Farrington (Harmondsworth: Penguin Books, 1967).

11. Karl Marx, *Capital* (London: Allen and Unwin, 1946), I, 789.

12. Fanon, p. 105.

13. P. 101.

14. P. 73.

15. Quoted in R. N. Berki, *Socialism* (London: J. M. Dent & Sons, 1975), p. 125.

16. Cranford Pratt, *The Critical Phase in Tanzania, 1945–68: Nyerere and the Emergence of a Socialist Strategy* (Cambridge: Cambridge University Press, 1976), p. 253.

17. Doreen Warriner, *Land Reform in Principle and Practice* (Oxford: Oxford University Press, 1960), pp. 70, 246. On the current disillusionment among observers of Tanzania's program of collective "Ujamaa villages," see Joel Samoff, "The Bureaucracy and the Bourgeoisie: Decentralisation and Class Structure in Tanzania," *Comparative Studies in Society and History*, 21 (1979), 31–37.

18. Jeffery M. Paige, *Agrarian Revolution: Social Movements and Export Agriculture in the Underdeveloped World* (New York: The Free Press, 1975), pp. 186, 286.

19. This is a point about which there is some dispute. According to Ghita Ionescu, the East European peasant movements should not be called "populist" but "peasantist," so that the former term can be reserved for the characteristic

doctrines of the Russian movement. However, Ionescu's article on what he calls "peasantism" appeared in a book entitled *Populism* ("Eastern Europe," in Ionescu and Gellner, eds., *Populism*, p. 98), while his terminological ruling has been challenged by Olga A. Narkiewicz in *The Green Flag: Polish Populist Politics, 1867–1970* (London: Croom Helm, 1976), p. 293, note 2.

20. See Teodor Shanin, ed., *Peasants and Peasant Societies*, (Harmondsworth: Penguin, 1971); Eric R. Wolf, *Peasants* (Englewood Cliffs, N.J.: Prentice-Hall, 1966); Henry A. Landsberger, "Peasant Unrest: Themes and Variations," in H. A. Landsberger, ed., *Rural Protest: Peasant Movements and Social Change* (New York: Macmillan, 1974).

21. For a good survey, see Hugh Seton-Watson, *Eastern Europe between the Wars, 1918–1941* (Cambridge: Cambridge University Press, 1946).

22. Seton-Watson, p. 75.

23. Philip Gabriel Eidelberg, *The Great Rumanian Peasant Revolt of 1907* (Leiden: E. J. Brill, 1974).

24. Nissan Oren, *Revolution Administered: Agrarianism and Communism in Bulgaria* (Baltimore: Johns Hopkins University Press, 1973), pp. 3–14; Nicos Mouzelis, "Greek and Bulgarian Peasants: Aspects of their Socio-political Situation during the Interwar Period," *Comparative Studies in Society and History*, 18, No. 1 (Jan. 1976), 95–102; and Bell, *Peasants in Power.*

25. For details, see David Mitrany, *Marx against the Peasant*, (London: University of North Carolina Press, 1951), p. 90.

26. For detailed information on the history of the various national peasant parties, see Mitrany, pp. 242–43; and George D. Jackson, Jr., "Peasant Political Movements in Eastern Europe," in Landsberger, p. 272.

27. Peter Brock, "Boleslaw Wyslouch, Founder of the Polish Peasant Party, 1855–1937," *Slavonic and East European Review*, 30 (1951–52), 146.

28. Brock, p. 148.
29. Narkiewicz, pp. 52–53.
30. Dyzma Galaj, "The Polish Peasant Movement in Politics: 1895–1969," in Landsberger, p. 322.
31. Bell, pp. 59–67.
32. Bell, p. 168.
33. Bell, pp. 171–75.
34. Bell, pp. 227–28.
35. Narkiewicz, p. 57.
36. Narkiewicz, p. 51.
37. Jackson, "Peasant Political Movements," pp. 294–95.
38. An attempt that—given the ethnic hostilities of Eastern Europe—usually had most chance of success among ethnic minorities. See George D. Jackson, Jr., *Comintern and Peasant in Eastern Europe, 1919–1930* (New York: Columbia University Press, 1966), pp. 171, 195, 246, 278.
39. Jackson, *Comintern and Peasant*, p. 42.
40. Jackson, *Comintern and Peasant*, p. 148.
41. Landsberger, p. 292.
42. Henry L. Roberts, *Rumania: Political Problems of an Agrarian State* (New Haven: Yale University Press, 1951), p. 144.
43. Landsberger, p. 43.
44. Mitrany, p. 126.
45. Roberts, p. 145.
46. Ionescu, p. 111. For more examples, see Mitrany, pp. 113–14, 240; Joso Tomasevich, *Peasants, Politics and Economic Change in Yugoslavia* (Stanford: Stanford University Press, 1955), p. 616.
47. Landsberger, p. 289.
48. See Tomasevich, p. 249.
49. Galaj, p. 334.
50. Mitrany, p. 106.
51. Ionescu, p. 110.
52. Tomasevich, p. 254.

53. Bell, Chapter 4.

54. Mitrany, p. 138.

55. Narkiewicz, p. 36.

56. Ionescu, p. 101.

57. Seton-Watson, p. 259.

58. Andrzej Walicki, *The Controversy over Capitalism* (Oxford: Oxford University Press, 1969), p. 12.

59. Proudhon's version of anarchism has many resemblances to the outlook of the Green movements. See *Selected Writings of Pierre-Joseph Proudhon*, ed. Stewart Edwards (New York: Macmillan, 1969). A romantic intellectuals' version of a similar outlook can be found in the "Distributism" preached by G. K. Chesterton and Hilaire Belloc in Britain in the 1920s; see Margaret Canovan: *G. K. Chesterton: Radical Populist* (New York: Harcourt Brace Jovanovich, 1977).

60. Which have frequently been associated with communal peasant traditions, since these form a basis for peasant organization and defense of their interests. See Wolf, *Peasant Wars*, pp. 28–31.

61. See Gerrit Huizer, *Peasant Rebellion in Latin America* (Harmondsworth: Penguin, 1973); John Womack, Jr., *Zapata and the Mexican Revolution* (New York: Vintage Books, Random House, 1968); Wolf, *Peasant Wars*.

62. Stuart R. Schram, *The Political Thought of Mao Tse-Tung*, revised ed. (New York: Praeger, 1969), p. 103; Maurice Meisner, "Leninism and Maoism: Some Populist Perspectives on Marxism-Leninism in China," *The China Quarterly*, 45 (Jan.–March, 1971).

63. Schram, p. 110.

64. See the symposium "To Define Populism," *Government and Opposition*, 3, Part 2, (Spring 1968), 153–55.

65. Schram, p. 316.

66. The countries that have most successfully implemented the ideals of the peasant movements have ceased to be peasant

countries. In Denmark, for instance, where small farmers united family production with cooperative marketing, and industry was subordinated to agriculture, by 1960 60 percent of the population were town dwellers, while those who remained on the land had long ceased to be peasants and become commercial farmers with a flourishing export industry. See Kenneth E. Millar, *Government and Politics in Denmark* (Boston: Houghton Mifflin Co., 1968), p. 4. See also S. H. Franklin, *The European Peasantry: The Final Phase* (London: Methuen, 1969).

67. Allcock, pp. 380–84.
68. Angus Stewart, "The Social Roots," in Ionescu and Gellner, eds., *Populism*, p. 180.

### 4. Populist Dictatorship

1. Giovanni Sartori, *Democratic Theory* (Detroit: Wayne State University Press, 1962), p. 86.
2. T. Harry Williams, *Huey Long* (London: Thames and Hudson, 1969), p. 762.
3. See Otto Kirchheimer, "The Transformation of the Western European Party Systems," in Joseph La Palombara and Myron Weiner, eds., *Political Parties and Political Development* (Princeton: Princeton University Press, 1966), p. 184.
4. See Christopher Mitchell, *The Legacy of Populism in Bolivia: From the MNR to Military Rule* (New York: Praeger, 1977), Gino Germani, *Authoritarianism, Fascism and National Populism* (New Brunswick, N.J.: Transaction Books, 1978), A. E. Van Niekerk, *Populism and Political Development in Latin America* (Rotterdam: Rotterdam University Press, 1974); Torcuato di Tella, "Populism and Reform in Latin America," in C. Veliz, ed., *Obstacles to Change in Latin America* (London: Oxford University Press, 1965); Alistair Hennessy, "Latin America," in Ionescu and Gellner, eds., *Populism*; Alan Angell, "Party

Systems in Latin America," *Political Quarterly* (1966);
Paul W. Drake, *Socialism and Populism in Chile, 1932–52*
(Urbana: University of Illinois Press, 1978); Gary W.
Wynia, *The Politics of Latin American Development*
(Cambridge: Cambridge University Press, 1978).

5. Drake, p. 2.
6. Van Niekerk, p. 206.
7. Di Tella, p. 47.
8. Di Tella, p. 47.
9. Germani, p. 88.
10. Germani, p. 95.
11. See Wynia, cited above; and K. P. Ericson, "Populism and
Political Control of the Working Class in Brazil," in June
Nash, Juan Corradi, and Hobart Spalding Jr., eds., *Ideology
and Social Change in Latin America* (New York: Gordon &
Breach, 1977).
12. Examples usually given include the P.R.I. in Mexico,
A.P.R.A. in Peru, and M.N.R. in Bolivia.
13. See di Tella and Mitchell.
14. Van Niekerk, p. 171.
15. Thus the M.N.R. in Bolivia; see Mitchell.
16. We shall take up the other side of Latin American populism, the politicians' catch-all party, in Chapter 7.
17. Jeane Kirkpatrick, *Leader and Vanguard in Mass Society:
A Study of Peronist Argentina* (Cambridge, Mass.: MIT
Press, 1971), p. 30.
18. On Peron and Peronism, see Germani; Kirkpatrick; G.
Blanksten, *Peron's Argentina* (Chicago: University of Chicago Press, 1953); Frank Owen, *Peron: His Rise and Fall*
(London: The Cresset Press, 1957); Joseph R. Barager,
"Argentina," in Martin C. Needler, ed., *Political Systems of
Latin America*, 2nd ed. (New York: Van Nostrand Rein-
hold Co., 1970), Wynia; Robert J. Alexander, *The Peron
Era* (London: Victor Gollancz, 1952).
19. Blanksten, p. 101.

20. Germani, p. 185.
21. Peron in 1950, quoted in Owen, p. 168.
22. Kirkpatrick, p. 37.
23. Blanksten, p. 107.
24. Kirkpatrick, p. 93.
25. Germani passim, but especially Chapters 3 and 4.
26. For a completely different and highly controversial account of fascism, see the work of A. James Gregor, e.g., *The Ideology of Fascism* (New York: The Free Press, 1969), and *The Fascist Persuasion in Radical Politics* (Princeton: Princeton University Press, 1974).
27. Vera Broido, *Apostles into Terrorists: Women and the Revolutionary Movement in the Russia of Alexander II* (New York: Viking Press, 1977), p. 10.
28. J. P. Stern, *Hitler: The Führer and the People* (London: Fontana, 1975), p. 18.
29. Gregor, *The Ideology of Fascism*, p. 232.
30. See Williams, cited above. Winn had long been a stronghold of agrarian protest. The Grange had been sufficiently successful there for Winnfield to house the longest surviving Grange cooperative store, still doing business in 1885 under the management of Huey Long's Uncle George. In 1890 the Winn Parish Farmers' Union established the first Populist newspaper in the South. See William Ivy Hair, *Bourbonism and Agrarian Protest* (Baton Rouge: Louisiana State University Press, 1969), pp. 67, 210, 212.
31. Williams, p. 416.
32. Williams, p. 188; Allan P. Sindler, *Huey Long's Louisiana: State Politics, 1920–52* (Baltimore: Johns Hopkins Press, 1956), passim.
33. Williams, p. 3.
34. Williams, p. 182.
35. Williams, p. 332.
36. Williams, p. 467.
37. Williams, p. 473.

38. Williams, p. 744.

39. Williams, p. 752.

40. Williams, p. 756.

41. Huey Long, *Every Man a King*, ed. T. Harry Williams (Chicago: Quadrangle Books, 1964), p. 290.

42. Sindler, p. 84; David H. Bennett, *Demagogues in the Depression: American Radicals and the Union Party, 1932–36* (New Brunswick: Rutgers University Press, 1969), p. 121.

43. On Coughlin, see Bennett; and James P. Shenton, "The Coughlin Movement and the New Deal," *Political Science Quarterly*, 73, No. 3 (1958).

44. The Democrats had been sufficiently nervous to commission a secret poll, which suggested that if Long stood for President in 1936 he might attract between 3,000,000 and 4,000,000 votes, drawn from the North as well as the South (Bennett, p. 127). After Long's death the organizer of his Share Our Wealth campaign, Gerald Smith, did join in the Union Party's campaign for the Presidency, headed by the Middle Western agrarian William Lemke and supported by Father Coughlin and Dr. Townsend, leader of a movement for old age pensions. In spite of the apparent strength of their combined followers, the bid failed miserably (See Bennett). Whether Long could have done better is a matter of speculation. It should be noted, however, that whereas in Louisiana Long had represented the *only* effective source of benefits for the poor farmers, on a national scale he would have been competing against the reform record of the New Deal as well as against Roosevelt's commanding personality.

45. Williams, p. 761.

46. *The Politics of Aristotle*, ed. Ernest Barker (Oxford: Oxford University Press, 1946), p. 216.

47. *The Republic of Plato*, ed. Francis Macdonald Cornford (Oxford: Oxford University Press, 1941), p. 286.

48. *Ibid.*, p. 289.

49. See John Duncan Powell, "Peasant Society and Clientelist Politics," *American Political Science Review*, 64 (1970), 411–25.

50. See J. Ortega y Gasset, *The Revolt of the Masses* (New York: Norton, 1940); William Kornhauser, *The Politics of Mass Society* (London: Routledge and Kegan Paul, 1960). Critical accounts of "mass" theory can be found in Salvador Giner, *Mass Society* (London: Martin Robertson, 1976); and Sandor Halebsky, *Mass Society and Political Conflict: Toward a Reconstruction of Theory* (Cambridge: Cambridge University Press, 1976). One of the most influential books applying mass-society concepts to the analysis of American politics was Daniel Bell, ed., *The New American Right*, retitled *The Radical Right* for the second edition (Garden City: Doubleday Anchor Books, 1964).

51. Philip Selznick, quoted in Giner, p. 146.

52. See particularly Kornhauser; also S. M. Lipset, *Political Man*, (London: Heinemann, 1960).

53. Kornhauser, p. 13.

54. Lipset, p. 97.

55. See Giner; Halebsky. See also Section IV of Maurice Pinard, *The Rise of a Third Party* (Englewood Cliffs, N.J.: Prentice-Hall, 1971).

56. See, for example, an attempt to test the applicability of mass-society theory to the followers of Enoch Powell, in Douglas E. Schoen, *Enoch Powell and the Powellites* (London: Macmillan, 1977), Chapter 9.

57. There was a long history of lower-class resentment against the Democratic oligarchy in Louisiana, and perfectly genuine grievances for Long to tap: see Sindler, p. 1. Many of the "mass" explanations for political movements seem unnecessarily complicated. Given that economic interests are more accessible to observation than psychological states, it seems reasonable, and in accordance with Occam's

razor, to accept economic explanations where plausible ones can be given. And yet, to cite just one example, David Bennett (p. 163) refuses to believe that it was "the material privations of the depression" that made old people such fervent supporters of Dr. Townsend's Old Age Pension plan, and seeks "deeper" causes related to alienation and loss of status. (It is hard not to suspect that some of those who reject material explanations so confidently have simply never been in a position where they had to worry about money.)

58. For a personal recollection of one such "redneck" Long supporter, see Robert Penn Warren, "All the King's Men: The Matrix of Experience," in John Lewis Longley, Jr., *Robert Penn Warren: A Collection of Critical Essays* (New York: New York University Press, 1965), p. 76.

59. Kirkpatrick, pp. 113, 153, 174. Between a quarter and a third were middle class.

60. Pp. 206–11.

61. P. 211.

62. P. 212.

63. Germani, pp. 185–88.

64. P. 230.

65. P. 240. Notice the similarities between Germani's account of Peronist participation and the description given by Goodwyn of participation in the U.S. Populist movement (Chapter 1 above). Is this evidence of a fundamental similarity between the two movements? Or just of the effects on academic interpretation of the Spirit of the Age?

66. P. 118.

67. P. 241.

68. Peter H. Smith, in "Social Mobilization, Political Participation, and the Rise of Juan Peron," *Political Science Quarterly*, 84 (March 1969), considers the beef consumers and packing-house workers of Buenos Aires, and shows why it made sense for them to support Peron's rise to

power. See also Smith's "The Social Base of Peronism," *Hispanic-American Historical Review*, 52, No. 1 (Feb. 1972), for an analysis of Peronist voting in the 1946 Presidential election.

69. Alexis de Tocqueville, *Democracy in America*, ed. Henry Steele Commager, (London: Oxford University Press, 1946), pp. 372–75.

70. Third World leaders brandishing anti-imperialist rhetoric are the obvious examples, but consider the case of Aberhard in Alberta (See Chapter 3 above). The quasi-colonial relation of the prairie farmers to Eastern markets in Canada produced a situation where not only radical solutions but a strong leader could be attractive to voters (though the fact that Saskatchewan, next door, did not produce a charismatic leader indicates that there is nothing inevitable about this).

## 5. Populist Democracy in Theory and Practice

1. Laura Tallian, *Direct Democracy: An Historical Analysis of the Initiative, Referendum and Recall Process* (Los Angeles: People's Lobby, Inc., 1977), p. 92.

2. *Memoir of Theophilus Parsons* (Boston, 1859), p. 109.

3. Joseph L. Blau, ed., *Social Theories of Jacksonian Democracy* (New York: Hafner, 1947), p. 22.

4. For an interesting discussion of "political distrust" which uses Kansas Populism as a case study, see Vivien Hart, *Distrust and Democracy: Political Distrust in Britain and America* (Cambridge: Cambridge University Press, 1978).

5. The fundamental distinction made in the present book between "agrarian" and "political" varieties of populism gains some support from the relation between the Populist and Progressive movements. As far as their *political* ideals went, both movements were at one in wishing to replace the influence of corporations and politicians with the power of the people, and, as George E. Mowry puts it, "the

real seedbed of Progressivism was of course Populism."
George E. Mowry, *Theodore Roosevelt and the Progressive
Movement*, (Madison: University of Wisconsin Press,
1947), p. 11. However, as Mowry himself remarks elsewhere, in terms of economic interests and social background the two movements were quite distinct. Far from
being a backwoods farmer, the typical Progressive was a
well-educated and comfortably off professional man, and
"most progressive leaders had been violently opposed to
the nineteenth-century agrarian radicalism of William
Jennings Bryan and the Populists." George E. Mowry,
*The California Progressives* (Berkeley: University of California Press, 1951), p. ix. The Progressive movement was
much less of a grass-roots upsurge than Populism, and the
successful campaigns in California, for instance, were the
work of a surprisingly small but highly organized minority
(*ibid.*, p. 86). In academic circles, the Progressives' stock
seems to be falling as that of the Populists rises: since
the latter became heroes of participatory democracy, the
former have been stamped as deplorably elitist. See Otis
L. Graham, *The Great Campaigns: Reform and War in
America, 1900–1928* (Englewood Cliffs, N.J.: Prentice-
Hall, 1971), pp. 28–29.

6. Edward N. Doan, *The La Folettes and the Wisconsin Idea*
(New York: Rinehart & Co., 1947), pp. 63, 81, 127.

7. For details, see Tallian, p. 45; Austin Ranney, "The
United States of America," in David Butler and Austin
Ranney, eds., *Referendums: A Comparative Study of
Practice and Theory*, (Washington, D.C.: American Enterprise Institute for Public Policy Research, 1978). I am
deeply indebted to this book, which is a gold mine of
information and statistics on referendums of all kinds.

8. Ranney, in Butler and Ranney, p. 73.

9. Marshall Stimson, speaking in Los Angeles in 1906, quoted
in Mowry, *California Progressives*, p. 91. See also Tallian,
especially Chapters 3 and 4.

10. For a classic statement of this program, see Walter E. Weyl, *The New Democracy*, revised ed. (New York: Macmillan, 1914), Chapter 18: "The Political Program of the Democracy."

11. The literature on the subject is vast. For samples of "elitist democratic theory," however, see G. Sartori, *Democratic Theory* (Detroit: Wayne State University Press, 1962); J. Schumpeter, *Capitalism, Socialism and Democracy*, (London: Allen and Unwin, 1943); B. R. Berelson, P. F. Lazarsfeld, and W. N. McPhee, *Voting* (Chicago: University of Chicago Press, 1954), Chapter 14: "Democratic Theory and Democratic Practice"; S. M. Lipset, *Political Man* (London: Heinemann, 1960). Examples of the critique of democratic elitism are: P. Bachrach, *The Theory of Democratic Elitism: A Critique* (Boston: Little, Brown & Co., 1967); Jack L. Walker: "A Critique of the Elitist Theory of Democracy," *American Political Science Review*, 60, No. 2 (1966); Barry Holden, *The Nature of Democracy* (London: Nelson, 1974); Duncan G., and S. Lukes: "The New Democracy," *Political Studies*, 11, (1963).

12. Schumpeter, p. 269.

13. See especially Berelson et al.

14. For a useful survey of this element in modern democratic theory see John Plamenatz, *Democracy and Illusion* (London: Longman, 1973), Chapter 3.

15. Lipset, p. 115. This attitude is also very strongly expressed in Sartori, passim.

16. Edward Shils, *The Torment of Secrecy* (London: Heinemann, 1956), p. 48.

17. P. 98

18. P. 99.

19. P. 103.

20. References are to the second edition, entitled *The Radical Right* (Garden City, N.Y.: Doubleday Anchor Books, 1964). See David Riesman and Nathan Glazer, "The Intel-

lectuals and the Discontented Classes," p. 112; Peter Viereck, "The Revolt against the Elite," passim; Talcott Parsons, "Social Strains in America," p. 255; S. M. Lipset, "The Sources of the 'Radical Right,'" p. 364.

21. Michael Paul Rogin, *The Intellectuals and McCarthy: The Radical Specter* (Cambridge, Mass.: M.I.T. Press, 1967), p. 6.

22. P. 48. For an opposing view, see David H. Bennett, *Demagogues in the Depression* (New Brunswick: Rutgers University Press, 1969), p. 65.

23. Terrence E. Cook and Patrick M. Morgan, *Participatory Democracy* (New York: Cranfield Press, 1972).

24. Kenneth A. Megill, *The New Democratic Theory* (New York: The Free Press, 1970), p. 44.

25. Robert J. Pranger, *The Eclipse of Citizenship* (New York: Holt, Rinehart & Winston, 1968), pp. 26, 69.

26. Cook and Morgan, p. 30.

27. One of the most interesting and least utopian discussions of such devolution of power is Milton Kotler, *Neighborhood Government: The Local Foundation of Political Life* (Indianapolis: Bobbs-Merrill, 1969). See also R. A. Dahl, *After the Revolution* (New Haven: Yale University Press, 1970).

28. Pranger, p. 18.

29. "Participatory Democracy: Lenin Updated," Cook and Morgan, p. 61.

30. Holden, p. 6.

31. See Carole Pateman, *Participation and Democratic Theory* (Cambridge: Cambridge University Press, 1970), Chapters 3 and 6; P. Bachrach and M. S. Baratz, *Power and Poverty* (New York: Oxford University Press, 1970), Appendix E.

32. See Dennis F. Thompson, *The Democratic Citizen* (Cambridge: Cambridge University Press, 1970); Vivien Hart, *Distrust and Democracy* (Cambridge: Cambridge University Press, 1978); Joseph V. Femia, "Elites, Participa-

tion and the Democratic Creed," *Political Studies*, 27, No. 1 (March 1979).

33. Eugene S. Lee, "California," in Butler and Ranney, p. 93.

34. Austin Ranney, "The United States of America," in Butler and Ranney, p. 75.

35. Tallian, pp. 138–39.

36. Pp. 75–76. Tallian maintains that "the middle class furnishes that solid foundation upon which society rests" (p. 76), and refers to "the poor" only as young people about to reach a middle-class income, and elderly people who once had one. Compare Weyl, *New Democracy*, pp. 237, 338, and Mowry, *California Progressives*, p. 97.

37. Alaska, Arizona, California, Colorado, Idaho, Kansas, Louisiana, Michigan, Nevada, North Dakota, Oregon, Washington, and Wisconsin (Tallian, p. 45).

38. Clyde E. Jacobs and Alvin D. Sokolow, *California Government: One among Fifty*, 2nd ed. (London: Collier Macmillan, 1970), p. 38.

39. Frederick L. Bird, "Recall," *Encyclopedia of the Social Sciences* (New York: Macmillan, 1949), p. 148. Ironically, Frazier was himself an agrarian populist, the candidate of the Nonpartisan League.

40. Henry A. Turner and John A. Vieg, *The Government and Politics of California*, 2nd ed. (New York: McGraw Hill, 1964), p. 80.

41. For a sympathetic account of this kind of political distrust see Hart, passim.

42. Switzerland, though the original home of the recall, makes very little use of it, in contrast to constant use of the initiative and referendum (Bird, p. 149).

43. Eugene C. Lee, "California," in Butler and Ranney, p. 99.

44. Lee, in Butler and Ranney, p. 92.

45. Apart from Switzerland and some U.S. states, the most notable modern case of use of the popular initiative is Italy. Recent referendums on popular initiative include

votes on the repeal of the divorce law, on the repeal of state financing of parties, and on antiterrorist legislation (Butler and Ranney, p. 13).

46. Butler and Ranney provide lists of referendums of all kinds. On terminology, the present work follows Butler and Ranney in using "referendums" rather than "referenda." (See Butler and Ranney, p. 4, for reasons backed by the authority of the editor of the *Oxford English Dictionary*.)

47. On the variations between referendums, see Gordon Smith, "The Functional Properties of the Referendum," *European Journal of Political Research*, 4, No. 1 (March 1976).

48. Butler and Ranney, p. 235. As these authors point out (p. 8), however, very large majorities are not always bogus. Some of the cases of honestly counted referendums revealing near-unanimity are Norway's 99.9 percent vote for separation from Sweden in 1905; Iceland's 99.5 percent for separation from Denmark in 1944; and Gibraltar's 99.6 percent for maintaining its ties with Britain in 1967.

49. See Vincent Wright, "France," in Butler and Ranney, and Henry W. Ehrmann, "Direct Democracy in France," *American Political Science Review*, 57 (1963).

50. Wright, p. 147.

51. David Butler, "United Kingdom," Butler and Ranney, p. 214.

52. Provisions of this kind have given rise to a very large number of referendums in Australia. See Don Aitkin, "Australia," in Butler and Ranney.

53. Maurice Manning, "Ireland," Butler and Ranney, p. 207.

54. For details, see Austin Ranney, "The United States of America," in Butler and Ranney, pp. 69–73.

55. Lee, "California," Butler and Ranney, pp. 92–93.

56. Jean-François Aubert, "Switzerland," Butler and Ranney, p. 43.

57. Hans Huber, *How Switzerland Is Governed*, 3rd ed. (Zurich: Schweizer Spiegel Verlag, 1974), p. 10.

58. In 1964, for instance, there was a large majority in favor of a Californian initiative to reverse legislation prohibiting racial discrimination in housing. A judicial battle between minority organizations and property interests followed, settled in 1967 when the U.S. Supreme Court declared the popular decision unconstitutional (Jacobs and Sokolow, p. 106).

59. Aubert, in Butler and Ranney, p. 40.

60. On the Swiss political system, see Christopher Hughes, *The Parliament of Switzerland* (London: Cassell, 1962); Hans Huber; Jurg Steiner, *Amicable Agreement Versus Majority Rule: Conflict Resolution in Switzerland* (Chapel Hill: University of North Carolina Press, 1974); Jonathan Steinberg, *Why Switzerland?* (Cambridge: Cambridge University Press, 1976); Henry H. Kerr, Jr., *Switzerland: Social Cleavages and Partisan Conflict* (London: Sage, 1974); Dusan Sidjanski, "The Swiss and Their Politics," *Government and Opposition*, II, Part 3 (Summer 1976); "The Everlasting League: A Survey of Switzerland," *The Economist* (London), February 3, 1979. For a Marxist critique which attacks the Swiss system for "spurious consensus," "pseudo-equality," and "symbolic violence," see Jean Ziegler, *Switzerland Exposed* (London: Allison and Busby, 1978).

61. Though not, at federal level, a law. As a result, matters which would otherwise be the subject of legislation find their way into the constitution.

62. Aubert, in Butler and Ranney, p. 49.

63. *Economist*, February 3, 1979, p. 10.

64. See the section on "Populist Democracy" in Robert A. Dahl, *A Preface to Democratic Theory* (Chicago: University of Chicago Press, 1956).

65. Kenneth Vickery, " 'Herrenvolk' Democracy and Egalitarianism in South Africa and the U.S. South," *Comparative Studies in Society and History*, 16, No. 3 (1974), 312.

66. Vickery, p. 322.

67. See Howard D. Hamilton, "Direct Legislation: Some Implications of Open Housing Referenda," *American Political Science Review*, 64 (1970), 124–37.

68. Given in somewhat compromising circumstances, to be sure, since Calhoun's purpose was to defend the interests of the slave-owning states before the Civil War. See John C. Calhoun, *A Disquisition on Government*, (Indianapolis: Bobbs-Merrill, 1953). Originally published in 1854.

69. This can be important in preventing the kind of arbitrary action of which populist democracy is often accused. For instance, the initiative vote in 1970 on the expulsion of foreigners (discussed below) came very near to a majority of voters (46 percent) but carried only seven of the cantons (Aubert, in Butler and Ranney, p. 61).

70. With the crucial exception, so far, of the small Communist Party (Steiner, p. 26).

71. See especially A. Lijphart, *Democracy in Plural Societies* (New Haven: Yale University Press, 1977). For a useful survey of the literature see Hans Daalder, "The Consociational Democracy Theme," *World Politics* 26 (1973–74).

72. Lijphart, p. 40.

73. In the French-speaking, largely Catholic Jura region, longstanding discontent at being part of the predominantly German and Protestant canton of Bern reached new levels with the formation of the separatist *Rassemblement Jurassien* in the 1950s. Referendums established that the Jura inhabitants were themselves split along religious lines over separation, and extremists who demanded a separate canton containing the whole Jura took to violence in the 1960s. With the recent establishment of the new canton of North Jura for those districts that opted to leave Bern, however, the issue seems to have been defused. See Steinberg, pp. 64–72.

74. "Obscurity works in the interest of special classes; clarity in the interest of the people" (Weyl, p. 310).

75. Tom Paine, *The Rights of Man* (London: Everyman's Library, Dent, 1915), p. 162; Edmund Burke, *Reflections on the French Revolution* (London: Everyman's Library, Dent, 1910), pp. 58–59.

76. Tallian, p. 61.

77. Sten Sparre Nilson, "Scandinavia," Butler and Ranney, p. 191.

78. Christopher Hughes, *Parliament of Switzerland*, p. 83. Laura Tallian also makes this point (p. 15).

79. Nilson, in Butler and Ranney, p. 185; Henry Valen, "National Conflict Structure and Foreign Politics: The Impact of the E.E.C. Issue on Perceived Cleavages in Norwegian Politics," *European Journal of Political Research*, 4, No. 1 (March 1976).

80. Butler and Ranney, p. 8.

81. Sidjanski, passim.

82. Steiner, p. 43.

83. Steiner, p. 165.

84. Tallian, p. 16.

85. For the use of this argument during the Progressive movement, see Delos F. Wilcox, *Government by All the People* (New York: Macmillan, 1912), pp. 77–79.

86. Aubert, in Butler and Ranney, p. 45.

87. Lee, in Butler and Ranney, pp. 108–09.

88. See Howard D. Hamilton, "Direct Legislation," passim. The fact that direct legislation often means "minority rule" because of low turnout is also stressed in James K. Pollock, *The Initiative and Referendum in Michigan* (Ann Arbor: University of Michigan Press, 1940), pp. 30–31; Joseph G. La Palombara, *The Initiative and Referendum in Oregon, 1938–48* (Corvallis: Oregon State College Press, 1950), p. 97.

89. Lee, in Butler and Ranney: Op Cit, p. 108.

90. Tallian, p. 62. Almost exactly the same position was stated in 1912 by Delos Wilcox, p. 238.

91. V. O. Key, Jr., and Winston W. Crouch, *The Initiative and the Referendum in California* (Berkeley: University of California Press, 1939), p. 572.

92. Key and Crouch, p. 573. See also Pollock and La Palombara, who support this thesis.

93. Lee, in Butler and Ranney, p. 97.

94. Lee, in Butler and Ranney, p. 101.

95. Steiner, p. 223.

96. Aubert, in Butler and Ranney, p. 49.

97. For a development of this aspect of Rousseau's position, see Brian Barry, "The Public Interest," in Anthony Quinton, ed., *Political Philosophy* (London: Oxford University Press, 1967).

98. The Progressives stressed the united interests of the people as consumers. See Weyl, *New Democracy*, p. 250.

99. After publishing *Unsafe at Any Speed*, a critique of car design directed particularly against the General Motors Corvair, Nader shot to fame in 1966 when, as a witness before a Senate subcommittee, he forced the President of G.M. to apologize for hiring detectives to investigate his personal life. Since then, Nader and his teams of "Raiders" have involved themselves in many areas of consumer protection, including food, air pollution, nuclear hazards, etc. See Charles McCarry, *Citizen Nader* (London: Jonathan Cape, 1972); Lucy Black Creighton, *Pretenders to the Throne: The Consumer Movement in the U.S.* (Lexington: Lexington Books, D. C. Heath, 1976).

100. Burke, whose conservatism has some populist elements, phrased it thus, à propos of the English radicals who supported the French Revolution: "Because half a dozen grasshoppers under a fern make the field ring with their importunate chink, whilst thousands of great cattle, reposed beneath the shadow of the British oak, chew the cud and are silent, pray do not imagine that those who make the noise are the only inhabitants of the field" (*Reflections*, p. 82).

101. Aubert, in Butler and Ranney, p. 47.
102. David Butler, "United Kingdom," in Butler and Ranney, p. 211. See also Philip Goodhart, *Referendum* (London: Tom Stacey Ltd., 1971).
103. Tallian, p. 16.
104. J. F. Aubert points out that although only about 5 to 10 percent of the Swiss population make a serious effort to inform themselves of the issues at stake in referendums, this does at least mean that there are between 200,000 and 300,000 people in this small country who are really politically educated (Aubert, in Butler and Ranney, p. 65).
105. P. 16.
106. P. 224.
107. Austin Ranney, "The United States of America," in Butler and Ranney, pp. 83–85.
108. Steinberg, pp. 90–91.
109. Steinberg, p. 92.
110. Steinberg, p. 93.

## 6. Reactionary Populism and the Dilemmas of Progress

1. Daniel Boorstin, *Democracy and Its Discontents* (New York: Random House, 1971), p. 15.
2. H. L. Mencken, *Notes on Democracy* (London: Jonathan Cape, 1927), p. 69.
3. S. M. Lipset and E. Raab, *The Politics of Unreason* (London: Heinemann, 1970), p. 342.
4. Lipset and Raab, p. 349.
5. Richard Scammon and Ben J. Wattenberg, *The Real Majority* (New York: Coward McCann, Inc., 1970), p. 62.
6. Scammon and Wattenberg, p. 21.
7. Douglas E. Schoen, *Enoch Powell and the Powellites* (London: Macmillan, 1977), p. 32.
8. Schoen, p. 33.
9. Schoen, pp. 37, 41.
10. According to Tolstoy, genuine art was to be found in myths and folk songs. He attempted to demonstrate the emptiness

of contemporary culture by means of a devastating description of Wagner's *Ring* as it would be seen through the eyes of a simple peasant. See Leo Tolstoy, *What is Art? and Essays on Art* (Oxford: Oxford University Press, 1930), p. 213.

11. For the claim that "people make culture," and a rejection of "the so-called cultural heritage" in favor of "community art," see Su Braden, *Artists and People* (London: Routledge and Kegan Paul, 1978).

12. See Richard Hofstadter, *Anti-Intellectualism in American Life* (London: Jonathan Cape, 1964).

13. Hofstadter, pp. 159, 162.

14. Mencken, pp. 60, 67.

15. See Norman F. Furniss, *The Fundamentalist Controversy, 1918–31* (New Haven: Yale University Press, 1954) ; Ray Ginger, *Six Days or Forever? Tennessee Versus John Thomas Scopes* (Boston: Beacon Press, 1958).

16. Furniss, p. 4.

17. Furniss, p. 40.

18. William Manchester, *The Sage of Baltimore* (London: Andrew Melrose, 1952), p. 144.

19. Hofstadter, p. 127. See also Paolo E. Coletta, *William Jennings Bryan*, III, *Political Puritan, 1915–1925* (Lincoln: University of Nebraska Press, 1969), 236.

20. On the relationship between theories of history and the development of a pedagogic conception of politics, see George Armstrong Kelly, *Idealism, Politics and History: Sources of Hegelian Thought* (Cambridge: Cambridge University Press, 1969).

21. A great many theorists of enlightenment have seen this clearly and been openly elitist: witness Voltaire's statement, *"quand la populace se mêle de raisonner, tout est perdu,"* quoted in Salvador Giner, *Mass Society* (London: Martin Robertson, 1976), p. 39; also the nineteenth-century positivists; Lenin; and the recently fashionable theories of

Herbert Marcuse, who preached the need for an "educational dictatorship" by the enlightened to lead Western populations to true consciousness. See Herbert Marcuse, *An Essay on Liberation* (London: Penguin, 1972), and *One Dimensional Man* (London: Abacus, 1972). John Stuart Mill saw and wrestled with the conflict between democracy and progress, criticizing American democratic institutions for giving U.S. citizens the false idea "that any one man (with a white skin) is as good as any other"; see J. S. Mill, "Representative Government," in *Utilitarianism, Liberty and Representative Government* (London: J. M. Dent, 1910), p. 196. He devised elaborate (and politically impossible) devices for multiple voting by the educated in order to safeguard enlightenment while allowing the masses the educative practice of voting (*ibid.*, p. 285).

22. On Rousseau's craving for authority, see Judith N. Shklar, *Men And Citizens: A Study of Rousseau's Social Theory* (London: Cambridge University Press, 1969), Chapter 4.

23. Jean-Jacques Rousseau, *The Social Contract and Discourses* (London: J. M. Dent, 1952), p. 129.

24. *The Social Contract and Discourses*, pp. 126, 142.

25. *The Works of Joseph de Maistre*, ed. Jack Lively (London: Allen and Unwin, 1965), p. 108.

26. There is an idyllic description in Rousseau's *Letter to d'Alembert* of a remote Swiss community where free and equal farmers spend their winters making watches, tools, scientific instruments, and painting, singing, and playing, all without the aid of teachers or "civilization." See Jean-Jacques Rousseau, *Politics and the Arts: Letter to M. d'Alembert on the Theatre*, ed. Allan Bloom (Glencoe: Free Press of Glencoe, 1960), p. 60.

27. Jean-Jacques Rousseau, *Emile*, trans. Barbara Foxley (London: J. M. Dent & Son, 1963), pp. 74, 147.

28. *Emile*, p. 167.

29. See *Social Contract and Discourses*, p. 85.

30. *The Social Contract and Discourses,* p. 31.
31. Two English examples of writers who shared populist views of the common man, had close links with agrarian populism of the "peasant" type, and were distrustful of "progress" and its elitist implications, are William Cobbett and G. K. Chesterton. On Chesterton, see Margaret Canovan, *G. K. Chesterton: Radical Populist* (New York: Harcourt Brace Jovanovich, 1977); on Cobbett, James Sambrook, *William Cobbett* (London: Routledge and Kegan Paul, 1973).
32. Andrzej Walicki, *The Controversy over Capitalism* (Oxford: Oxford University Press, 1969), p. 34. On Lavrov, see also Philip Pomper, *Peter Lavrov and the Russian Revolutionary Movement* (Chicago: University of Chicago Press, 1972).
33. Pomper, p. 146.
34. Pomper, p. 187.
35. On Tkachev, see Walicki; also F. Venturi, *The Roots of Revolution* (London: Weidenfeld and Nicholson, 1950), Chapter 6.
36. Walicki, p. 39.
37. Walicki, p. 42.
38. Venturi, p. 407.
39. On Mikhailovsky, see James H. Billington, *Mikhailovsky and Russian Populism* (Oxford: Oxford University Press, 1958); Walicki; Arthur P. Mendel, *Dilemmas of Progress in Tsarist Russia: Legal Marxism and Legal Populism* (Cambridge, Mass.: Harvard University Press, 1961).
40. Mendel, p. 24.
41. Billington, p. 32.
42. Billington, p. 93.
43. Billington, p. 94.
44. Billington, p. 91.
45. Mendel, p. 11.
46. Mendel, p. 78.

47. L. Schapiro, "The Role of Jews in the Russian Revolutionary Movement," *Slavonic and East European Review,* 40 (1961–62), 154.

48. Quoted in Adam B. Ulam, *In the Name of the People: Prophets and Conspirators in Pre-Revolutionary Russia* (New York: Viking Press, 1977), p. 371.

49. Richard Wortman, *The Crisis of Russian Populism* (Cambridge: Cambridge University Press, 1967), p. 135.

50. A. Walicki, pp. 67, 76.

51. For a recent example of a populist argument of this kind, see Peter Berger, *Pyramids of Sacrifice* (London: Allen Lane, 1976).

52. Brecht's *Mother Courage*—on one reading of the play, at any rate—is an example of this.

53. Philip Goodhart, *Full-Hearted Consent* (London: Davis-Poynter, 1976), p. 21. Tolstoy's position on this issue was an interesting one. In some ways, his outlook was that of an extreme *narodnik.* Having become convinced that the life of the rich was parasitic upon that of the workers, he suffered torments of guilt, since he could not accept that upper-class culture contributed anything at all to the welfare of the poor. Eventually he rejected art, science, leisure, and luxury in favor of the simple life of manual labor and peasant diversions. *But* for all his praise of the peasant, he held firmly to the conviction that he himself and others who reached spiritual enlightenment were in the vanguard of moral progress. In other words, his position was a long way from simple deference toward popular views.

In this connection, see also the controversy over law and morality set off by Lord Devlin. See Patrick Devlin, *The Enforcement of Morals* (London: Oxford University Press, 1965); H. L. A. Hart, *Law, Liberty and Morality* (London: Oxford University Press, 1963). Many liberals were alarmed not only by Lord Devlin's view that the law should enforce morality in, for instance, sexual matters, but even more by his "moral populism" (Hart, p. 79)—his view that, for practical purposes, the arbiter of morality must be "the man in the jury box" rather than the "Superior Person" (Devlin, pp. 90–93).

54. Norman Cohn, *Europe's Inner Demons* (London: Sussex University Press, 1975), pp. 251–62; Keith Thomas, *Religion and the Decline of Magic* (Harmondsworth: Penguin Books, 1971), pp. 521–25.

55. On the Eugenics Movement in Britain, its original home, see C. P. Blacker, *Eugenics: Galton and After* (London: Gerald Duckworth, 1952); G. R. Searle, *Eugenics and Politics in Britain, 1900–14* (Leyden, Nordhoff, 1976); also the most revealing source, the journal of the Eugenics Society, *The Eugenics Review.*

56. William Kornhauser, *The Politics of Mass Society* (London: Routledge and Kegan Paul, 1960), p. 188.

57. The claims of populist intellectuals to represent "the people" are often dubious. Consider, for example, recent demands by members of the populistic Left for schooling which would be "relevant" to proletarian life—and which would (contrary to the desires of many "proletarian" parents) make upward social mobility more difficult.

## 7. *Politicians' Populism*

1. Presented at the party's conference in Lagos, December 1978. I owe this reference to Martin Dent of Keele University.

2. Advertisement in the *American Political Science Review* (1964), p. 244.

3. E. E. Schattschneider, *The Semisovereign People* (New York: Holt, Rinehart & Winston, 1960), p. 71.

4. Otto Kirchheimer, "The Transformation of the Western European Party Systems," in Joseph LaPalombara and Myron Weiner, eds., *Political Parties and Political Development* (Princeton: Princeton University Press, 1966), p. 184.

5. Henry St. John, Viscount Bolingbroke, *Letters on the Spirit of Patriotism; On the Idea of a Patriot King, etc.* (London, 1775), pp. 141, 218. Bolingbroke is often called a Tory. Donald Greene, however—in *The Politics of Samuel Johnson* (New Haven: Yale University Press, 1960)—refers to his "manifestly insincere nonpartisanship" (p. 236) and is inclined to deny him this title (pp. 11, 247).

6. Alexander Werth, *De Gaulle* (Harmondsworth: Penguin, 1965), p. 37. De Gaulle is also said to have denied ideological ties to Right, Left, or even Center, on the grounds that his only position was *"au-dessus"*—Ernest Mignon, *Les Mots du Général* (Paris: Librairie Arthème Fayard, 1962), p. 41.

7. Peter Worsley, *The Third World*, revised ed. (London: Weidenfeld and Nicholson, 1967), pp. 165, 166.

8. Analyzed in terms of the categories adopted here, Worsley's populism consists of politicians' populism, plus a large admixture of peasant populism and dashes of both farmers' populism and *narodnichestvo*.

9. See especially Chapters 4 and 5 of Worsley.

10. At any rate in the first edition. For a rather more disillusioned view, see Chapter 7 of the second edition.

11. Worsley, p. 227.

12. See Giovanni Sartori, *Parties and Party Systems*, I (Cambridge: Cambridge University Press, 1976), 253–54; Immanuel Wallerstein, "The Decline of the Party in Single-Party African States," in LaPalombara and Weiner.

13. John S. Saul, "On African Populism," in Giovanni Arrighi and John S. Saul, *Essays on the Political Economy of Africa* (New York: Monthly Review Press, 1973), p. 173. Saul remarks on the need for clarification of the concept of populism, and goes some way toward this by distinguishing between "Populism as the Will of the People," "Populism and the Defense against Capitalism," and "Populism and the Aspiration for Solidarity." His own socialist outlook is in

some ways reminiscent of *narodnik* ideas: see his discussion (in the same volume) of Tanzania's chances of avoiding capitalism and building a socialist society, which echoes the Russian idea that backwardness can be an advantage. Tanzania, being comparatively undeveloped, "experienced some of the benefits of being a *tabula rasa*—less distorted and therefore more open-ended" ("Socialism in One Country: Tanzania," p. 256).

14. C. B. Macpherson, *Democracy in Alberta: The Theory and Practice of a Quasi-Party System* (Toronto: University of Toronto Press, 1953). See above, Chapter 3.

15. Macpherson, p. 21. For an alternative analysis which does not rest upon the assumption of class homogeneity, see Maurice Pinard, *The Rise of a Third Party: A Study in Crisis Politics* (Englewood Cliffs, N.J.: Prentice-Hall, 1971), p. 69.

16. James Wooten, *Dasher: The Roots and the Rising of Jimmy Carter* (London: Weidenfeld and Nicholson, 1978), p. 71.

17. Wooten, p. 288.

18. *The Presidential Campaign 1976* (Washington: U.S. Government Printing Office, 1978), passim.

19. Speech accepting the Democratic nomination, July 15, 1976. *Ibid.*, I, Part 1, 349.

20. *Ibid.*, p. 472.

21. *Ibid.*, p. 349.

22. *Ibid.*, p. 735.

23. *Ibid.*, p. 209.

24. *Ibid.*, p. 720.

25. Alistair Hennessy, "Latin America," Ionescu and Gellner, eds., *Populism*, p. 29.

26. See L. Vincent Padgett, *The Mexican Political System*, 2nd ed. (Boston: Houghton Mifflin Co., 1976).

27. An interesting example is the People's Redemption Party of Nigeria, whose 1978 program continually contrasts the privileged "elite" of Nigeria with "the people." As the

quotation at the head of this chapter shows, "the people" includes virtually everyone except the politicians and administrators at present in power. A definition of the people that can include "big businessmen, and traditional rulers with a social conscience" is obviously not a very radical one, and seems in fact to be simply an invocation of the outs against the ins.

28. See Alan Angell, "Party Systems in Latin America," *Political Quarterly*, 37 (1966), 315–19; Paul W. Drake, *Socialism and Populism in Chile, 1932–52*, (Urbana: University of Illinois Press, 1978), especially the Introduction; Christopher Mitchell, *The Legacy of Populism in Bolivia: From the M.N.R. to Military Rule* (New York: Praeger, 1977).

29. See Herbert S. Klein, *Parties and Political Change in Bolivia, 1880–1952* (Cambridge: Cambridge University Press, 1969); C. Mitchell; Jorge Dandler, " 'Low Classness' or Wavering Populism? A Peasant Movement in Bolivia (1952–3)," in June Nash, Juan Corradi, and Hobart Spalding Jr., eds., *Ideology and Social Class in Latin America* (New York: Gordon and Breach, 1977); Robert J. Alexander, "Bolivia—the National Revolution," in Martin C. Needler, *Political Systems of Latin America*, 2nd ed. (New York: Van Nostrand Reinhold, 1970).

30. "Populism and Reform in Latin America," in C. Veliz, ed., *Obstacles to Change in Latin America* (London: Oxford University Press, 1965), p. 50.

31. *Ibid.*, p. 47.

32. H. J. Hanham, *Scottish Nationalism* (London: Faber and Faber, 1969), pp. 204–05.

33. See Iain McLean, "The Politics of Nationalism and Devolution," *Political Studies*, 25, No. 3 (September 1977), 428. On Scottish Nationalism, see also Christopher Harvie, *Scotland and Nationalism* (London: Allen and Unwin, 1977); Jack Brand, *The National Movement in Scotland* (London: Routledge and Kegan Paul, 1978). Both the

latter authors deny that S.N.P. is a populist movement
(Brand, p. 279; Harvie, p. 254), but the senses in which
they use the word remain vague and unanalyzed.

34. *A Populist Manifesto: The Making of a New Majority*
(New York: Praeger, 1972), p. 9.

35. *Ibid.*, p. 175.

36. Padgett, p. 13.

*Conclusion*

1. Peter Wiles, "A Syndrome, Not a Doctrine: Some Elementary Theses on Populism," in Ionescu and Gellner, *Populism*, p. 166.

2. Wiles, p. 171.

3. P. 172.

4. See the chapters on Norway by Stein Rokkan in R. A. Dahl, ed., *Political Oppositions in Western Democracies* (New Haven: Yale University Press, 1966) ; S. M. Lipset and Stein Rokkan, eds., *Party Systems and Voter Alignments: Cross-National Perspectives* (New York: The Free Press, 1967).

5. One example is G. K. Chesterton. See Margaret Canovan, *G. K. Chesterton: Radical Populist* (New York: Harcourt Brace Jovanovich, 1977).

6. This seems to be the connotation of the term in the Nigerian People's Redemption Party program quoted at the head of Chapter 7 on p. 260.

7. Richard L. Sklar, in *Nigerian Political Parties* (Princeton: Princeton University Press, 1963), seems to mean little more than this when he applies the term to parties; see his Chapter 8.

8. This is the strongest objection to the sophisticated attempt to establish a Marxist theory of populism recently made by Ernesto Laclau. ("Towards a Theory of Populism," in E. Laclau, *Politics and Ideology in Marxist Theory: Capitalism—Fascism—Populism* (London, NLB, 1977). Laclau's great strength is that he is much more willing than previous

theorists to recognize the diversity of populism. He argues that the defining characteristic of populist movements is not that they all arise on the basis of the same class or at a particular stage in social development, but rather that they all make use of "popular-democratic interpellations" (p. 172). Alongside the "class contradictions" of all societies, according to Laclau, runs another "objective contradiction," that between "people" and "power bloc," which gives rise to its own ideological vocabulary. "Populism starts at the point where popular-democratic elements are presented as an antagonistic option against the ideology of the dominant bloc" (p. 173).

Laclau's terminology is rebarbative, but what his position seems to amount to is a stress upon the anti-elitist rhetoric of "the people," which provides a store of distinctive motifs that can be adopted by different groups for different purposes. Having first placed a much-needed stress upon the diversity of populisms, however, Laclau then goes on to claim that they are systematically related to one another via their dependence upon socio-economic conditions.

There are two aspects to this. Firstly, he claims that populism in all its varieties emerges during "a crisis of the dominant ideological discourse, which is in turn part of a more general social crisis" (p. 175)—a formula which is too all-embracing to be helpful. Secondly, he argues that the specific form populism takes depends upon the class or complex of classes by which "popular-democratic interpellations" are adopted. In many cases this line of argument is illuminating (as Laclau's own analysis of the class-setting of Peronism shows), but unfortunately Laclau's determination to make his theory Marxist by tying particular types of populism to particular classes prevents him from doing justice to important aspects of the subject.

He claims, for instance, that the full development of "the 'people'/power bloc contradiction," that is, "the suppression

of the State as an antagonistic force with respect to the
people" (which is surely the very ideal of Populist Democracy) can be aspired to only by the proletariat and in
conjunction with socialism (p. 196). This blatantly ignores
non-proletarian movements for direct democracy, as in the
United States and Switzerland. Similarly, Laclau pays no
serious attention to Reactionary Populism at the grass roots
(see p. 174). He seems to be misled partly by his Marxist
commitments but also by his wish for greater theoretical
symmetry than the phenomena of populism allow.

9. See Ionescu and Gellner, eds., *Populism*, "Introduction,"
   p. 3.

# Index

345